Hatching Twitter

Hatching Twitter

A True Story of Money, Power,
Friendship, and Betrayal

NICK BILTON

Portfolio / Penguin

PORTFOLIO / PENGUIN
Published by the Penguin Group
Penguin Group (USA) LLC
375 Hudson Street
New York, New York 10014

USA | Canada | UK | Ireland | Australia | New Zealand | India | South Africa | China
penguin.com
A Penguin Random House Company

First published by Portfolio / Penguin, a member of Penguin Group (USA) LLC, 2013

Photograph credits
Insert page 1 (top and bottom), 2 (top and middle): Dom Sagolla
2 (bottom): Ray McClure
3 (top), 4 (top): Scott Beale
3 (bottom), 5 (bottom): Sara Morishige Williams
4 (bottom), 6 (middle and bottom): Twitter, Inc.
5 (top): Scott Heiferman
6 (top): Dustin Diaz / Twitter, Inc.
7 (top), 8 (bottom): Jillian West / Twitter, Inc.
7 (bottom): Geoff Livingston
8 (top): Tim Trueman / Twitter, Inc.

ISBN 978-1-59184-601-7

Printed in the United States of America
10 9 8 7 6 5 4 3 2 1

Set in Mercury Text G1
Designed by Daniel Lagin

For Sandra, Terry, Leanne, Elissa,
their respective families,
and Pixel

Author's Note

The author Julian Barnes once wrote, "History is that certainty produced at the point where the imperfections of memory meet the inadequacies of documentation."

What you are about to read is the result of several hundred hours of interviews with current and former employees of Twitter and Odeo, government officials, Twitter executives' friends and significant others, and people at competing companies, as well as discussions with almost everyone mentioned in the book. While Twitter, the company, declined to give me official access for the book, Twitter's current and former board members and all four cofounders of the company agreed to sit for, collectively, more than sixty-five hours of interviews. Although most interviews were recorded to ensure accuracy of dialogue, all of these conversations, while on the record to be used within this book, were conducted on "background," with the understanding that material would not be explicitly attributed to specific sources within this book. There are only a couple of people mentioned in this book who declined to be interviewed.

It became apparent in the interviews for the book that people's memories of past events have changed over time. During only a select few occasions two people agreed that a meeting took place, but their recollections of the location or timing were drastically different. In every instance possible I have tried to triangulate timing and location of events using documents I obtained and, of course, social media. There may be some occurrences where this was not possible; in these instances I have done my best to estimate timing. I chose to leave out of this narrative moments of the story for which accounts were too different. In some areas of the book events are referred to a few months earlier than they occur to help the reader understand the overall significance of a moment.

The book is also based on more than a thousand documents I obtained or reviewed during my reporting, including employee e-mails, boardroom presentations, investment filings, contracts, employee calendars, partnership documents, government-level communications, instant-messenger correspondence, newspaper articles, blog posts, and highly confidential Twitter legal notices and internal e-mails. In moments of the book where scenes are described in exact detail, I have often personally visited the location. Any instance of a character's inner monologue or emotional state is based on interviews with that individual and not assumed.

Even with the hundreds of hours of interviews and the internal documents, the most exact location of memory I found was strewn about the Internet on social-media Web sites. With a researcher, I pored through tens of thousands of tweets, photos, and videos.

It became clear in the reporting of this book that the imperfections of memory of those I spoke with have sometimes become more pronounced over the past decade. But what has remained intact are the hundreds of thousands of photos, videos, and tweets they all shared over the years, helping to pinpoint exact moments in time, clothing, conversation, and mood. Unbeknownst to the people in the book at the time, their use of the tools they created, especially Twitter, ensured there were very few inadequacies of documentation to deteriorate the true events that make up this history.

Contents

Author's Note ix

#START 1

I. #FOUNDERS 7

@Ev 9
@Noah 17
@Jack 28
@Biz 37

II. #NOAH 43

Troubled Waters 45
Status 52
Twitter 60
Just Setting Up My Twttr 66
The Cowboy at the Rodeo 70
The Green Benches 75

III. #JACK 81

A Bloody Mess 83
Chaos Again 90
And the Winner Is . . . 96

The First CEO   102
The Hundred-Million-Dollar Offer   107
Is Twitter Down?   114
The Dressmaker   120
Rumors   126
Fuck Fuck Fuck . . .   130
Building Sand Castles Underwater   139
Calling My Parents   143

IV. #EV   159

The Third Twitter Leader   161
Fight or Flight   167
The Marathon Man   173
Dinner with Al   177
Oprah   182
Spiraling into Iraq   190
The *Time* 101   197
Iranian Revolution   205
The Accidental Billionaire   212
The Coach and the Comedian   219
Jack's Gone Rogue   226
Steve Jobs 2.0   231
Russian-Roulette Relations   237
Secret Meetings   244
The Clown Car in the Gold Mine   248
A Sunday Storm   262

V. #DICK   273

No Adult Supervision   275
Jack's Back!   281
Make Better Mistakes Tomorrow   286
What's Happening?   290

Acknowledgments   301

Hatching Twitter

#START

October 4, 2010, 10:43 A.M.

The Twitter Office

Get out," Evan Williams said to the woman standing in his office doorway. "I'm going to throw up."

She stepped backward, pulling the door closed, a metal clicking sound reverberating through the room as he grabbed the black wastebasket in the corner of his office, his hands now shaking and clammy.

This was it. His last act as the CEO of Twitter would be throwing up into a garbage can.

He knelt there for a moment, his dark jeans resting on the rough carpeted floor, then leaned back against the wall. Outside, the cold October air rustled the trees that lined Folsom Street below. Violin-like noises of traffic mingled with a muffled din of conversation near his office doorway.

Moments later, someone informed his wife, Sara, who also worked at Twitter, "Something is wrong with Ev." She rushed up to his corner office, her rich, black, curly hair wobbling slightly as she walked.

Sara checked her watch, realizing that Ev had only forty-five minutes before he would have to address the three hundred Twitter employees and break the news. She opened the door and went inside.

Down the hall, the Twitter public-relations team reviewed the blog post that would go up on the Web site at 11:40 A.M., the moment Ev would finish addressing the company and hand the microphone to the new CEO, passing power in a gesture as simple as handing off the baton in a relay race.

The blog post, which would be picked up by thousands of press outlets and blogs from around the world, gleefully announced that Twitter, the four-year-old social network, now had 165 million registered people on the service who sent an astounding 90 million tweets each day. Five paragraphs down, it noted that Evan Williams, the current CEO, was stepping down of his own volition.

"I have decided to ask our COO, Dick Costolo, to become Twitter's CEO," said the post, allegedly written by Ev.

Of course, that wasn't true.

Ev, seated on the floor of his office with his hands wrapped around a garbage can, had absolutely no desire to say that. A farmer's son from Nebraska who had arrived in San Francisco a decade earlier with nothing more than a couple of bags of cheap, raggedy, oversized clothes and tens of thousands of dollars in credit-card debt, Ev wanted to remain chief of the company he had cofounded. But that wasn't going to happen. It didn't matter that he was now worth more than a billion dollars or that he had poured his life into Twitter. He didn't have a choice: He had been forced out of the company in a malicious, bloody boardroom coup carried out by the people he had hired, some of whom had once been his closest friends, and by some of the investors who had financed the company.

Ev looked up as he heard Sara come in. He wiped the sleeve of his sweater across the dark stubble on his chin.

"How are you feeling?" Sara asked.

"Fuck," he said, unsure if it was his nerves or if he was coming down with something. Or both.

Down the hall, through the doors that led to the Twitter office's main foyer, copies of the *New Yorker*, the *Economist*, and the *New York Times* were fanned out on the white square coffee table in the waiting area. Each publication contained articles about Twitter's role in the revolutions now taking place in the Middle East—rebellions that, through Twitter and other social networks, would eventually see the fall of dictators in Tunisia, Egypt, Libya, and Yemen and spark massive protests in Bahrain, Syria, and Iran.

Around the corner, Biz Stone, another of Twitter's four cofounders, finalized an e-mail telling the employees that there would be an all-hands meeting in the cafeteria at 11:30 A.M. Attendance was mandatory; no guests were allowed. There would be no hummus, just important news. He hit "send" and stood up from his desk, heading for Ev's office to try to cheer up his friend and boss of nearly a decade.

Jason Goldman, who oversaw Twitter's product development and was one of Ev's few allies on the company's seven-person board, was already sitting on the couch when Biz arrived and dropped down next to him. Ev was now quietly sipping from a bottle of water, despondently staring off into the distance, the turmoil and madness of the past week playing over in his mind.

"Remember when . . . ," Goldman and Biz chorused, trying to cheer Ev up with humorous memories of the last several years at Twitter. There were lots of stories to tell. Like the time Ev had nervously been a guest on the *Oprah Winfrey Show*, fumbling in front of millions of viewers. Or the time the Russian president showed up to the office, with snipers and the Secret Service, to send his first tweet, right at the moment the site stopped working. Or when Biz and Ev went to Al Gore's apartment at the St. Regis for dinner and got "shit-faced drunk" as the former vice president of the United States tried to convince them to sell him part of Twitter. Or other bizarre acquisition attempts by Ashton Kutcher at his pool in Los Angeles and by Mark Zuckerberg at awkward meetings at his sparsely furnished house. Or when Kanye West, will.i.am, Lady Gaga, Arnold Schwarzenegger, John McCain, and countless other celebrities and politicians had arrived, sometimes unannounced, at the office, rapping, singing, preaching, tweeting (some others were even high or drunk), trying to understand how this bizarre thing that was changing society could be controlled and how they could own a piece of it.

Ev struggled to smile as his friends spoke, trying his best to hide the sadness and defeat on his face.

There was one person who might have been successful at making Ev smile: the man who was now pacing in the office directly next door, his bald head bowed, his phone cupped to his ear. Dick Costolo, once a well-known improv comedian who had graced the stage with Steve Carell and Tina Fey. The same Dick Costolo Ev had "decided to ask" to become Twitter's new CEO, the third of a company that was only four years old.

Yet Dick wasn't in a jovial mood either. He was talking to the board members who had been involved in the coup, confirming the wording of the blog post that would soon go out to the media, and also what he would say to the hundreds of Twitter employees when he took the mic from Ev.

He paced as they plotted what would happen next: the return of Jack Dorsey.

Jack had been the first CEO of Twitter and another cofounder. He had been pushed out of the company by Ev in a similar power struggle in 2008. On this particular morning, he'd been expecting to make a triumphant return to the company he had obsessively built before his own ousting.

As Jack had been informed by the board a few hours earlier, though, his return to Twitter would not happen today; it would be delayed again. Jack was only a few blocks away as the scene unfolded that morning, pacing in his office at Square, a mobile payments company he'd recently started.

He had woken up in his wall-to-wall-concrete penthouse apartment in Mint Plaza and dressed for work in his now-signature several-thousand-dollar outfit of fancy Dior shirt, dark suit blazer, and Rolex watch. It was a very different ensemble from the unkempt T-shirt and black beanie hat he had worn two years earlier when he was ousted from Twitter.

But although he wore a different uniform that morning, he was equally disdainful of Ev, his once friend and forever cofounder, who had foiled Jack's planned return to Twitter. Although Ev had been successfully removed as the CEO, he had not, as was originally sup-posed to unfold, been publicly fired from the company. At least not yet.

Back in the Twitter office, Ev looked up as the clock approached 11:30 A.M. Time to go.

Ev had no idea that within just a few months he would be com-pletely out of a job at Twitter. Biz and Jason followed Ev out the door and down the halls, as they had for years, clueless that they would also be pushed out of the company in due time.

They walked silently toward the company's cafeteria, past the col-orful walls and white sleigh rocking chairs and the confused employees who were grabbing their seats. None of Twitter's staff members knew what they were about to hear from their beloved boss, Evan Williams. They had no idea that the company they worked for, a company that had changed the world in countless ways, was itself about to change forever.

I.
#FOUNDERS

@Ev

Ev's bicycle tires crunched on the gravel as he drifted along the dirt road, past the endless rows of green and yellow grapevines. The orange glow of the morning California sun warmed his back, his bright orange sneakers pressing down on the pedals as he picked up speed to begin his dreaded daily four-mile bike ride to work.

As he approached Sebastopol's Morris Street, cars swooshed by, leaving pockets of moving air in their wake, which helped dry the small droplets of sweat that had gathered on his brow from the morning commute. This was the moment in the ride when he once again told himself that one day soon he would be able to afford to buy a car to get to work, rather than have to use an old bicycle borrowed from a coworker.

Of course, he had never imagined people needed to own a car in San Francisco, where he had thought he was moving when he arrived in California earlier that year. It was 1997, the middle of the modern-day gold rush called the tech boom. Young, nerdy tech enthusiasts like Ev, along with designers and programmers, had set out for the area in pursuit of a new dream where, rumor had it, you could get rich by selling ones and zeros rather than nuggets of shiny yellow gold.

He had arrived a twenty-five-year-old with empty pockets and fierce idealism, only to find that the job he had been hired for, writing marketing material for a company called O'Reilly Media, was in Sebastopol, a small, quiet hippie town fifty-five miles north of San Francisco.

When viewed on a map spread out on his mother's small kitchen table in Nebraska, it had looked much closer to the big city. Ev decided he didn't have much of a choice but to keep the job. He had no college degree and no idea how to write code. The odds of finding work elsewhere were slim to none. Plus O'Reilly was paying him $48,500 a year, which would help deplete his tens of thousands of dollars in credit-card debt and student loans from the single year he had made it through college. He also reasoned that his new employer, which published technology how-to books, would be the perfect place to learn how to program. So he settled in on the outskirts of town, renting a six-hundred-dollar-a-month shoebox that sat atop a stranger's garage.

Ev felt a surprising sense of comfort in the solitude of Sebastopol, surrounded by the sounds of nothingness. It reminded him of the farm in Clarks, Nebraska, where he had grown up. The day he left for California, Clarks's population went from 374 people to 373.

At his new office, he often sat quietly at his computer, wearing baggy, cheap jeans, an oversized T-shirt—almost always tucked in—and, if the day afforded it, a strange hat.

When your parents are farmers, style isn't usually part of the morning breakfast discussion. Neither is talk of tech start-ups and San Francisco, which is why his father, Monte, hadn't quite understood why young Ev was heading to California to play with computers rather than tending to the family farm. But the Williams family had never really understood Ev.

From the time he could walk he was a daydreamer. As a young boy, he would sit on the side of the family's green tractor in the deep fields and stare up into space. He was shy and sometimes socially awkward and rarely fit in, often spending hours alone with his thoughts. As he grew up, normal life in Clarks required that he go hunting with his dad and brother. Like all midwestern boys, he was supposed to learn to fire rifles, shoot a bow, gut a deer, and fish for bass or trout in the Nebraska lakes. He was also expected to fall in love with football. And, of course, all of these things should be done while driving a very large pickup truck. All part of the American Dream.

Yet Ev preferred to sit in his bedroom and glue together plastic models, or spend hours taking apart his bikes before painstakingly putting them back together, or draw ideas for video games he wanted to make when he was older—when he could afford to buy a computer. Guns, football, and hunting were simply not his thing.

When Ev grew up and it was time to buy his first car, rather than procure a big, brawny truck, he opted for a bright yellow BMW. Owning four wheels and four doors helped catapult him to high-school popularity. A car in the Midwest for a teenager is like a watercooler in the middle of the desert. He was soon whisking his new friends to parties, where he started hooking up with girls and drinking beer out of red plastic cups.

But his carefree new lifestyle came to a halt when his parents got divorced during his senior year. The small-town gossips whispered that his mother later fell for the fertilizer guy. Ev was dragged over to a different town and a different high school, where he once again fell into obscurity and isolation.

His mind was always filling up with wacky business schemes. Most of them never quite clicked, especially with the local Nebraskans. As the Internet stared to gain speed on the coasts, Ev came up with the idea of making a VHS tape explaining what this Internet thing was. He then spent a summer driving around in his yellow Beemer trying to convince local businesses to buy the tapes. He didn't sell many.

But once Ev got an idea in his mind, he was determined to make it a reality. You might have had better luck stopping the earth from spinning than barring Evan Williams from raising one of his idea hatchlings.

After high school he didn't stray far from home and attended the University of Nebraska at Lincoln, but after a year and a half he felt that college and his professors were a waste of time. One afternoon in 1992 he was sitting in his dorm room reading, when he came across an obscure article about an advertising guru who lived and worked in

Florida. Ev was so taken by the subject of the article that he tried to call the man to ask if he was hiring. After a few conversations with an answering machine, Ev said "Fuck it!" and got into the family's old Chevy van. He drove the two thousand miles to Key West, Florida. As a runaway student he was flat broke. He paid for gas with plastic and slept in the van. In the morning, as the southern sun woke him, he would pop an audiobook tape into the car's cassette deck—often a marketing or business book—and listen as he coasted along the empty roads. When he arrived in Florida, he knocked on the advertising exec's door, demanding a job. Impressed by Ev's tenacity and persuasiveness, the exec hired Ev on the spot. Yet after several months Ev realized the man was more bullshit artist than advertising artist. So, playing everything in reverse—with a brief stay in Texas—he drove back to Nebraska.

His determination often rubbed people the wrong way. At O'Reilly Media he was once asked to compose the marketing material for one of the company's latest products. Ev responded by e-mailing the entire company that he wouldn't write it, because the product "was a piece of shit."

His abrasiveness didn't help win many friends when he arrived in California, either, so each night he would ride his borrowed bicycle home, back past the vines of grapes that would soon end up in a bottle of something he couldn't afford. Once atop the garage, he would sit and sip cheap beers alone in a single room that was large enough for a mattress, a small brown kitchenette, and Ev's prized possession: his computer.

There he would teach himself how to write code, his only friends the crickets he could hear gathered around the garage cheering him on as he learned to speak a language only computers could understand.

He eventually escaped the confines of the sleepy northern California town and darted south to Palo Alto to work for Intel and later Hewlett-Packard, building mundane software and slowly making friends who worked in the industry. On weekends he would take the train to San Francisco, where his new buddies took him to start-up parties. The draw of the city eventually enticed him to rent an inexpensive, crooked apartment in the Mission area of San Francisco.

He met a girl, Meg Hourihan, a sprightly programmer who shared Ev's passion for opinion and computers, and the two began a brief love affair. Although the relationship didn't last long, they decided to start a company together. They set off with a small group of friends, and opened a bare-bones start-up called Pyra Labs that operated out of Ev's apartment. The group planned to build software to increase workplace productivity. But, starting a pattern that would follow Ev through his career, something better accidentally grew out of Pyra.

Ev and an employee had built a simple internal diary Web site that would help Pyra employees keep up to date about work progress. Meg didn't like the side project and was not shy in expressing her views, calling it just another Ev distraction. One week in the summer of 1999, while she was away on vacation, Ev released the diary Web site to the world. He called it Blogger, a word that had not existed until then. He believed it would allow people without any computer-programming knowledge to create a Web log, or blog.

After Blogger rose in popularity among the tech nerds, Meg eventually came around to its potential, but not Ev's. Meg was concerned that he didn't have the skills to run a business, as paperwork was piling up and bills going unpaid. A mini power struggle quickly ensued, wherein Meg tried to take control of the company and Ev refused to step down. In the end, the five-person Pyra team disbanded, leaving Ev friendless, single, and running a company out of his living room.

At around the same time, the tech boom, which had since turned into a tech bubble, went *pop*. The stock market started to spiral down, with trillions of dollars eventually falling out of the NASDAQ. Within months the parties disappeared. Jobs became sparse. Start-ups closed down. And most of the people who had come to the Valley in search of wealth left the area, broke.

Ev wasn't going anywhere, though. He had a vision for Blogger, where anyone could have their own blog, the equivalent of their own online newspaper. Unlike his lonely high-school days, Ev's seclusion was relieved by a connection to the world through the hundreds of blogs that were popping up in this town he had laid the foundation for: Blogger, population tens of thousands.

On his own blog, *EvHead*, he forged digital friendships with other people. By day he wrote code by the pound, often for fourteen or sixteen hours at a time, expanding Blogger and building new features for the service. At night he wrote on his blog about the "electronica" he was listening to, recent movies he had seen, a run-in with the IRS for some back taxes. Then, as the moon crested in the sky, he checked the blogs one last time, said good night to the people of the Internet, scrunched up into a ball on his couch surrounded by week-old pizza boxes and empty Snapple bottles, and fell asleep. No friends, no employees, no money. Just Ev.

He soon learned that if you give a microphone to enough people, someone will yell something into it that will offend someone else. Complaints flowed into Blogger constantly. People were vexed by political blogs, religious blogs, Nazi blogs, blogs that used the words "nigger" and "spic" and "kike" and "retard" and "whitey." Ev realized it would be impossible to police all of the posts that were shared on the site, so as a rule, he opted for an anything-goes mentality.

As Blogger, and the art of blogging, continued to seep into everyday society, Ev started making just enough money, through ads and donations from people who used the site, to gradually hire a small gaggle of programmers. In 2002 they moved into a tiny four-hundred-dollar-a-month space that looked eerily like an old detective office.

By then, Blogger had grown to house nearly a million people's blogs from around the world, with close to ninety million blog posts—both huge numbers in 2002. Yet the "office" was no bigger than a New York City studio apartment: a meager twelve feet by twelve feet. The room was dark and dank. One of the three small white clocks that hung on the wall had stopped ticking a long time ago, looking as if it had simply fallen asleep, the little hand napping on the seven, the large hibernating near the ten.

It soon became apparent that Ev needed an office manager to handle all the mundane tasks, like bills and paychecks and the onslaught of complaints about the content of the site. So he hired Jason Goldman, an already-balding twenty-six-year-old who had studied astrophysics at Princeton University but dropped out for the tech promised land and was now willing to work for the cash-strapped start-up for twenty dollars an hour.

Jason Goldman wasn't the first Jason in the six-person start-up. He was the third. To avoid having three people looking in his direction when he called for one of them, Ev referred to all the Jasons by their last names. Jason Sutter, Jason Shellen, and Jason Goldman were Sutter, Shellen, and Goldman.

"Goldman!" Sutter barked in a playful tone on one of Goldman's first afternoons at work. "You're going to be in charge of the customer-service e-mail."

"What's that?" Goldman responded, peering up at him through his glasses in confusion. "And why are you grinning?" Goldman was tall and wiry with an egg-shaped head. As unstylish as Ev at the time, he often wore clothes a little too wide for his shoulders and pants a little too long for his legs.

"Oh, you'll see. It's the e-mail address we use on the site where people complain about other blogs." Slight laughter came from others in the room as Sutter showed Goldman how to check the account. "Start with that message," he said, pointing to the computer screen. Goldman clicked on the e-mail, which was a complaint from a woman in the Midwest who had come across a blog that she demanded be taken down immediately. He opened the link in the message and his screen was quickly filled with an animated picture of a group of naked men having sex on a trampoline.

"Ahhhh . . . man. . . . What . . . what, what am I supposed to do about this?" Goldman asked with an uncomfortable laugh, as they all giggled. He squinted at the screen, his head half turned away, trying to understand what the men were doing and who, if anyone, would be interested in such bizarreness.

"Nothing," Ev said. "Push-button publishing for the people." It was Blogger's motto and meant that anyone should be able to publish whatever they wanted. There were mugs around the room that declared this statement, brown coffee stains dribbled over big, bold letters that laid out the moral code of Blogger: PUSH-BUTTON PUBLISHING FOR THE PEOPLE. And it was a motto Ev was determined to stand by. In one instance, a coal-mining company in Scotland threatened to sue Blogger if it didn't take down a union blog that was being used to show a coal mine's wrongdoings. Ev always stood his ground, preferring to go out of business rather than to give in to corporate pressure. Eventually, the coal mine gave up.

Blogging had an unintended side effect for Ev. As the company grew, along with other blogging services, Ev was written about in the technology trade press, and he started to grow slightly popular in Silicon Valley. Soon his endless nights on his couch alone with his computer started to change; his personal life started to grow. Just as in his early days with a car in high school, he was now being whisked off to the few tech parties that still existed in the area, hooking up with girls, and drinking beer out of red plastic cups.

Outside the small enclave of the Valley, most people didn't believe in the promise of this weird blogging thing. Some called it "stupid" and "infantile." Others asked why anyone would care to share anything about themselves so publicly.

But not Ev. Ev was determined to see Blogger grow, to allow anyone with a computer to publish anything they wanted. To disrupt the publishing world. To disrupt the world in general. One line of code at a time.

@Noah

Noah Glass almost dropped the issue of *Forbes* when he saw the picture on the page. Like two magnets coming together, he pulled the magazine toward his face and his face toward the magazine, the gravitational pull of curiosity at work.

It was a warm summer afternoon in 2002 and he had been lounging around his apartment, the chatter of traffic and derelicts from Church Street below floating up through the window like an inescapable smell. Flip, flip, flip, through the pages, when he stopped at a profile of a twentysomething man who was behind a burgeoning Web site called Blogger.

As Noah looked at the picture, it wasn't the words that made him almost fall from his chair to the earth. It was the picture of Evan Williams, the Pied Piper of Blogger, proudly posing for the photographer in front of a computer with a bright orange Blogger sticker stuck to the bottom corner of the screen. In the distance, past a smiling Ev, through a window, was a kitchen. The same kitchen that Noah was sitting in at that very moment.

Noah spun around in his chair and held the magazine up in the air, peering through the window and into the apartment directly across the way, where the same exact computer from the magazine sat at the same exact desk in real life. The same orange sticker was stuck to the bottom corner of the screen, and there was the man featured in the article in his hand: Evan Williams, sitting at his desk.

"Whoaaaa, holy shit!" Noah said aloud as a giant smile spread across his face. He stood there for a second, doing a double take between the photo and real life.

The magazine looked particularly small in Noah's hand, given his size. He was large in every way: tall and broad, with a wide, boxy face and droopy eyes like a sad puppy's. And like a puppy, he had the energy of a nuclear power plant.

He quickly opened the back door to his kitchen and rushed out onto the balcony. "Hey. Blogger!" Noah yelled. Ev turned around, confused and a little startled by the noise. "You're Evan Williams, from Blogger, right?" Noah said. "I'm Noah. Noah Glass."

"Yeah, that's me," Ev said cautiously as he walked out onto his balcony.

Noah looked over Ev's shoulder and into the distance of the apartment. Earlier in the summer he remembered seeing as many as five people stuffed into the space, often sitting in the kitchen at computers, working away. A set of servers, which were barely indistinguishable from pizza boxes, sat on the countertop above Ev's kitchen sink powering all of Blogger. But today the makeshift workplace was empty except for Ev.

"Are you blogging? Are you blogging right now?" Noah asked excitedly between their two respective balconies.

"Yes," Ev said, then let out a small burst of laughter. They stood there talking for a while, Noah continually laughing and clapping with amazement, proud that they were neighbors.

At the time, Noah's head was shaved bald. When his hair grew, it was often scraggly and wild, like a surfer who lived on the beach, which is exactly where Noah had grown up. He was born in a small, decrepit house next to an even more decrepit barn that was home to a hippie commune in Santa Cruz, in northern California. His mother and the other commune residents made candles and other trinkets by hand to pay the bills.

His dad left the house for a quart of milk one morning shortly after Noah was born, and he never returned.

The commune life didn't last long, and soon Noah ended up living with his grandparents nearby. One of his relatives, a tough mountain man, took on the role of father figure and directed Noah into adulthood. In one memorable lesson, one of the horses on his grandfather's property kicked Noah's brother in the leg. To teach them how to control such a situation, Noah's relative grabbed a pipe and beat the horse to death. "That's how you stand up for yourself," the man told the boys afterward, the pipe dripping with blood in his hands. Noah just stood there in utter shock. He had a gentle soul and was not wired to be so tough and rugged. He was more artist than revolutionary, often preferring to escape into his creative and zippy mind.

Although Ev was more standoffish and hushed, he was drawn to Noah's effervescent personality, and they quickly became close friends. In an earlier era they could have been an odd-couple TV show, two polar-opposite neighbors who met regularly to share a beer or two on their abutting porches, Noah mostly speaking, Ev mostly listening. Their friendship continued to grow and intertwine, moving from their porches to coffees at nearby cafés, lunches at Barney's Burgers down the street, late-night parties, and before long they spent more time together than apart.

Goldman, who had developed a strong friendship with Ev, often joined them on their outings.

Noah was always glancing out his kitchen window to see if his new friend was home. Sometimes he showed up randomly, knocking on the door erratically—more than once while Ev was enjoying the company of a girl—and turbulently entering the apartment.

Noah was always offering to help too. One afternoon Goldman and Ev were struggling to lug a couch up the stairs of Ev's apartment building. When they stopped to rest for a moment, they turned around to see Noah standing there, pushing them aside, no questions asked, as he dragged the large sofa up through the stairwell practically alone.

Toward the end of 2002 Blogger moved out of its rented detective's office and temporarily back into Ev's apartment. Noah would wake in the morning, sip his coffee by the window, and watch the programmers in Ev's kitchen with admiration. It was something he wanted to be a part of. Sure, Blogger wasn't a traditional start-up: It didn't have a pool table, a fridge full of beer, or rambunctious parties—and people's paychecks sometimes bounced because the company had trouble paying the bills—but Noah yearned to join a group of friends huddling together trying to change the world with code.

Noah had been working from home for nearly two years on a pirate-radio project, hacking together tools that would allow anyone to set up a pirate station subverting government rules and regulations. But he often found himself lonely with no one to talk to about his ideas. Erin, his wife, was often nowhere to be found, attending law school at all hours of the day and night. Noah was like an only child playing alone in a giant sandbox.

Across the way, inside Ev's messy apartment, that wasn't the case.

When Noah arrived at Ev's place, they would listen to music together, sharing this idea for that and that idea for this. Often Ev just watched and smiled, his head moving side to side like a windshield wiper as this animated character paced in his living room discussing concepts that could eventually turn into real things.

As their friendship progressed, Ev confided to Noah why Blogger was now working out of Ev's kitchen and not the office that it had graduated to earlier that year.

"You can't tell anyone," Ev said.

"Of course, of course, I won't!" Noah replied with glee. "I promise."

Ev explained that Google had approached Ev to buy Blogger. There were over one million blogs hosted on Blogger at the time, and Ev was at a crossroads: He could either take investment money from people in Silicon Valley or, if Google really followed through with the deal, sell for "potentially millions of dollars." As the lease to the detective's office had ended, Ev and his employees decided to move back to his apartment before deciding what to do next.

Noah was brimming with pride and excitement at the news. It meant that Ev, who was often so broke he could barely afford to eat, would become so rich he would never have to worry about a meal again. Over the next few months Noah watched Ev anxiously signing papers—with Goldman helping him—waiting to hear if the deal would go through.

Then, on February 15, 2003, he got the call. Evan Williams had found gold. Tens of millions of dollars in ones and zeros.

"The buyout is a huge boost to an enormously diverse genre of online publishing that has begun to change the equations of online news and information," wrote the *San Jose Mercury News* reporter who broke the news of the deal. "Part of that vision, shared by other blogging pioneers, has been to help democratize the creation and flow of news in a world where giant companies control so much of what most people see."

Although Ev wouldn't receive the millions of dollars from the buyout straightaway, he was given a small check to start that was just enough to buy a flashy new Subaru (again, bright yellow). Before he drove away from the car dealership he slapped a square orange Blogger sticker on the rear bumper.

The Blogger team moved to Google's fancy campus, with free food galore, and Ev became famous. At least slightly nerd-famous among an esoteric group of San Franciscans. People started to recognize him at tech events as he was featured in more blogs and news articles.

Noah had since taken his pirate-radio project and refocused it to work with Blogger, writing an application called AudBlog, or audio blogger, that allowed anyone to post voice-based posts to blogs from a phone. Google's acquisition meant more attention for Noah's project too.

Before long, through discussions with friends, Noah decided to turn AudBlog into a start-up, and as soon as Ev started cashing out his Google stock, Noah asked if he would invest a few thousand dollars to help kick-start the idea.

"I'm happy to," Ev said sincerely, "but I really appreciate our friendship and don't want me investing, or us working together, to affect us being friends." After all, Ev had been down this road before, losing all of his friends when Pyra and Blogger had imploded a few years earlier.

"Come on!" Noah said confidently. "We can work together and be friends too."

He finally wore Ev down, convincing him to fork over the money he needed to get started. Noah took off on the project, posting a freelance job listing for a start-up called Citizenware. A few e-mails started to trickle in from programmers applying for the gig, but one stood out. It was from a hacker who knew "Ruby on Rails," a hip new programming language. After a few back-and-forth e-mails, an interview was arranged at a coffee shop in the Mission.

The interviewee introduced himself as Rabble, even though his real name was Evan Henshaw-Plath. He was tall, his head and shoulders leaning forward slightly as a drunk slouches on a pole to keep from falling to the ground. "Tell me about yourself," Noah said, his arms crossed. Rabble explained that he was only in San Francisco for a short time with his fiancée, Gabba, so they could save money to continue traveling and going to political demonstrations and protests around the world. This, Rabble explained, was their "full-time" job. But they were not your traditional protesters: They were hacktivists, part of an emerging group of protesters who used laptops instead of picket signs and blogs instead of bullhorns and who marched down the Internet instead of paved streets. Rabble told Noah he planned to work for only a few weeks, then hit the road again, looking for another protest to join and another way to tell "the man" to go fuck himself. He had just wrapped up assisting protesters involved in the 2004 presidential elections, he explained, and once he saved money from this new gig, he would set out for South America to wreak digital havoc on a government there.

Noah wasted no time talking excitedly about his new audio-blogging project, which was a musiclike service that would make it simple for anyone to make and share podcasts, which could be downloaded to the relatively nascent Apple iPod. Noah also spent a solid part of the interview speaking effusively about Ev, his involvement, and how he was the real deal.

Rabble had a thick, long, reddish beard with strands that seemed, like Rabble, to go in any direction they pleased. As Noah spoke, Rabble listened, caressing his messy whiskers tightly with his left hand—a Rabble trait—moving his fingers downward from his chin like a baker squeezing the last drop of frosting out of an icing bag.

Rabble told more stories of his protests and hacking over the past few years: of Boston, New York, Italy, Seattle; about his assistance with May Day, the anticapitalist riots in London where protesters had constantly evaded police using mobile tools Rabble had helped build. He hadn't actually gone to London, of course, especially after being arrested and deported from Prague for protesting there. Instead he had assisted with May Day from the comfort of a cubicle at Palm, Inc., the maker of the PalmPilot, where he was freelancing, using the company's servers and computers (without his supervisors' knowledge, of course) to cause havoc for the bankers, who used, well, PalmPilots.

Story time was interrupted when Ev showed up. He slid over a chair and sat quietly watching Noah, who became self-conscious and straightened his back. Ev interjected a few times with questions about Rabble's coding skills and work habits. As Ev stood up to leave, he pursed his lips and gave Noah a blasé nod of approval.

Rabble and Noah stayed and talked for a while longer. As they wrapped up, Rabble asked why the new company was called Citizenware.

"Oh," Noah said, pausing momentarily, then leaning forward. "The project is really called Odeo; 'Citizenware' is just a code name," he whispered. "Ev's pretty high profile, so we don't want anyone to know what we're working on."

Rabble left the coffee shop, certain he would be hired for the job, then went home to tell Gabba about the plan. As expected, Rabble's "home" wasn't traditional. The couple lived in a two-hundred-dollar Volkswagen van that was parked on Valencia Street. It had a dented, decaying yellow exterior, where each day the rust spread like an unrelenting ivy.

For the first few weeks the official Odeo office wasn't very official. Coffee shops around the city became the vagabond start-up's makeshift workplaces.

Building a start-up is a lot like building a house, as Noah soon learned, so he recruited more laborers to help. Noah outlined the site's business plan: He was the house's architect. Rabble wrote the back-end code, the equivalent of the house's plumbing and electrical. Then Gabba was recruited to help, building a desktop version of Odeo, essentially the house's driveway and garage; and finally Ray McClure, a small, soft-spoken Flash developer who looked like he was in elementary school, was hired to work on the tools for the Web site—an interior designer, if you will.

At night, after a long day coding, Rabble and Gabba would leave the coffee shop of the day and become invisible as they slowly opened the squeaky door to the van and quietly slipped inside, climbing over a jungle gym of ripped black leather seats and stained carpets. They would sleep on a makeshift bed built of plywood and rusty nails until the sun rose a few hours later, ushering in another day of tireless hacking.

As soon as Ev had managed to off-load all his Google stock, he quit with the goal of never returning to the company, or any like it. The Blogger team had been stuffed into a windowless conference room that was called "Drano" because it was so close to the bathrooms. He didn't fit in with his programmer cohorts, who spent their lunch hours bragging about their degrees from prestigious schools. Those same programmers didn't understand blogging, and Ev soon learned that the acquisition of Blogger was facilitated simply to place ads next to people's blogs, not to try to further the cause of push-button publishing for the people.

But after Google, Ev wasn't anywhere to be found at Odeo, either. He soon semiretired at thirty-two years old. His bank account had gone from a three-figure balance—often barely enough to cover his rent—to double-digit millions of dollars. For Ev, it was time to enjoy the good life, not get involved in another start-up. He began taking Italian cooking classes and exploring museums. He bought a house worthy of a millionaire with wide windows that overlooked San Francisco like a perched owl and a fast new car to put in the millionaire's garage. He went on expensive vacations with his new girlfriend, Sara, whom he had met at Google during an office party.

But while Sara and Ev were becoming proficient in the art of spaghetti making, Noah and his troupe of programmers were toiling away, scrunched in the corners of coffee shops around the city, sitting on mismatched chairs, computer power cords weaving among mugs and torn sugar packets. A modern-day Beatles. Their instruments, laptops; their music, code.

Noah's mind often moved frantically. His thoughts zipped around with the speed of a single firefly trying to light an entire darkened football stadium with its movement. Some thought it could be ADD, ADHD, OCD, or an alphabet soup of all three; it didn't really matter: This was Noah. He had always been this way.

Once, in his late teens, he was picked up by the police in Bakersfield, California, because he was acting erratically. The cops believed he was tripping on mushrooms and methamphetamines. They cuffed him and threw him in a cruiser. Although Noah denied consuming anything more than a few cups of coffee, the police booked him and tested him for every drug imaginable. Then he was stuffed into a jail cell for the night. The next morning the police found Noah in his cell, acting exactly the same as he had been the day before. He hadn't done any drugs; he had been arrested for being Noah.

Every once in a while, Ev would appear in the coffee shop of the day and start asking questions. Noah, who was indebted to Ev for the money that had so far financed Odeo, had no choice but to answer. Before long, that fear of business ruining friendship started to come true.

Eventually band Odeo had moved to Noah's small apartment. It took some convincing to get Noah's wife, Erin, on board, but it would only be temporary, he assured her. She was not timid in showing her displeasure at the fact that her living room now housed a collection of unkempt programmers. (Rabble often sat programming with one hand, scratching his testicles with the other.)

Some mornings, the smell, the hand on the balls, the noise would percolate into a boiling fury for Erin. "Noah, in the bedroom," she would bark. "Now!"

Like a child in trouble for not taking out the garbage, he would follow behind, his head dropped, his heart sad. There would follow a series of shouts from her, apologies from him, her heels banging down the hallway like mallets, the door slamming behind her as she left. He would always reappear in the living room as if nothing had happened, smiling, telling jokes, encouraging everyone to "keep kicking ass!"

As the year drew on, the Web-based podcasting site started to come together, yet the rest of the business quickly began to fall apart. Finances turned into fumes. The apartment situation also worsened, threatening Noah's marriage, and before Noah knew it, he found himself with two options: either stop development of Odeo or ask Ev for more money.

Noah approached Ev again, asking for two hundred thousand dollars to take Odeo from an idea to a real business. Ev agreed to finance more of the project and eventually help secure funding from other venture capitalists, but only on one condition: that Ev become CEO. It wasn't a coup as much as a compromise. For Noah, who was still very much a no-name in tech, it would mean that Ev, well-known and with tech street cred, would now be permanently attached to Odeo. To sweeten the deal, Ev offered to continuing paying the rent for his old apartment, which could become Odeo's first real office.

For Ev it was a paradox. He had no interest in podcasting, but he had started to enjoy the label given to him by bloggers and the media: one of the new up-and-coming tech pioneers who had helped take blogging mainstream. Now here was an opportunity to do the same for podcasting.

It was time for Ev to prove that he wasn't a one-hit wonder. And if

Noah wanted to succeed, to break radio and put it back together again, he knew he needed to let the farm boy from Nebraska run the show.

His hands tied, Noah sadly had no choice but to agree, trading the CEO role at Odeo to Ev for a two-hundred-thousand-dollar investment and keys to Ev's old apartment that he once saw in a picture in *Forbes* magazine.

@Jack

ew people noticed the twenty-eight-year-old man sitting in the window of Caffe Centro coffee shop day after day. People shuffled in to get lunch or wandered by the window outside, but few saw or talked to him. He liked it that way, often preferring to sit with his headphones on, a faint hum of obscure punk music streaming into his ears while his fingers massaged his computer keyboard.

He often looked out of the window, which he had spent most of his life doing. To many people he was one: a clear piece of glass, see-through, an invisible man. He was born with a speech impediment, which made it difficult for him to speak as a child—he was unable to pronounce more than one syllable. "Hello" came out as "hel." "Good-bye" sounded more like a muffled "goo." When people asked his name, rather than reply "Jack Dorsey," he said "Ja." Although he had overcome his speech problem with therapy, it had left an indelible dent in his communication skills.

Jack's inability to talk did have its benefits. In St. Louis, where he was raised, he enjoyed riding around on the city's buses, taking in the vast expanse of the blue-collar neighborhood he lived in, his imagination wandering with each twist and turn. His speech impediment also helped him find one friend: a computer that arrived in his house as he turned eight years old, an IBM PC Junior. He soon fell in love with its monochrome screen and learned to speak to it in code.

On weekends his computer time was interrupted by his mother, Marcia, who would drag Jack and his brothers through the streets of St. Louis in search of the ultimate purse, "the one true bag," as she called it. Jack would sit quietly in the aisles of women's clothing stores while Marcia shopped. There he also started to develop a fascination with bags himself. Rather than opting for purses, though, Jack found comfort in messenger bags.

In San Francisco years later, he wore one daily. A light-colored Filson bag that contrasted with his dark clothing: black T-shirts, zip-up sweaters and jeans, bulky sneakers to match. His shoulders, which sloped down steeply, made his jackets hang on his skinny and lanky frame. He sometimes played with a silver nose ring that hugged his nostril.

He loved that nose ring. At one freelance job a couple of years earlier, where he wrote software for a system that was used to sell tickets to tourists visiting Alcatraz prison, he was told by his employer that he couldn't wear it to work. Rather than take it out, he chose to conceal it under a large beige Band-Aid. As a result he had trouble breathing in the office and often walked around with his mouth agape. He reasoned that it was better to stand up for his right to wear a nose ring and struggle to breathe than to take it out at the behest of his employer.

As he sat in Caffe Centro, his current employer wasn't much better. He was working at a nondescript ticketing company writing low-level code, which felt, to him, like a prison. Whenever possible, he would escape the office with his laptop or sketchbook and wander over to an area of San Francisco called South Park. There he would slip his headphones over his scraggly, dark hair and find refuge among the local cafés and sandwich shops. But this area of the city wasn't just any ordinary park. This was nerd Mecca.

Each day, he spent as much time there as possible. On gloomy afternoons, the glow of his laptop would light his face like a flashlight in a dark basement. Sometimes he sat and sketched in his notepad, staring out the window as bike messengers and start-up founders streamed by. Other times he hung out in the 550-foot-long park, an ovate patch of grass that looked like it belonged in front of the royal palace in London, not in San Francisco's warehouse district. In the center of the park was a rickety old brown swing set.

South Park had played a crucial role in the late nineties as home to many of the now-defunct start-ups that quickly wilted away after the technology bubble burst. Pets.com and other start-ups that had collectively squandered hundreds of millions of dollars on ridiculous parties, asinine salaries, and expensive TV ads met their timely demise overlooking South Park.

It hadn't always been the epicenter of tech. Before the start-ups had moved in, the park had been home to brothels, drug dealers, dive bars, and sordid hotels. After the bubble had gone *pop*, it had almost returned to its Seedyville roots, but in mid-2005 South Park and the Web were making a comeback. To the north side of the park, companies like PCWorld and VideoEgg had started to rent office spaces. To the south, *Wired* magazine, the arbiter of tech cool, had moved into a large, raw loft space. And close by, nestled among the sweet-and-sour backdrop of sports bars and homeless inhabitants, was a small audio-podcasting company called Odeo.

Jack had always been a big fan of routine, so each day when he arrived at Caffe Centro, he sat in the same place, butted up against the window on a rickety wooden chair, able to watch the world float by like a silent movie.

On sunny days he sat in the park, his computer half buried in the grass like a predator as he tried to mooch wireless Internet from a company that left its network open. But as the saying goes, the coldest winter you will ever spend is a summer in San Francisco, which was true on a gloomy June day in 2005 as Jack found himself confined to the great indoors.

He was particularly melancholy on this afternoon as he sat looking out at the sparse park. The life he was living in San Francisco wasn't exactly what he had expected. When he'd left St. Louis years earlier, eventually landing in San Francisco after a stint in New York City working for a bicycle-messenger company, he'd hoped desperately to work for a real start-up, yet he hadn't had much luck.

As he sat calculating how he could get out of his dead-end job, he noticed someone familiar walk by the window. Jack had never actually met the man before, but he recognized that short black hair, the pointed nose, the slightly square stubbly chin, and those signature bright-colored sneakers. There were numerous stories on the Internet about him and the company he had sold for millions of dollars. The man continued to walk past Jack's window, then, to Jack's surprise, he wandered into the café and stood waiting in line to order.

The man didn't notice Jack staring at him, methodically studying his every move; if he had seen the visual intrusion, he might have felt slightly violated. But Jack saw it as a sign and quickly opened his computer, popped open a Web browser, and searched for "Evan Williams e-mail" address in Google.

Jack didn't have a traditional résumé. His most recent CV had been used to apply for a job at Camper, the shoe store. He had spent hours tweaking and designing the red and black lettering, choosing the spiky yet elegant Futura typeface to represent himself. He split his résumé up into three sections: Jack. Life. Love. There was no last name. Just Jack. Camper never offered him the job. But still, he pulled the résumé up on his computer, took out any references to shoes, and sent a near replica to Ev saying that he had just seen him at the café and was he hiring? A few back-and-forth e-mails later, Jack was told to come in for an interview.

Odeo had since stopped using Ev's old apartment in the Mission and now lived in a larger space a few blocks from the park off Third Street. The space was wide and open, but it still had the telltale signs of a scrappy Ev and Noah production.

The desks in the new office were cheap and rickety, with Formica tops and metal legs. (Some of the furniture Ev had purchased from a sidewalk sale of an old church that had closed down.) Although there was a large arched window at one end of the room, it managed to brighten only a few feet of the loft. It was as if the light were afraid to come too close to the grimy Odeo hackers. A small, tattered Oriental rug had been placed on the floor, seemingly to brighten the area. The worst part about the entire space was the shared bathroom down the hall. It smelled so bad that people would place their T-shirts over their faces as they shuffled inside to avoid the vile odor. The stairwell stank too, as it had become an impromptu shelter for a number of homeless people who lived in the area.

When Jack stepped out of the building's creaky old elevator into the Odeo offices, it was eerily quiet. A few scruffy geeks tapped on their keyboards. White IKEA curtains hung from the ceiling to cordon off sections of the large room. Jack was directed to the conference room.

When Ev walked in, he pulled up a chair and began with the usual banal questions about Jack's past employment, where he was from, and how he'd ended up in San Francisco. But before long the interview was interrupted by a series of loud thuds that could be heard coming down the hall. Then the door swung open, slamming into the wall, and a large man came bustling in. "Hey! What's going on, guys?" he said with verve and excitement. "Hey! Hey. I'm Noah!" he said to Jack. "Noah Glass."

Noah was carrying a huge bowl that was brimming with salad; as he charged into the room, pieces of lettuce fell haphazardly from the bowl to the floor. He settled in at the far end of the table, several seats away from Jack and Ev.

"So, you do dispatch?" Noah said to Jack, as though Ev were not there.

Jack, a bit confused by the spectacle, looked over at Ev, who had a strained look on his face. They both peered back at Noah. "Yes, I used to write code on dispatch systems for bike messengers," Jack said.

"That's cool, that's cool," Noah said, nodding his head. "Well, what we do here, that's kind of like dispatch," he said while taking a giant bite from the salad bowl, lettuce hanging from his mouth like fangs. "Yeah, we make sounds, as a podcast, and then"—another pause as his brain calculated what he would say next—"then, these podcasts are dispatched to users!"

Ev stewed silently as Noah rambled. The relationship between the two had become increasingly strained. It was unclear who was making the decisions, and Ev, often the recluse, would sometimes be overshadowed by Noah, who tended to be the most boisterous voice in the room. Of course, Jack didn't know any of this yet.

When the interviewed ended, Jack was introduced to Rabble, who asked a few pertinent questions about his programming skills but really wanted to know his political biases.

While Ev and Noah had been sparring over who made the decisions in the company, Rabble had recruited most of the engineers at Odeo, often hiring friends, typically those who had the same fuck-the-man, hacker mentality that he did. One friend, Blaine Cook, a slim twenty-four-year-old Canadian hacker with long blond hair, had come on board to help with the back-end programming code. Another former hacktivist who had helped with antigovernment protests had also joined, working remotely to help set up the servers that would store all the Odeo podcasts.

Some of Rabble's friends were too antiestablishment even to work for Rabble. When he called one, Moxie Marlinspike, a lanky security researcher and hacker with long, thick, shaggy dreadlocks, he blatantly refused to join the clan. "I'm not working for you fucking dot-coms," Moxie told him.

But given the choice between hiring a hacker and hiring a hack, Rabble always chose the former. On one occasion someone with a corporate background had applied for a job at Odeo. Although Ev wanted to hire him, Noah and Rabble were petrified that he would set up a lot of meetings. ("I don't want to have to go to meetings," Noah had pleaded.)

So Jack, who had tattoos and a nose ring and openly talked about his time in St. Louis spending every waking hour plodding through hacker message boards online, was a perfect fit.

Jack also had an anarchist background. One of his tattoos, on his right leg, was a black and orange star, which was a symbol for an anarchist group. He had been vociferous for years online about his contempt for war and corporations. He'd written about these issues on his own personal Web site, which he called gu.st, and also posted some rants about the perils of capitalism, his disdain for banking institutions, and Americans' thirst for oil. He also frequented message boards promoting feminism.

As Jack walked out of the building, playing the interview back over in his head, he knew he would get the job. Bumping into Ev in the coffee shop was a sign, he thought.

Jack had an uncanny ability to tie moments and things like this together, even if they had nothing to do with each other. His other tattoo was a perfect example of this trait. A black, long blob of ink in the shape of an *S* covered most of his left forearm, but underneath there was a hidden story. Under the dark, curvy *S*, the tattoo had originally read, "0daemon!?"

The meanings of the tattoo were endless. The word "daemon," he explained, refers to a computer program that lives in the background. To Jack, this signified what he saw in himself, a person who lived "behind the curtain" and had little influence. The exclamation mark on the tattoo was meant to show his excitement for life. The question mark, his level of curiosity with the world. He also had chosen to have the word placed on his arm upside down.

But that tattoo had since been covered up. He'd explored multiple career paths and at one point worked as a massage therapist. While people had lain half naked on his massage table, peering up at his arm, they had thought "daemon" had actually said "demon," and that Jack the masseuse was into devil worship. Needless to say, most people had come for a massage only once.

Jack was hired as a freelancer almost immediately and fit into the culture of Odeo seamlessly. He had a hacker mentality, no degree, and a love for programming. He also had a solid work ethic and completed any given task with speed and accuracy.

He had learned to program young, helping his father, Tim, with work-related projects. As a child, rather than ask for toy guns or cars, Jack had stared longingly at RadioShack fliers, cutting out clippings to hang in his room of the calculator he wanted to get as a Christmas gift. He had also dabbled in his own fair share of hacking, once getting a job in New York City by breaking into a company's Web site to show how vulnerable it was. Jack programming the Odeo Web site was like a seasoned car mechanic fixing a lawnmower.

Still, he was methodical in his work. His headphones would go on, a programming book spread open on his desk, and code would start raining down from his computer monitor. Before long he began winning the Getting Shit Done Award, a contest that Ev set up to reward the hardest worker of the week. On Fridays a hat would be passed around the office and everyone would drop in the name of the most productive employee of the week. After Ev and Noah tallied the votes, the winner would be announced.

"The Getting Shit Done Award goes to . . . ," Ev would say, pausing for dramatic effect, "Jack!" Then people would clap and Jack would smile, brimming with pride as he stood up to accept his reward. Some prizes were monetary; others were gadgets.

Though most people in the office liked Jack, they weren't shy about telling him his ideas were a bit strange. He was always experimenting with peculiar concepts. One day he showed up to work with a white T-shirt that had his cell-phone number sewn onto the front in giant, dark numerals. He explained to a coworker that it was an experiment. He planned to walk around the streets of San Francisco with his phone number on display like a walking billboard, waiting for people to call. Although most people ignored the walking number, a few people decided to dial it.

"Hello?" one person said.

"Hello," Jack replied, monotone.

"Who is this?"

"This is Jack. Who is this?"

The conversations soon devolved into the awkward banter that is usually reserved for the moment you run into an ex on the street. Needless to say, the calls ended quickly.

Jack had done similar bizarre experiments before joining Odeo. In 2002, in his early twenties, he had become enamored with eBay. At the time, he was destitute and didn't have anything to sell, so he set up auctions where he offered to read the famous children's book *Goodnight Moon* over the phone to the highest bidder. He somehow managed to sell his reading service to four different people—one of whom paid one hundred dollars to listen to Jack, a perfect stranger, read. "Goodnight clocks and goodnight socks," he said into the phone. "Goodnight little house and goodnight mouse." He finished, "Goodnight stars. Goodnight air. Goodnight noises everywhere."

Yet even with his proclivity for weirdness, he quickly bonded with several of his new coworkers. Most nights he would venture out with Noah, Ray, and a few other Odeo programmers, exploring the city on bikes together or sometimes setting out on foot. They would dip in and out of clubs, music shows, and hookah lounges or go on unmethodical explorations of the city's wine bars, sake dens, and art galleries. Almost every morning was met with a hangover.

But for now, Jack had found what he had spent his life looking for. A job with someone he looked up to: Ev. A group of coworkers who had a hacker spirit: Rabble and company. And a new friend: Noah.

@Biz

It was early October 2005 when Biz Stone sat down in a small conference room with his boss at Google. The company's logo was spelled out in bright blue, yellow, green, and red letters on the wall behind him, as if it belonged in a kid's play den. Red beanbag chairs sat close by. Biz's smile seemed appropriate in the room's festive atmosphere as his tousled blond hair fluttered atop his head.

"I'm quitting!" Biz said with a giant grin.

His boss looked at him, unsure if Biz, the Google jester, was joking or serious.

"Nope," Biz continued. "I'm quitting."

"You don't care about money?" his boss asked.

"Yes. I *do* care about money."

"Biz, you do realize that if you quit now you have to give up all your stock options?" his boss said. He reminded him that he had only been at Google for two years, which meant his stock had not vested and wouldn't for another two years.

"How much am I leaving on the table?" Biz asked.

"More than two million dollars," his boss said, confident that such a number would sway the young employee's decision. For most people two million dollars or zero dollars was an easy financial equation. It was for Biz too. He just did the math a little differently.

Biz was far from rich. He had finally paid off fifty thousand dollars in credit-card debt he had been battling for years and was now living month to month in a small Palo Alto apartment with his wife, Livia, and their ark of rescued dogs and cats.

Yet having zero dollars in the bank, while he worked at Google—where even the chef was worth several million dollars—wasn't a new experience for Biz. That was, after all, exactly how he had been raised: poor among the rich.

He had grown up in Wellesley, an affluent suburb of Boston, where the town's median family income was well into the six figures. Though Biz's neighbors were often absurdly wealthy, the Stone family's life was rather different.

Biz was raised on food stamps.

His mother had been adopted by a kind Swiss couple as a child, and when they passed away, their large house was left to Biz's mother and her children.

Feeding several hungry mouths was difficult as a single mother, so she developed a plan: Sell the house they owned every few years and downgrade to a smaller place in Wellesley. This way her children could take advantage of the county's fancy schools, and they could use the money from the house sale to pay the bills. Four years later, do it all again. Sell and downgrade.

So Biz was raised in houses that shrank as he grew. Everything was rationed. Haircuts, for example, happened at home, with his mother placing a round bowl atop his mopey head and snipping anything that hung below the edge.

As a boy, Biz was a little idea generator. On weekends he would often visit a family friend who was an electrician, and he spent hours in the man's basement building strange gizmos. In one instance, Biz rigged a doormat with a buzzer that blared when someone came to the front door. Another endeavor, which failed, was an attempt to build his own scuba gear out of Coke bottles and rubber tubes.

But most of Biz's time was spent with his best friend from third grade, Marc Ginsberg, whose father was wealthy enough to own a computer. Biz spent days on end at Marc's house, staring through his round Coke-bottle glasses as he used the Ginsberg family's Apple II machine, playing video games and drawing on the built-in graphics program.

As Biz grew up, his father, a Boston car mechanic, turned absentee and on the rare occasions he did come home he would spiral into a drunken rage on Biz's mother—on more than one occasion she ended up in the hospital. She eventually kicked him out of the house, and he was only allowed to see his kids on Sundays; Biz decided to stop the weekly visits soon after his sixteenth birthday.

Such a traumatic upbringing would normally turn a young boy into a recluse, maybe someone who needed decades of therapy. But not young Christopher "Biz" Stone. No, it made Biz into a complete and utter goofball. From early on he was cracking jokes to make his mom and sisters feel better after one of his father's drunken tirades. He was the class clown in high school. He dropped out of college twice, from Northeastern University and from the University of Massachusetts, but while at each school he spent his time making his university friends laugh, rather than focusing on homework. The jokes continued into every meeting at Google.

While Biz's sense of humor helped him in his career and in social settings, the jokes were also used to avoided conflict at all costs, which allowed people to take advantage of him at times, especially in the workplace. Between 1999 and 2001 he worked at a blogging network called Xanga. His coworkers there walked all over him as they took the company in a direction Biz thought was unethical by deceiving people who used the service and harvesting private information about them for profit. Rather than stand up and fight, Biz chose to quit.

After racking up bills and hanging out in his mother's basement, he eventually went in search of a job at Blogger. At that time, in the summer of 2003, Ev had been working at Google for a few months, trying to settle into the giant company. Biz had read about Ev and his "push-button publishing for the people" philosophy and wanted to help spread the word about blogging too.

In mid-2003 Biz sent Ev an e-mail to say that he, Biz Stone, was the "missing member of the band." After a few phone interviews, some jokes, and ethical discussions of the importance of blogging and how it allowed anyone with a computer to publish content, Ev decided he wanted to hire Biz. But Google didn't feel the same way; Biz had no programming experience and was a college dropout. It took some convincing and politicking, but Ev was finally able to offer him the job.

After Biz received the offer letter from the search giant, the deal almost crumbled. At some point in his childhood, Biz had developed an inordinate fear of flying. He would go between Boston and New York City only on a multihour train or bus ride, rather than hop on a short fifty-minute flight. When he realized he would have to fly out to Mountain View, he declined without giving the real reason. Google, which at first had said no, did not like to be turned down, and the company kept adding money and stock options to woo him. When Biz explained the situation to a friend, the friend replied with one simple word: "Valium."

"What's that?" Biz asked.

"Let's just say you won't be afraid of flying."

He accepted the job and popped a giant, round antianxiety pill as he boarded the plane. On the flight, half-dazed and half-ecstatic that he had "overcome" his phobia of flying, he spent most of time slurry and chatting excitedly with any passenger who would listen to him.

Biz's jovial mentality became apparent to Google executives the moment he officially started at the company. He didn't just come to Google and slip into the company's culture of quiet and insular engineers. Instead, Biz held his own ticker-tape parade in the form of a fake press release on the Internet to announce his new job.

"Google Inc. has acquired the entire staff and some of the intellectual property of Genius Labs, a Boston-based blogging entity comprised entirely of Biz Stone," he wrote on his personal Web site on October 7, 2003, in a post titled "Google Acquires Genius Labs." "Financial terms of the deal were not disclosed." He concluded his fake release with a joke at his new employer's expense. "Google's free snack and coffee program has drawn accolades from industry elite and their innovative search technologies are also very nice."

When he arrived at the search engine, his comic routines saw him shuffle between bosses. Like Ev, Goldman, and the rest of the Blogger team, Biz often felt out of place amid the company's cutthroat, business-like mentality. Like a group of unpopular kids at school, the Blogger misfits would eat together in the company's cafeterias, drink in their own corner during the company's weekly Friday addresses, and crack jokes at the expense of the straitlaced programmers.

Ev wasn't like any traditional boss Biz had worked under before. When Ev hired someone new, rather than wait to trust them with confidential information or important tasks, he chose to trust them immediately. Biz felt a sense of confidence and pride that Ev treated him this way, and the bond between the two quickly tightened. Before long, fueled by their collective comic relief, Biz, Ev, and Goldman became best friends.

After Ev left Google in 2004, Biz was miserable, as his new bosses at Google didn't trust him or treat him with respect. So in 2005 he decided he had had enough and wanted to follow Ev to his next project. This came with a conundrum: He would have to leave millions of dollars on the shiny Google table in order to take a new job at the grimy podcasting start-up Odeo, working with Ev again and his new, wacky business partner, Noah.

"We didn't move out to California so I could work at Google," Biz told Livia as they discussed the millions of dollars they would be throwing away. "We moved out here so I could work with Ev."

Given how close their friendship had grown over the past two years, the decision was easy. He went into work the following day and turned over his white Google employee ID, and the money that came with it, in exchange for the freedom of start-up life.

When he started at Odeo on September 6, 2005, he quickly realized it was a much bigger change than he had anticipated. His unlimited free meals, free snacks, free buses to work, and free inexhaustible everything at Google were now replaced with an office where homeless people slept in the stairwell, the only free transportation was his two feet, and the only free food or drink was a beer after work if Ev picked up the tab.

The cultural difference was incalculable. The sterile, robotic culture of Google, with its know-it-all engineers and bossy bosses, was now replaced with tattooed hackers with a do-what-you-want mentality. A group of people who had nothing but disdain for the Googlers of the world, who made a point to always tout their degrees from Stanford and MIT, the Odeo employees were all dropouts from midtier colleges.

And Biz, working alongside his best friend and former boss, among the homeless people and the chaos, the grime and grunge, felt right at home.

II.

#NOAH

Troubled Waters

It was late 2005 as the boat emerged from the thick fog and the Odeo employees looked out at the view. The Golden Gate Bridge glowed orange in the distance as the sails clanked against the mast as the wind thrust them forward.

"We're about to head to the Tiburon Marina," Ariel Poler, one of the Odeo investors, said as he steered his boat through the salty air and across the San Francisco Bay. "Sam's is open; that's excellent," he added, squinting into the distance.

Noah was hyperactively filming as he interrogated his coworkers for another short video he would later post to his blog. He butted the lens of the camera up against people's faces like a child showing off a lollipop. "Tell us about it?" Noah asked Biz, looking for a play-by-play of the relatively uneventful boat outing.

"It's good. We didn't lose anyone on the way over here, but maybe on the way back, one or two guys," Biz said to the camera, scrunched up to keep warm as the wind scraped across his orange jacket. Ev, who was sitting to his right, his eyes concealed behind his dark sunglasses, said, "We can afford to lose one."

Ev was joking, mostly. Although he wouldn't throw him over the side of the boat, Ev would have happily thrust Noah over the rails of Odeo.

Ev and Noah were at odds on almost everything. The colors of logos.

The type of products they should focus on. Who was in charge. They couldn't even agree on when to open Odeo to the public.

"No. It's not ready!" Ev had said one afternoon earlier in the year, shaking his head from side to side as Noah tried to negotiate with him. "I'm telling you, I'm CEO; I've done this before; I don't want to put the site up yet!"

Rabble and Ray, the young Flash designer who had been hired while Odeo was working out of coffee shops, leaned back in their chairs to get comfortable for the next Noah-versus-Ev debate. Ev wasn't ready to announce his new disruption to the world just yet. He had always had a difficult time making decisions and pressing the final launch button. Noah, brimming with excitement and eagerness, had not.

Unbeknownst to them, the winner of this debate wouldn't count. Rabble decided. "It's live," Rabble told them, a mischievous grin on his face, his chaotic hair pulled back in a ponytail. Ev and Noah continued to bicker. Again Rabble told them, "It's live, guys," now speaking up to ensure that they stopped talking. "I just turned the site on."

They stopped arguing and looked over at him. Noah smiled from ear to ear. "No way!" he said. Ev just shook his head.

The site they had just unintentionally launched hoped to be the Web's central destination for podcasts. It would allow people to create and record audio files, then share them with other people on the Web using an Adobe Flash–based widget called Odeo Studio. All of this would be completely free.

With Ev's name attached to the company, Odeo had received press and awareness throughout 2005 that had brought the attention of investors, including Ariel Poler, who presumed that podcasting could become a competitor to radio, just as blogging had done to publishing. In August 2005, with no business model, Odeo had received five million dollars in funding from Charles River Ventures and a number of other smaller investors—a bet on podcasting and Ev, not necessarily on the company or the people working for it.

With a slew of money in the bank to hire new engineers and take the company in any number of podcasting-related directions, Noah and Ev hadn't been able to agree on anything. As the first month flush with cash had passed, Noah had started complaining to the board, calling George Zachary, the lead investor in Odeo, to voice his displeasure with Ev's lack of leadership and inability to make decisions. On several occasions Noah had tried to stage a mutiny and suggested that the board remove Ev as CEO and install Noah as the new captain. Ev, who had an aversion to conflict, decided to deal with the contention by simply ignoring it. On most days he skipped going into the office altogether, rather than face the wrath of frenetic Noah.

"Who would you lose? Who could you afford to lose the most?" Noah asked Biz and Ev on the boat as they floated through the chilly water, smiling, as he already knew the answer.

"Oh, that's a tough choice," Biz said as he looked over at Ev, who didn't answer.

"Probably me," Noah said sarcastically, then flipped the camera around to document his own face, his broad smile filling the frame, buglike sunglasses wrapped around his eyes. "Probably me, probably me," he said, laughing slightly.

Biz and Ev didn't disagree.

Noah set off like a rogue Ping-Pong ball, bouncing around the boat to film everyone else.

Jack was standing on the bow in a uniform of denim—dark jeans and a matching jean jacket. His messy, dark hair slapped around in the wind as he stood daydreaming. He loved to sail, and the day trip reminded him of an earlier goal he had set for himself, to soon buy a boat and skipper it, alone, to Hawaii: a 2,400-mile journey that, according to his research, would take about a month.

As Ariel's boat slowed at the dock, the group stepped onto the rustic planks, stretching their legs and collectively looking like a giant caterpillar waking from a nap.

Although this was the first boat outing for the Odeo crew, it was another field trip for a small group of mismatched employees who, for a brief moment, were becoming close friends—at least some of them were.

As on most of their excursions, alcohol would be used to help lubricate the afternoon's conversation. They soon found themselves rocking back and forth on the white plastic chairs outside Sam's Anchor Cafe, seagulls sniping at their food. They sipped glasses of wine, telling nerdy jokes and laughing at one another.

Jack sat quietly listening. He never really said much. When he did speak, it was in two- or three-syllable sentences, as if he were rationing how much he could say aloud during a single day. It wasn't clear anyone would have listened to him anyway. He was, after all, one of the most junior people at Odeo. The deckhand on a boat; a lowly private in the army; a contract programmer at a start-up. Although Ev rarely interacted with Jack, he referred to him in the office as "the idea guy" because of his wacky concepts. Some were totally bizarre, like his suggestion to create a start-up that would allow programmers to team up and work together, but not in a traditional way. The idea was that while one person wrote code, the other programmer would massage his or her shoulders; then they would switch.

Jack often told his coworkers about a new movie, book, or album they should watch, read, or listen to or about an upcoming art show or party they could all attend, helping sew together friendships between his office mates.

Often, though, Jack would simply sit quietly, absorbed in his own thoughts. But his daydreaming inevitably hit a dead end as the group of beer-sipping geeks' conversation quickly arrived at its final destination: work. This was often the case. Breakfasts, lunches, dinners, drinks, dancing in clubs were often punctured by work-related chatter.

It was these conversations—Noah, Ev, Biz, Rabble, Jack, and a handful of other Odeo engineers talking about the past and the future—where a potion started to stir together that would ultimately transform the podcasting company, which was going nowhere, into one that would change the world and all of the people gathered on the dock at Sam's that day.

At times Ev and Biz talked about their days at Blogger and how people used the service to share news. To tell stories. To disrupt media.

On one of the group's outings, Rabble and Blaine shared tales of their hacker days using mobile phones to help antiwar and antigovern-ment demonstrations evade the police. Noah talked about pirate radio stations. Jack mentioned his days as a bike messenger.

Others discussed competitors, including Dodgeball, a location-based messaging service that had started to gain a lot of traction in New York City.

Jack took it all in, processing the ideas he heard and he sat silently, as usual. But that was all about to change in the office. There was a new Odeo employee starting the following week.

A girl.

"Oh, that's Crystal," Jack was told when he asked about the woman in the office. "Not gonna happen; she has a boyfriend." Still, Jack was immediately smitten. And understandably so. Crystal Taylor had pin-straight black hair, deep welcoming eyes, and a smile that could stop traffic. Her slight frame made her seem like a pixie from a children's fairy tale.

During her first week at Odeo, Jack made endless excuses to talk to her. He would stand nervously fidgeting with something on her desk, staring at her at lunch, awkwardly playing with his nose ring. He even-tually picked up the courage to ask Crystal what kind of music she was listening to on her headphones. The conversation quickly led to the type of bands they both enjoyed, and Crystal asked him if he wanted to join her and a group of friends to see a show.

"Yeah, I'd love to," Jack said, excited, nervously peering away from her. "I'll call you later to figure out where to meet."

"Call me?" Crystal said, confused. "I don't really use the phone. Can you just text me?"

"Umm, what's a text?" Jack asked, slightly embarrassed.

"Um, text messages, helloooooo? You've never used text before?"

In today's age, such a conversation might be like asking someone if they had ever heard of the Internet, or cars, or this giant ball of fire in the sky called the sun. But in 2005, although it had taken off in other countries and with teenage girls in the United States, text messaging was a relatively esoteric form of communication for most of America.

"No," Jack said solemnly. "I've never heard of texting. What is it?"

"Here, let me show you," Crystal told him as he stood nervously watching her explain how to send an SMS from a phone with a tiny two-inch black-and-white screen, a form of communication that until then had been lost on Jack but had spread in the rest of society like an epidemic that afflicted only girls with cell phones.

Jack was a quiet engineer at the time, and with his Raggedy Andy hair and fear of face-to-face communications he had not had the opportunity to interact with too many girls, most of whom texted. That was, until he met Crystal.

Although she told him she had a boyfriend, Jack was obsessed. He soon found out she liked juice, so at lunchtime he would show up with a bottle and place it on Crystal's desk to surprise her. But when that didn't garner much response, his head hanging, he tried one of his signature moves with the ladies: making the perfect origami crane.

He had first learned how to make the perfect paper version of the long-necked and long-tailed bird after he decided to craft one thousand of them as a gift for a friend's wedding. He had meticulously folded each one, on his own, until he was so perfect at crane making that he could do it from memory with his eyes closed. He decided such a gift was now worthy of Crystal.

One morning he rushed into the office early and placed a crane on her keyboard. He then slyly sat at his desk, silently pretending to work when she arrived with her cup of Tully's coffee to be met by a little paper bird staring up longingly from her computer. At first Crystal put the crane to the side, smiling at it and moving on with her day. Then she received another the next day. And another the day after that, until finally she grew upset at Jack's relentless passes, especially given that she had a boyfriend.

"You don't need to get me juice," she said to Jack as she stormed over to his desk, reminding him that she was in a relationship. "And it's really sweet that you're putting the cranes on my keyboard, but you can stop now."

"Did you see which letter I put them on?" Jack said excitedly, almost ignoring her request to respect her boundaries. She had not seen that the cranes had each been placed on different letters, which were going to spell out her name. "No!" she said, annoyed, and turned around to leave. But he pressed on, determined that something would eventually happen with Crystal.

He was more successful with the friendships he forged with his coworkers.

With each social event, flocks were being shaped, people bonding like some sort of strange chemical concoction separating and coagulating back together again. At one end of the spectrum there was the Blaine and Rabble posse, sticking to their anarchistic, antieverything mentality. At the other end were Ev and Biz, dinner-party mavens who enjoyed a quiet evening of wine around a long wooden table. And in the middle were Noah, Jack, Crystal, and the rest of the mess, who soon became an inseparable group of friends. Sometimes they went to music shows together or foreign films. To wine bars and dive bars. For long walks and short bike rides. They were best-friend club kids who enjoyed drinking sake out of square boxes and dancing long into the night to music that sounded like a fax machine.

Although the groups sometimes overlapped, with Noah going to Ev's parties and Ev getting beers with Noah, they mostly kept to their own boats in the same waters. And although they didn't know it yet, the waters they were in were about to become even more fraught with mayhem and chaos. These waters would eventually see half of the crew of the HMS *Odeo* thrown overboard.

Status

I think I'm going to leave Odeo," Jack said as Noah pulled his car over to the side of Valencia Street. The rain was falling so heavily against the window that it sounded like buckets of marbles slamming against the glass. As the car came to a stop, the street was completely desolate. A faint blue light hovered on the stereo, reminding them both it was approaching 2:00 A.M. and sleep deprivation followed by the usual intense hangover would greet them in a few short hours when they awoke.

It was late February 2006 and they were nearing the end of another long night of dancing, vodka and Red Bulls, and long conversations about love, loss, and loneliness.

Noah's relationship with his wife, Erin, was breaking apart. She was a lawyer and he was an artist: two fundamentally different outlooks on life. The foundation of their marriage was caving in on itself, and he had confided to Jack how lonely and sad he felt. Jack could relate. Although he had friends in San Francisco, he was lost too, half punk rocker, half engineer, with dreams of sailing and hopes that Crystal might still fall in love with him. Or that he could quit his computer life altogether.

"What do you want to do?" Noah asked as he looked out at the empty street, the stench of vodka soaking his breath.

"I'm going to quit tech and become a fashion designer," Jack said. "Plus, Odeo is a fucking mess." No one who worked there even used it, Jack noted.

Noah sighed, unable to argue with the statement. He had been trying to get people to use Odeo more, setting up Ev's old beige couch in the center of the room for employees to spew platitudes into a microphone. But the mics just sat there, ignored, relics of the past inside a company that was trying to reinvent the future.

Jack's statement that the company was a fucking mess went beyond the sad reality that none of the employees of Odeo were actually using the service they were building. There were far bigger problems.

For one, the tension between Ev and Noah had worsened. The personality conflicts between the two had boiled over on several occasions, erupting in the office for all to see.

"I should be running this fucking company," Noah had barked at Ev in front of employees more than once. "I could do a much better job than you! You don't know what the fuck you're doing." Ev's aversion to conflict resulted in his simply standing there and taking it, trying to calm his turbulent cofounder with silence but often ending up pummeled by one of Noah's tirades. The investors were in a tizzy too, not sure who was running the company, an absent Ev or an erratic Noah, and petrified that the five million dollars they had invested in Odeo to build a site that could be the central hub of podcasts on the Web was about to slip away into the start-up sewers.

The only thing Noah and Ev had been able to agree upon over the past several months was the move to a new, large street-level office at 164 South Park, just off the park.

But the cofounders' spats were only one aspect of the drama at Odeo. The other element was the anarchist culture that had been in the DNA of Odeo since day one, special thanks to the hackers who had been hired to program the Web site. Rabble and Blaine had been labeled "the Anarchists" in the office, a name they proudly answered to, as their lawlessness could not be controlled.

Attempts to quell the chaos often went nowhere.

One of the more corporate employees, Dom Sagolla, had been hired in October 2005 to help test new podcasting products. He had previously worked at the software giant Adobe and often used corporate jargon at Odeo, trying his best to help institute some organization. In one effort he created a grid of index cards on the wall near his desk. The top row listed all the employees' names, then, trickling down, more index cards listed each person's designated tasks for the week. As soon as Dom stepped away from his desk, engineers would slyly walk by, kneel over pretending to tie a shoelace or pick something up, and switch the cards around, placing jobs they didn't want to do under someone else's name.

A daily morning "stand-up" meeting was scheduled by Tim Roberts, a vice president at Odeo. Yet two people always remained seated: Rabble and Blaine. "I'm not standing at your fucking meetings," Rabble blared when asked to get up out of his chair with everyone else.

The Anarchists defied any directive. One morning Tim decided to one-up them and announced that stand-up meetings would now be "sit-down meetings, and everyone should take a seat." As the dozen employees grabbed chairs and settled in for the morning meeting, Blaine and Rabble, without skipping a beat, stood up and proudly remained standing. Everyone else, now seated, started giggling at them.

But worse than the anarchy inside was the fact that Apple Computer had recently torn a hole in the hull of the company.

On a Tuesday morning several months earlier, Odeo employees had gathered around their computers to watch Steve Jobs, the venerable CEO of Apple, announce the latest iPod.

But stunned silence had enveloped them when Jobs declared that Apple was adding podcasts to iTunes. At the end of the announcements, the tech giant sent a brief press release across the news wires with the ominous headline, APPLE TAKES PODCASTING MAINSTREAM. In that brief moment podcasting, which had been the entire company thesis for Odeo, had become a simple add-on for Apple. Ev had known almost immediately that this was a fatal blow for Odeo. How could they beat Apple, which owned iTunes, the biggest music service in the world, at podcasting? They couldn't. It would be like a tricycle racing a Formula One race car.

None of this needed to be discussed in the car that night, as the rain fell and the smell of alcohol lingered in the air. Noah continued to talk about the past few months as Jack sat silently staring at the desolate street. This was how most affairs between the two worked: Noah talking enthusiastically, while Jack responded in monosyllables. "So what excites you?" Noah asked again. "What do you want, *really* want, to do?"

"I want to go into fashion," Jack said quietly. "I want to make jeans."

"Okay, great, we're getting somewhere. Tell me what else you're interested in," Noah said. "What else do you want to do?"

Although Jack and the others didn't know it, Ev had been talking to Noah about shutting everything down, throwing in the dirty Odeo towel. Ev was tired and saw no solution for Odeo. But Noah was trying desperately to sift ideas out of the employees to save the company. Or at least the people in it.

Jack listed a few items he liked, including music, sailing, and programming. Then he mentioned his "status" concept.

Several months earlier, Jack had raised the idea with Crystal and Noah on one of their drunken outings. He'd originally come up with it in early 2000 when he was living in a dingy building called the Biscuit Factory, situated in a deep, dangerous part of Oakland.

At the time, Jack had been using a blogging service called LiveJournal, which was a competitor to Blogger. One of the features LiveJournal offered was the ability for people to show small status messages on their blogs to say what they were doing at that moment. Most bloggers used the feature to write pithy updates about themselves.

The idea of displaying a status on a computer had come into the public light in 1997 when AOL introduced its instant-messenger service. The company had come across a unique challenge at the time with the way people communicate: How do you let others know that you have stepped away from your computer when they can't actually see you? The solution was a feature AOL called the "away message." In a small snippet of text, people could note if they were available, in a meeting, or just busy, so their online friends knew their whereabouts. When teens started using the "away" feature, they took a different approach, often typing in their mood or the music that was currently playing on their computer. Soon nerds like Jack, Crystal, and Noah were copying teenagers and also making their away messages reflect the music they were listening to.

Unable to sleep one night in the Biscuit Factory, Jack had thought about the quickly evolving status genre, which he was now using with his LiveJournal blog, and wondered if it could be sifted out to be its own Web site. He had gotten out of bed and begun taking notes on the concept, even building a very crude prototype.

Now, six years later, sitting in the car with Noah, he again mentioned the concept of a one-off site that people could use to share their current status. "You could say what music you're listening to," Jack said, "or tell people you're at work."

Noah had always thought that Jack's idea sounded very clinical. The updates, like Jack's voice, sounded too brief and monotone to Noah. The idea also sounded similar to Dodgeball, which had launched in 2000 and allowed people to share their location with friends by text message. Plus, there was Facebook, which was starting to circulate through college campuses.

Noah stared out the window, processing. The alcohol was starting to wear off. He thought about Erin and their failed marriage. About Crystal and how he wished she were there with him and Jack in the car. A part of him also wanted Ev there; he yearned for the friendship he had lost. He wished they could all be there together, sharing in melancholic talk of loss and failure amid the rain and the empty street, and then it hit him. "I get it!" Noah exclaimed.

This status thing could help connect people to those who weren't there. It wasn't just about sharing what kind of music you were listening to or where you were at that moment; it was about connecting people and making them feel less alone. It could be a technology that would erase a feeling that an entire generation felt while staring into their computer screens. An emotion that Noah and Jack and Biz and Ev had grown up feeling, finding solace in a monitor. An emotion that Noah felt night after night as his marriage and company fell apart: loneliness.

It was the same sentiment that had driven Ev to feel so passionate about Blogger, sitting there in his apartment, alone, with no friends, able to connect to the world through his keyboard. It was the reason Biz had started blogging from his mother's basement years ago. The same reason Jack had started a LiveJournal account in St. Louis, spending hours alone in coffee shops talking to people who lurked on message boards, all looking for connections. This status idea could be the antidote to all of this, a cure for feeling lonely, Noah thought.

"What if it had audio!" Noah said with excitement. "Or what if"—he paused—"it was text messaging instead of e-mail?" Ideas sprang into view. "What if . . . What if . . . What if . . ."

Jack started to grow excited by the suggestions too. He proposed integrating the idea into Odeo: voice-based status updates. "Maybe it would work if there was the ability to attach an audio file," Jack said. Then more "what ifs."

"Let's talk to Ev and the others about this tomorrow," Noah said as Jack got out of the car to stagger home. Then he peeled off into the wet night, his mind buzzing with a vision for the future.

On February 27, 2006, a Monday, they both hobbled into work, heads pounding from a night of very little sleep. Noah immediately dragged Ev and Biz into a conference room to tell them about his drunken discussion with Jack the night before. Jack watched Noah explain the "status thing" to Ev and Biz.

"It lines up with the other things we've been talking about!" Noah proclaimed.

They had known since January that Odeo was not going to work. Although people had signed up for the site, they rarely returned. Ev and Noah's bickering had stalled any new product developments, leaving them in a perpetual stalemate. Then Apple's entering the podcasting fray had placed one hundred nails in the Odeo coffin. Still, Ev and Noah had known they had to do something, so they'd held a number of meetings with Jeremy LaTrasse, a senior Odeo engineer, and Tim Roberts to try to find a new direction for the dying company—or possibly even scrap the entire company and start anew.

Changing the focus of a start-up is not like the metamorphosis of a traditional business—like trying to turn a high-end clothing store into a construction company. Instead it is more akin to altering the type of food a restaurant serves. Although the cuisine the customers are served changes, sometimes drastically, the same chefs and waitstaff can be used to make and serve it. Or, in Odeo's case, the same programmers, designers, and managers.

The meetings had often taken place at Ev's apartment, where, sitting at his kitchen table, Jeremy, Tim, Noah, and Ev would sip beers and endlessly throw out suggestions for what to do next.

Ev's worst fear was about to be realized: Odeo was going to fail, which meant Ev, the blogging phenomenon, was actually a one-hit wonder. But he reasoned that if he could pivot Odeo into something else, he could save his name in Silicon Valley.

"What if we killed the audio part of Odeo?" Ev had suggested a few weeks earlier. "Or what if we make it a messaging platform, where you can leave a message for a group of friends to hear?" The conversations about the reinvention of Odeo had been focused on the concept of friends following one another on a messaging platform. The big question Ev, Noah, Jeremy, and Tim were unable to answer in those discussions was what these groups of people would actually want to share with one another. This was where Jack's status idea fit perfectly.

When Biz heard the concept, it reminded him of an idea he had been obsessed with at Google. He had owned a phone called a Treo at the time, which had a crude black-and-white screen and was half Palm-Pilot, half cell phone. He had started suggesting to coworkers that Google should build its own "Phone-ternet."

"What the hell is a Phone-ternet?" people would reply.

"It's like an Internet, but for your phone!" Biz told those who would listen. "Get it? Phone plus Internet. Phone-ternet?" People just rolled their eyes.

But now, hearing about Jack's status concept—mixed with mobile phones, groups of friends, and Noah's human explanation of it all—Biz, like Ev, was smitten.

As the meeting wrapped up, Noah had to run to take a phone call, and Ev quickly gave Jack and Biz their orders. "Look," Ev said as he leaned in to the table and began to whisper to his employees. "I like this idea, but I don't want Noah getting distracted by something else." He continued in a low tone. "So I want you two to go off and quietly start working on sketches for this status thing. But don't tell anyone," Ev said to Jack and Biz, who were now talking enthusiastically about their secret assignment. "And don't let Noah get too involved."

But it was too late. The idea had been planted in Noah's mind. The idea had been planted in all of their minds. And together they were about to build something that would change their lives forever.

Twitter

The book's pages silently fell through the air as Noah flipped with his thumb. He had been at it for hours, turning each leaf with the care of a heart surgeon as he studied every word.

When he came across one that might make sense, he muttered it to himself to see how it sounded aloud. "Worship." "Quickly." "Tremble." Then, shaking his head with disapproval, he continued to flip through the dictionary.

As the day drew on, he left the office and went home to continue his search for a name to give to the new side project. Finally he stopped, frozen as he stared down at a word, instantly knowing that this might be it. He read the definition, reread it, then quickly dashed off an e-mail to the group.

Ev's efforts to keep Noah out of the status project had lasted about twenty minutes. Just as in the early days of Odeo, if Ev said one thing, Noah would do exactly the opposite.

Ev also had other problems to worry about that week: He was busy pulling together documents for the next board meeting, where he planned to suggest selling Odeo to the highest bidder. Or any bidder, for that matter.

All the other engineers not involved in Status were busy reluctantly working on what was left of Odeo. The small group immersed in the new project had been throwing around name ideas for a couple of days, though they couldn't agree on something that worked. Jack suggested the name Status, which others said was "too engineer sounding." Biz suggested Smssy. "Cute, but no." Ev had come up with Friendstalker, which was instantly nixed as sure to drive away anyone who wasn't eighteen years old, male, and very single.

Although the rest of the group didn't seem as concerned with the name, Noah had been obsessing about it since the drunken talk in his car with Jack. Sunday, Monday, Tuesday, and now Wednesday had found Noah searching for a word that made sense. He had skipped lunch with his coworkers all week, burrowed in the back of the office.

When he arrived at his apartment on Wednesday night, he again sat flipping through the dictionary. But his thoughts kept getting inter-rupted by text messages, which would trigger a loud dinging noise on his mobile phone. Frustrated by the intrusion, he reached over and flipped the switch to silent, causing his cell phone to vibrate slightly on the table. Noah stopped what he was doing and stared at the phone, then picked it back up again and held it in his hand as he flipped it on and off, watching it quietly shake. *Vibrate*, he thought, and quickly looked up the word in the dictionary. "Shake, quiver, or throb; move back and forth rapidly." This immediately got Noah excited.

Although the status updater was intriguing to everyone, for Noah it had a more personal meaning. As he had explained to Jack in his car in the rain, Status could make people feel "less alone." Noah's love life, business, and now friendships, which were all woven into Odeo, were falling apart. This new invention could glue them all back together again, and he reasoned that the project needed a name that could explain such an idea.

His vibrating phone led him to think of the brain impulses that cause a muscle to twitch. "Twitch!" *No, that would never work,* he thought. So he continued flipping through the *tw*'s in the dictionary. Twister. Twist tie. Twit. Twitch. Twitcher. Twitchy. Twite. And then, there it was.

"The light chirping sound made by certain birds." Noah's heart started to pound as he continued to read. "A similar sound, especially light, tremulous speech or laughter." *This is it,* he thought. "Agitation or excitement; flutter."

A verb. Twitter.

Twitter. Twittered. Twittering. Twitters.

As the sun started to set, dimming Noah's apartment, he wrote a quick e-mail to Ev. "What are your thoughts on the domain name twitter?" he said, then, noting what the tagline could be, he added, "A whole new level of connection. Or something like that."

As the name made it to the group, it took some convincing, each person secretly thinking their own name suggestion was the best; they finally all agreed that Twitter was the right choice, and Biz started mocking up logos.

Since the new site would allow people to share updates via text message, Jack suggested removing the vowels, a theme circulating through the Valley at the time, thanks to the photo-sharing site Flickr. This way Twitter, or Twttr, could use a special five-digit phone number called a short code to send messages. The domain name was available too.

As they revved the engine to begin development of Twitter, Tim Roberts, who was still director of product at Odeo, quickly put up a giant red STOP sign. In a meeting with Ev to explain Twitter, Tim voiced concerns. "First, we will need a lot of people in order for this to work properly," Tim said, also following up his concerns with an e-mail. But more aptly, he warned, "explaining what this is" was going to be very difficult.

Ev reluctantly agreed and, after a long discussion, decided it was best to explore other ideas in the office before focusing exclusively on Twitter. While Jack, Biz, and Noah continued talking about the Status idea, Ev decided to hold one last "hack day."

They had first organized a hack day, or hackathon, in early February, when Odeo was truly going sideways. Ev presented the idea as follows:

"Ladies and Gentlemen, It is my pleasure to announce to you Odeo's first Hackathon," Ev wrote in an e-mail to the company on February 6,

2006. "A hackathon is a day-long event where everyone cranks on something valuable to the company, but not what you're 'supposed' to be working on."

The ground rules were laid out: Hacking would begin at 9:30 A.M. and would stop at 6:30 P.M. when Ev rang a bell. Afterward, over beer and takeout, people would present their hackathon projects. Collaboration was encouraged, but there were some rules, specifically that certain people (like the office troublemakers) should try not to work together. "What should you work on? More or less, anything you want," Ev wrote. "This means it should be conceivably related to Odeo—something we would consider shipping. But that leaves a pretty wide berth."

During the first hack day in early February, Jack had been out of the office for the week and was unable to attend. There had been others since, but the following week's would be the last hackathon. As people zigzagged between one another's desks the next day inquiring about teams, the office felt like an elementary school when students are told to grab a partner and a coloring book.

As the hack day began, groups ventured into their own corners, flush with ideas. The hackers were all trying to answer the basic question Ev had asked: If you were to start a new company today, or reinvent Odeo, what would you build?

Florian Weber, a young German contract programmer who had been hired temporarily to help with Odeo, grabbed Jack and Dom, and the three ventured to get burritos at Mexico Au Parc at the end of South Park. They then wandered over to the old brown rickety swing set to eat and pass around ideas. Jack pulled his black beanie a little tighter around his ears to fight off the cold as he mentioned the idea for the status updater to Dom and Florian, who until then had never heard of it.

"Why wouldn't you just use voice?" Dom asked.

"Well, you could," Jack said, but then explained that via text message, people could send their status from a noisy club, where it's almost impossible to make a voice call.

Florian, who, like Jack, often enjoyed going to all-night raves, nodded enthusiastically. "Then we'll be able to know when parties are going off," he said.

"What are other use cases?" Dom asked.

"My mom could use it too," Jack said, so she could see what he was up to.

Eventually, everyone meandered back to their desks to sketch out their respective ideas. Mouses skimmed across the table. Keys tapped. As the haze of the San Francisco night started coloring the sky, the *ding* of a loud bell broke the silence, announcing that it was 6:30 P.M. Everyone shuffled into the front room, beer cans cracked open, bottle tops hitting the floor, and people began presenting their concepts.

All of the final hack-day projects ended up looking sort of similar. Twitter was presented, as well as Off the Chains, Ketchup, ShoutOut, and a few other ideas, each with similar aspects of sharing and friends and text messaging. After the presentations concluded, people left for the day and Ev said he would mull over the projects.

A few days went by and Ev composed an e-mail to Noah and a couple of other Odeo execs. Jack was so low within the company, he wasn't included in the message.

"In terms of our new projects, I feel most strongly about Twitter (aka, Twttr). We could have a lot more discussion, and I may change my mind, but I think I just need to make a call at this point, and my gut is pulling me to Twitter," Ev wrote in the e-mail. "Jack is chomping at the bit to build the thing."

Ev then gave the go-ahead to start building.

("The light chirping sound made by certain birds.")

It was agreed that Jack and Biz could take two weeks to pull together a prototype. Florian would be the main engineer. Noah would oversee development of everything. Jeremy could help with Twitter when needed. Everyone else, including Rabble, Dom, Crystal, and Blaine, should stay focused on Odeo as they continued to search for someone to buy the podcasting company.

("A similar sound, especially light, tremulous speech or laughter.")

Tim Roberts still wasn't sold on the idea. "I feel like i am a dissenting voice here, which is awkward," he wrote in an e-mail. "But I continue to have some very fundamental questions around Twitter and its chances for success."

("Agitation or excitement; flutter.")

But it was too late for dissension or questions of chances for success. Ev, Noah, Biz, and Jack had a new obsession. This was what they wanted to build.

(Twitter.)

Just Setting Up
My Twttr

Jack stood up, thrusting his arms into the air like Superman about to take flight as he shouted, "Yessssssssss!"

Rabble and Blaine, sitting close by, looked up at Jack as if he had lost his mind. Mr. Quiet never yelled or stood up abruptly, but something had catapulted him out of his seat like a zap of electricity. Jack looked back at them with an animated grin as he quickly settled back into his chair and began coding again.

"What?" Rabble asked him, annoyed. At the time, Rabble was essentially sitting around waiting to get fired—which wasn't far off—and writing code for his next hacktivist project.

"I got the site hooked up to update a status," Jack replied as he fidgeted with his computer. Their conversation was interrupted by another loud "Yessssssss!" from the back room as Noah jumped up, his arms thrusting in the air too. "I saw the update! I saw the update!"

Technically, this wasn't the first status update. Before the hack day, Ev had decided to build his own crude version of Twitter using some old Blogger code and his personal *EvHead* blog. He called his experiment a "Twitlog," and although it was a rudimentary version of the concept, it gave him a glimpse into what a Twitter-like experience would be. For his first update he wrote, "setting up my twitlog," a few minutes later adding, "hmmm ... will it work?" He then spent the next few days updating pithy Twitlogs from his phone. "Eating a vegan peanut butter cookie. Mmm." "Wishing Sara was here." "Walking to work." "Eating a vegan burger in Salt Lake airport."

While employees watched Ev's Twitlog experiment to see if these updates were interesting, Jack and Biz dove in headfirst on the real Twitter, Florian building the back end of the site, Jack working on the front end, and Biz designing the look and feel. Noah set out to oversee the development of a Twttr logo, which, after days of trivial iterations, ended up looking like a hideous green blob of goo. Jeremy, Blaine, and Tim helped with code problems when needed.

To keep the site simple and clean, Jack's original status concept had envisioned that, as with instant messenger, people would have only one status message visible at a time. If a person updated their status, the previous update would vanish forever and be replaced with the new Twitter message. But Ev had argued that like blogs, status updates should be in a stream format, showing up chronologically. After Noah spent a few days following Ev's Twitlog, he also suggested adding a time stamp to each update so people would know when it had been posted.

For several days Noah, Biz, Jack, and Florian worked away. There were bugs. Problems. Roadblocks. Things were digitally taped together, held in place with makeshift snippets of code. Then finally, two weeks later, Jack sent what would be the first official Twitter update. On March 21, 2006, at 11:50 A.M., Jack tweeted, "just setting up my twttr," like the first message Ev had sent on his Twitlog a few days earlier.

And with this collaboration, it all started to come together. Jack's concept of people sharing their status updates; Ev's and Biz's suggestion to make sure updates flowed into a stream, similar to Blogger; Noah adding timestamps, coming up with the name, and verbalizing how to humanize status by "connecting" people; and finally, friendships and the idea of sharing with groups that had percolated out of Odeo and all the people who had worked there.

Biz was working from home in Berkeley that day. But he was on instant messenger and saw the words "just setting up my twttr" appear on his cell phone. He quickly messaged Jack. "Just got your status on my phone!" he said, then, giving a nod to Alexander Graham Bell when he demonstrated the telephone for the first time in 1876, Biz wrote: "Watson, come in here please!" They started talking on instant messenger:

Jack: Nice! Update yours. I'm following

Biz: Hey, that makes me think of a good tagline for twitter "do you follow me?"

Then Biz signed up and sent his first tweet: "just setting up my twttr."

"Got it!" Jack replied. Then nine minutes later, it was Noah's turn: "just setting up my twttr." Then Crystal and Jeremy thirty seconds later. Then Tony Stubblebine, another senior Odeo engineer. Florian. Ev. And the other employees started to follow along.

Jack tweeted again: "Inviting coworkers." Biz: "Getting my odeo folks on this deal." Dom joined. Rabble. As everyone peered at their phones and computers trying to decide what to type, Dom excitedly tweeted, "oooooooh," followed by Jeremy: "Oh shit, I just twittered a little."

Each update was followed by a chorus of other phones vibrating as everyone simultaneously felt the messages. Tim Roberts joined. "Oh this is going to be addictive," Dom wrote. "Wishing I had another sammich," Biz wrote. "Lunch," Jack typed. "checking out twttr," Ev said. "Oh man, this twitter tickles my nose," Jeremy said.

And that was it. A spark of life. Tweets.

"using twttr.com," Biz wrote as he continued to test the site. The first version of the Web site was crude and simple. "What's your status?" sat at the top with a rectangular box below, then an "update" button that allowed people to share their status. Like a blog, a stream of updates flowed below.

Jack left the office at around six o'clock that evening, walking over to his evening drawing class, excited that Twitter was working, and announced that he was "Drawing naked people." Then for the following few hours they were like a bunch of children at a sleepover wishing each other good night. Like a group of friends talking about what they had done that evening, they all sat separately, together, having a conversation. Tweeting.

Adam: "pumping iron."

Noah: "Oh crap, I think I might be getting that f'in cold."

Jeremy: "fantasizing about jack drawing naked people mmmmmmmmmmmmm. . . . naked people."

Dom: "Heading home."

Jack: "sleep."

Ev: "wondering if updates are working."

Ev: "happy that they are."

Biz: "having some coffee."

Tony: "thinking about polyphasic sleep."

Noah: "biz wont leave me alone."

Crystal: "Aerobics Supah Star."

Jack: "n bd readn, wrtng txt spk."

Biz: "accessing twttr on my treo web browser."

Jack: "sleep."

Noah: "late night at the office. missed lost :-("

Crystal: "cleaned the bathroom, ate a salad, going to bed soon!"

Noah: "bed time for me. goodnight."

The Cowboy at the Rodeo

It was late in the evening when the door to the Odeo offices burst open and Noah stumbled in, drunk.

"Jack!" he bellowed across the room, barreling toward him with the elation of a child just home from school but with the pungent smell of a drunk. Jack slipped his headphones off and looked up with a tired expression. "Hey, Noah."

"I might have just fucked up," Noah said, clapping his hands in the air and dropping into a chair next to Jack. "You guys might be kinda pissed at me."

"What'd you do?" Jack asked, unsure how this particular Noah production would play out.

"I think I just announced Twitter to the media," Noah said, spiraling into a ramble about this great party, Om Malik, cigarettes, free drinks, and a mechanical bull.

It was mid-July 2006, and the Valley had the feel of an amusement park that had just reopened for business. Exciting new social rides were being built on the plots that had once belonged to pet-food Web sites and other pedestrian ideas from the late nineties. And now admission was free. You simply paid in privacy by giving up your personal information for access.

The new Valley had a new name too. Web 2.0! New and improved:

the social Web. MySpace and Friendster were the chatter of the late-teen world, and this nascent thing called Facebook was spreading around college dorm rooms with the velocity of a common cold. Flickr, the social photo site, had recently been purchased by Yahoo! for almost forty million dollars, a small gold mine in those days.

Like children mesmerized by an enigmatic snow globe, people outside the Valley were once again peering in, wondering how they could become part of this wonderland, how they could own a snow globe that, if shaken properly, would send not snowflakes but money fluttering down to land neatly in their hands.

But among the boundless wealth beginning to swirl around the Valley there was also a slew of broken start-ups, like Odeo, that were going out of business. Which is how Noah had ended up drunk at a party, extolling himself as one of the creators of Twitter.

A couple of Valley entrepreneurs with a witty sense of humor about the roller-coaster mentality of the tech scene decided to capitalize on the demise of these start-ups and started a monthly club called "Valleyschwag," where people would pay a twenty dollars a month to receive a bag of random swag. Each month's goodies, wrapped in brown burlap, included T-shirts, stickers, pens, and mouse pads from the companies that were about to disappear in an elaborate magic trick of their own making.

To help commemorate these dying companies, there was a party called the "Valleyschwag Hoedown." Earlier in the day, before the festivities began, the Valleyschwag organizers needed more junk to hand out at the hoedown. It was no secret that Odeo was dying, so one schwag organizer stopped at its offices, where Ev led him into a closet filled with gray T-shirts with pink Odeo logos. "Can I take some for the party?" the organizer asked.

"Sure," Ev replied in a chagrinned tone. "Take as many as you want."

As the hoedown got under way, bales of hay sat in the corner of the room and Noah arrived, gleeful about Twitter, a product that until that evening very few people knew about. After swigging shots of vodka with well-knowns from the tech scene, eating a dry piece of hoedown cake, dancing with girls in cowboy hats, and riding the rented mechanical bull with a cardboard horse head taped to the front, Noah found himself standing outside, drunk and smoking cigarettes with Om Malik, a blogger who covered the tech scene. They leaned up against a large yellow school bus called "Lola" that had been brought in for the party.

Noah, unable to contain himself, took a few manic drags of his cigarette and excitedly told Om everything about the new site. "It came out of a chat in my car on Valencia and Fourteenth after a night of heavy vodka drinking," he slurred. "Give me your phone. I'll sign you up!" Noah said, a cigarette now hanging from his mouth like James Dean. He pressed a few buttons, then handed the phone back, briefly explaining how Twitter worked.

"Looking 4 food," Om tweeted, then inhaled a last puff of smoke and stuffed his phone back in his pocket.

After pulling the cat out of the bag by its tail, Noah decided it would be best to sign others up too, and he turned into a traveling salesman at the hoedown. "Give me your phone! I'll sign you up!" he yelled to people over the sound of country music. Before he knew it, he was standing there, drunk, in the middle of the hoedown, people swirling around him in cowboy hats, a tiny ocean of alcohol in his little plastic cup. He soon realized he should tell Jack and the others back at the office about his impromptu media conference.

Noah's excitement about Twitter had been palpable for weeks. A few days earlier the Odeo board members had arrived in the office to attend a quarterly board meeting and hear updates about potentially selling the podcasting service. But before the meeting began, Noah and Ev wanted to demo Twitter to the investors. Jack came into the conference room for the show-and-tell, which was his first time attending a board meeting, and sat dead silent as Noah gave an impassioned demonstration of Twitter.

"What do you think?" Noah asked George Zachary, the lead Odeo investor, after his demonstration. "It's amazing, right? It can allow you to connect with your friends!"

George stared at Noah with a confused look, quietly wondering to himself why anyone would want to "connect with their friends" when those friends were sitting right there. He thought the group of programmers had smoked something before the meeting and looked around uncertainly. Still, Noah continued with animated examples of Twitter's ability to connect people.

A few days later, when Noah stumbled in from the hoedown and announced that he had told the blogosphere, Jack acknowledged that it wasn't a big deal, brushed it off, and got back to work. Like Ev, Jack was grossly averse to conflict, at least the kind that happened in plain sight.

Secretly, Jack was furious.

His friendship with Noah had already started to wane after a recent discussion about Crystal.

Over the past year, Noah, Jack, and Crystal had become best friends, eating breakfast, lunch, and dinner together several times a week, drinking excessively at night, and on weekends dancing late into the morning. In April they had all set out with some friends to Coachella, a massive music festival seven hours south of San Francisco. They danced in the desert to the Chemical Brothers, Girl Talk, and Imogen Heap and slept next to one another in the desert. But Noah had noticed Jack's increased obsession with Crystal as he followed her around the concert like a security guard.

One evening Noah pulled Jack aside and told him the obsession with Crystal was unhealthy and he should "chill" a bit. Jack became defensive and accused Noah of trying to push Jack aside so he could be with Crystal instead. "Huh? I love Crystal, but I don't want to date her," Noah protested, a look of total bewilderment on his face. But Jack's mind was already made up.

Now, as Noah sat in the office, drunkenly describing how he had signed people up for Twitter and pulled back the curtains on the top-secret project, Jack was again upset that Noah was meddling. First Crystal, now Twitter. Jack's feelings toward Noah were turning from love to disdain.

And he wasn't alone.

The following morning the Odeo and Twitter employees came in to work to discover a handful of blog posts discussing this new strange thing called Twitter.

Mike Arrington, who ran *TechCrunch*, a popular Valley tech blog, wrote that Twitter had launched officially and "a few select insiders were playing with the service at the Valleyschwag party in San Francisco last night." But Arrington didn't seem too impressed by the new service. He questioned its privacy issues and, in a direct slam to Ev, wondered why Odeo, a podcasting company, was wasting its time on side projects.

Although Om Malik's blog post was kinder, showing interest in the new Twitter contraption, he gave all the credit to a certain drunk cofounder he had shared cigarettes and vodka with the night before. "A new mobile social networking application written by Noah Glass (and team)," Om wrote.

Ev tried to fix the press afterward, but it was too late. And although Noah didn't know it yet, his drunken media announcements were about to have serious consequences.

The Green Benches

S outh Park was eerily still and quiet in the dark. There were no children playing on the swing sets. The green park benches were empty. The lights of the matchbox-shaped buildings that surround the park were all off, their cafés, restaurants, and offices long since closed for the day. The sole exception was number 164, where a dim yellow glow whispered through the cubed windows that faced the street.

Inside, the clocks on the walls swept silently past midnight. Yet in the rear of the building, past the empty desks with darkened computer monitors, was Noah, doing what he now did on most nights. Sitting alone.

It had become an evening routine. Some nights he cried while painting large, elaborate murals. Other times he played music, rattling his fingers against the strings of his guitar while he sang melancholy music. He often sang about love into his webcam, a dark-brimmed hat covering his welled-up eyes.

His marriage was essentially over; his start-up, Odeo, a decomposing corpse. His relationship with his closest friends, who were also his coworkers, was in complete tatters too.

So Noah did what Noah did best. He turned to the magical Internet in search of solace. He talked to his webcam. His blog. And, of course, Twitter.

He was using Twitter for exactly what he had hoped it might be used for: curing loneliness. Noah had understood the concept well before everyone else had. "It can be whatever you want it to be," he had written on his blog a few days earlier. "The fact that I could find out what my friends were doing at any moment of the day made me feel closer to them and, quite honestly, a little less alone." Sadly, of course, his hypothesis had proven false and his sadness wasn't being lessened by friends far away. Which was why he had been spending night after night solitarily hiding in the back of the office, unwanted.

His state of affairs was mostly his own doing.

In early June, Crystal had started helping with Twitter, adding her support prowess and answering questions from early testers of the site. Although it was still secret at the time, employees were allowed to give out private invites to close friends and family.

At around lunchtime on July 5, Dennis Crowley, a well-known entrepreneur who ran Dodgeball, which had recently been acquired by Google, e-mailed Twitter asking if he could join. Crystal, unaware of who Dennis was, happily responded with a code that activated his account. Moments later, when Noah saw Dennis's name stream across his computer monitor with the usual first tweet, "just setting up my twttr," Noah became enraged, storming out of his office like a wrestler into a ring.

"What the fuck is going on?" he bellowed as everyone's head's snapped around, startled. "Why the fuck did we approve Dennis Crowley's account?!"

"I don't know who he is. . . . ," Crystal said, a timid look of shock and fear in her eyes as she stared back at Noah.

Noah tore into a rampage. "You have no idea what you've just fucking done," he yelled, pacing erratically. Crystal burst into tears.

"Calm down, Noah," employees said to him. "You're overreacting. It's not that big of a deal."

"This is fucking war!" Noah yelled as Jack also tried unsuccessfully to pacify him. "This is fucking war! This is our enemy. We need a war map. They're going to attack us; we need to destroy them."

Everyone tried again to mollify Noah, but he continued yelling, a panic saturating him as he eventually stormed back into his office.

A few days later he had another outburst, sending an almost frantic e-mail to George Zachary, an investor in the company and a member of the Odeo board: "I would like to talk with you about twttr," Noah wrote in the e-mail. "It is important that I speak to you as soon as possible." Noah had been arguing that Twitter should be spun out as its own company and he should be the CEO. Technically, what happened to Twitter was up to the investors who had originally financed Odeo, as they were now unintentionally paying for the development of this experiment.

Ev hadn't originally been against the idea. He knew Noah had given everything to the new project. Two months earlier, in May 2006, Ev had even e-mailed the Odeo board suggesting that they spin Twitter out into its own company with Noah at the helm: "Why not set up Twttr, Inc. as a separate company—perhaps not wholly owned, but mirrored ownership, seed it with $500k or so and let Noah see what he can do," Ev had written enthusiastically. But the board was not interested in Twitter; if Ev and Noah didn't want to continue with Odeo, the investors wanted to sell it to the highest bidder and get their money back. They saw the side project as just another Ev distraction.

"Ev, we are going to have a disaster situation occur shortly if we slow down selling the company," George Zachary had responded. "My patience is really getting pushed here and I am close to out of it."

Now, as the discussion was being raised again about spinning out Twitter, Noah's erratic and manic behavior had slowly chipped away at the prospect of his running it—or even Odeo.

Noah was also becoming paranoid about Ev. On more than one occasion he solemnly pulled Jack aside and confessed his fears. "Ev's trying to push me out of the company. I can feel it. We should get out of here and start our own thing," he whispered to Jack. "We should go off and start our own Twitter."

But Jack knew what was going to happen next and told Noah to stay put and see how things unfolded before doing anything. "Wait," Jack said. "Don't do anything yet. Let's just wait."

"But Ev is trying to kick me out of the company," Noah replied.

Noah's hunch was only half-correct: It wasn't just Ev who wanted to kick Noah out of the company. It was everyone else too.

Twitter was barely a newborn at the time, but there was already squabbling over who had fed it, who had let others go near it. For a while the entire site had existed solely on Noah's IBM laptop. Then Jack had taken charge of the engineering side of Twitter and, each morning, assigned programming tasks to Florian, who was now working remotely from Germany. But late at night, while Noah was sitting alone in his office catching ideas that were falling out of the dark, brief stints of passion amid his depressed state, he was also telling Florian what to work on. Jack would arrive in the office the next morning to find a list of tasks completed, but not his list: Noah's.

Ev was torn over what to do about Noah's outbursts and media hijacking. Jack helped him decide. One afternoon Jack asked Ev if they could talk privately. "You can't tell Noah about this conversation," Jack said. They were, after all, still "friends." Jack said that Noah was interfering with Twitter, that he couldn't work with him anymore, and that Jack was thinking about quitting. When Ev asked where he would go, he proclaimed that he would happily leave and go into the fashion industry. Then Jack threw down the gauntlet: "If Noah stays, I'm going to leave. I can't work with him anymore."

For Ev the answer was simple. He knew Noah's life was falling apart, but he also saw that he was scrambling to hold onto anything tangible as he fell, and he risked taking the dying Odeo and the newborn Twitter with him.

So after conferring with the board, at around 6:00 P.M. on Wednesday, July 26, Ev and Noah walked outside to the park benches. Noah knew exactly what was going to happen next. The park benches were an Ev tell.

Although Ev's gut told him Twitter was going to be something, at the time it was still just a side project. Odeo, on the other hand, was dead on arrival. As a result, Ev had started laying people off over the past months.

Layoffs always followed the same pattern. At this point Ev had it down to a science: He would walk over, tap someone on the shoulder, and quietly say, "Hey, let's go for a walk." He'd said it to Rabble, Dom, and a few others on separate occasions. His hands were often half in his pockets, his elbows slightly bent. He would slowly move his head at an angle, back and slightly to the right, to motion toward the door.

Together they'd walk out of the building and cut left, taking the few brief steps to South Park. There they would sit on a green park bench and Ev would deliver his eulogy.

"Things have been rough at Odeo lately," he would say. A sort of "It's not you, it's me" breakup. Some people cried; some felt relieved. (Rabble had been elated when he was let go by the Man.) But there was one person who was angry.

"I won't fucking leave," Noah barked at Ev as they sat on a bench. Noah then spun into a tirade about Odeo and about Ev's rarely being present at the company, about Noah's overseeing Twitter, nurturing it, feeding it, helping realize its ideas along with everyone else.

"I don't see a role for you moving forward," Ev explained. "If we don't sell Odeo, Twitter will become our main focus, and I don't think we can work together well on it."

Noah tried to plead, arguing that he wanted to oversee Twitter, but Ev knew it wasn't possible. Everyone was fed up. They had long since reached their limits. And Jack, the most important developer on the Twitter team, would leave if Noah stayed. Ev had already decided, and that decision was the only one that counted. When Noah had agreed to make Ev the CEO in exchange for the early funding for the podcasting start-up, he had also given Ev the ability to make carte blanche decisions. Noah had never anticipated that the power he'd handed to his friend and neighbor would be used to fire him, the founder of Odeo, from the company.

Ev gave Noah an ultimatum: six months' severance and six months' vesting of his Odeo stock, or he would be fired and the story would not be pretty publicly. He didn't mention Jack's ultimatum; he didn't even mention Jack's name. "Take the rest of the week to think about what you want to do," Ev said.

Noah left the office that evening, sullen and sad, angry and defeated, believing Ev was kicking him out of the company to conserve control of Twitter. Noah needed to douse his sadness in liquor. He met up with Jack and another friend at a nearby club, where they drank and danced late into the night.

As they stood at the bar ordering drinks, Noah told Jack what had happened. Jack appeared dumbfounded by the fact that his friend had been pushed out. He never mentioned that he had handed Ev the gun with which the final shot was fired. As the night came to a close, Noah hugged Jack good-bye and went home alone.

Noah spent the next few days riding his bike around San Francisco trying to calculate what to do. He cycled along the Embarcadero, watching the boats as they bobbed in the bay. He wrote in his journal as he lay in Dolores Park, the movie *Raiders of the Lost Ark* playing in the background. And he sat along the edge of the world as people played with massive kites in the wind. "Watching colorful parachutes trace the shape of infinity as they fall to earth," he tweeted.

Ev had expected Noah to battle for power and control of Twitter. But no matter how much Noah wanted to be a fighter, he wasn't. He didn't fight because he didn't know how. When he was kicked by a horse, he just walked away.

Noah didn't fight because he realized it wasn't power that he had been after when he started Odeo. More than fame and more than fortune, he had just wanted friends.

Two weeks later, faced with no other choice and no one in his corner, Noah resigned. He stopped by the desolate office on a Saturday afternoon, packed his life into cardboard boxes, and let the beige door slam behind him, no longer an employee of two companies he helped start.

III.
#JACK

A Bloody Mess

A crimson stream of blood flowed down Jack's cheek, past the drunken grin on his face, turning left onto the crest of his black T-shirt and finally stopping, in small red pools, on the white sheets of the hospital bed. A sour smell of alcohol lingered in the air.

The room swayed a little, moving to and fro like a boat at sea, sloshing around in the countless vodka and Red Bulls Jack had drunk throughout the evening.

It wasn't how the grand public launch of Twitter was supposed to end up: Jack in the hospital at around 2:00 A.M., covered in blood, and Noah, Ray, and a few others still dancing at a rave a few blocks away. But in hindsight, it was as predictable as nightfall that the public debut of this tiny social start-up would end this way.

It had all begun before Noah had been fired from Twitter. One evening, while out drinking and dancing, Jack and Noah tried to explain Twitter to a DJ friend of Crystal's. "It can be used in clubs, for finding out what your friends are up to or what they're listening to; it was great at Coachella," they said while sipping sake in a dark San Francisco bar.

"Oh, you guys should totally launch it at the Love Parade in September," the friend replied, excited by his own epiphany. "I'm throwing a party there and you can set up a booth."

Although Noah and Jack had been planning to attend Love Parade, the burgeoning techno-music festival that would soon land in San Francisco, Jack was skeptical of the idea, doubting whether the rave was the right venue to use as bait for luring the nontech public to Twitter.

"This is why we built this thing!" Noah told Jack before he was let go from the company. "For concerts and music shows!" And, as he noted, what better place to launch it than the biggest rave in San Francisco?

It was the summer of 2006 and Twitter was just a speck of dust at the time, a small town in a big city of bigger start-ups. Barely 4,500 people had signed up for the site since Noah had first announced it a few months earlier at the hoedown—a smaller portion of whom were actually tweeting on a daily basis. It was a bare-bones operation too—still a vestige of Odeo, which had been reduced to a half a dozen employees.

Although it wasn't an official company yet, Twitter had been growing slowly over the summer with a lot of "firsts." There was the first tweet of a car crash. (Not to worry, everyone was okay.) A blogger announced that he had been fired from his job. (He soon found new employment.) In August, Ev tweeted that he had asked Sara to marry him. (She said yes!) And there was a lot of egotistical banter among the Twitterers. People had been sharing their lunches, dinners, and breakfasts. Cappuccinos, sake, and wine. Uncouth first tweets about sex, masturbation, bathroom schedules, drunk epiphanies, and several other topics flew out of people's phones and into plain sight.

But still, this repartee hadn't moved beyond the tech nerds. So Jack followed through on Noah's suggestion and decided the Love Parade would be the perfect venue to bring awareness of Twitter to the music-loving mainstream.

The group quickly set to work.

Ray, the young designer from Odeo, who had been spared in the layoffs, made a flyer that they would hand out to the ravers providing instructions on how to sign up for Twitter. Jeremy and Blaine prepared the servers, ensuring that the site could handle the flood of new sign-ups. On the day of the event, Jack procured a large folding picnic table that he set up near the entrance of the Bill Graham Civic Auditorium, home of the main Love Parade dance party. As night started to fall, Ray, who had donned a black top hat with his white T-shirt for the occasion, hooked up his laptop to a pathetically dim projector that would show people's tweets using a little animated character called Celly. Jack rushed back and forth to a liquor store around the corner to buy cheap bottles of vodka and plastic cups.

Although Noah no longer worked for Twitter, or even what was left of Odeo, he was still friendly with some of his former coworkers and was happy to help in any way he could. But on that night he was there more for the rave than for Twitter and dressed appropriately, looking as if he had just walked out of a haunted house, wearing pink bands around his wrists and neck and painted black stripes across his lips.

When everything was almost set and ready to go, Jack pulled his phone out of his pocket and tweeted: "At the love parade after party setting up the twitter booth!"

The plan was to give out free drinks, along with the Twitter flyers, to get people to sign up for the service. Their first tweets would be proclamations that Massive Attack, Junkie XL, and DJ Shadow were currently playing music at the Love Parade. Exactly what Twitter was originally designed for. But the idea soon turned into a disaster.

Strangely dressed and half-naked ravers, many tripping on various drugs—mushrooms, ecstasy, acid—twirled by the Twitter booth, grabbing free drink concoctions that Jack mixed, in exchange for a Twitter flyer being thrust into their hand. But that was about as far as the transaction went. The few people wearing enough clothes to actually put the flyer somewhere likely lost it during the night. The flyers given to others, some wearing nothing more than underwear and large platform boots that raised them off the ground nearly a foot, ended up scrunched into tiny meteors on the floor of the theater.

Every time Jack looked up at the computer to see how many new people had started tweeting, he saw barely a trickle of sign-ups. The evening wasn't going as planned. Still, he continued to mix drinks, hand out flyers, and check the screen.

While Jack played bartender, a raver wandered over to Ray's

computer, dancing and watching the animation of Twitter on the projector, then bumped into the table and accidentally poured an entire cocktail onto the computer's keyboard. Fade to black. The computer was dead. Ray was distraught, and after friends tried to console him, he wandered outside to cool off, only to find that his brand-new bicycle had been stolen.

Then things went from bad to worse to fucking terrible. Jack had spent most of the day running around setting up the grand Twitter unveiling, and as he had been doing all of this on his own, he had been exhausted and flustered. To calm his nerves, he had downed one vodka and Red Bull after another. Later in the evening, when Jeremy arrived to help hand out flyers, Jack was so drunk he was wobbling.

As the last of the leaflets were thrust into people's hands, the vodka bottles now pouring out mere drops of liquid, Jack and his merry group of ravers moved inside the theater. A solid day's work complete, they danced to the repetitive beats of techno, their arms reaching toward the sky, hoping to touch the laser lights that melted like drunken stars in the air above them. More vodka, more Red Bull, the digital music sounding like a tempo for each drink. Jack was more drunk than he had been moments earlier. More drunk than he had ever been before in his life.

As they danced, a girl walked up with sloshed excitement and placed her arm around Jack. Disoriented, he threw his arm around her in response. And just like that, they both came tumbling down to the ground, Jack cracking his head on the concrete floor as he gave a drunken bow.

When he finally got up, blood was pouring from his brow. He laughed as everyone stared at him, their mouths agape. His coworkers had never seen Jack "let go" like that before. He beamed as Ray snapped a quick picture of the blood streaming down his cheeks.

Noah, who was also wasted beyond comprehension, immediately came running over. "Lay down! You have to lay down," he yelled at Jack in a slight panic, "You might have damaged your head." He rushed off to get a medic. In a matter of minutes Jack was placed in a neck brace on a stretcher and rushed out of the theater, into an ambulance, and off to the hospital. Red lights flashed on the windows like the laser lights on the walls at the rave a few minutes earlier.

It might have turned out differently if a more seasoned manager had supervised the grand unveiling of Twitter. But instead it had just been Jack, Ray, and a couple of other very junior employees.

Biz was not a fan of techno music, so had chosen to stay at home in Berkeley with Livy and their rescued pets. They were also completely broke, as credit-card debt had started to pile up again, forcing them to break into a coffee-can piggy bank they used to collect change. Florian was in Germany, held back by delays with his work visa. Crystal was at a wedding, dressed as a bridesmaid with flowers in her hands. Most of the other employees who had originally been hired to work at Odeo had since been laid off.

Ev was finally taking some time off from work and had set off with Sara on vacation. And Twitter wasn't top of mind for him. He was in the process of off-loading some of his remaining Google stock so he could buy out the Odeo investors. The prospect of a sale to MySpace or Real-Networks, two of the companies interested in buying Odeo, had gone from freeways to dead-end streets. In the end Ev opted to buy the start-up back from the investors with millions of the dollars he had made from the sale of Blogger—mostly with the hope of preserving his name.

Earlier in the month, at a Web conference, he had publicly admitted that Odeo had been a terrible mistake and said that he had been lured into the podcasting company by outside forces that would boost his self-image, including an offer to give a talk at TED, one of the world's premiere technology conferences, and the temptation of being included in a front page business article in the *New York Times*. "I got sucked in for numerous reasons, including my own ego," Ev had written in a blog post.

But as he noted, he wasn't buying Odeo back to spin off Twitter. Instead he planned to begin a start-up incubator called Obvious Corporation, an idea factory for someone with too many ideas. He didn't want investment money, he said, because he believed that in such a setting, where he was throwing sloppy ideas against a wall, investors would only get in the way.

"It may be stupid. It may be naive. It may be selfish and undisciplined. And, frankly, it may not work," Ev wrote on his blog. "All I know is I'm more excited about work than I've been in a long time. And from excitement and bold moves, great things often happen."

But such "excitement" diverted his attention from something that was already on its way to greatness, which left young Jack Dorsey, with no management experience or leadership skills, in charge of Twitter. The same Jack Dorsey who was now lying on a hospital bed getting five stitches across his right eyebrow as blood flowed down his face onto the white hospital sheets.

As the clock neared 2:00 A.M., Jack emerged from the emergency-room doors onto the sleeping streets of San Francisco, his head throbbing. Although the alcohol had now started to wear off, the caffeine in the Red Bull had not, and he was wide awake, his adrenalized heart pounding. So he wandered back to the Bill Graham Civic Auditorium in a daze and walked back inside, past the slapdash Twitter booth he had set up earlier in the day.

Crystal had since arrived at the show, shedding her bridesmaid dress for an almost-naked outfit of raver clothes. "What the hell happened to you?" she said to Jack as everyone rushed over to hug him. Jack started to offer his version of the story, then Noah jumped in with his view of the events. Before long, they were quarreling about where, why, and how Jack had fallen.

"Boys! Boys! Enough!" Crystal said, interrupting them both. "You're bickering over the same little details."

Eventually everyone packed up, beaten, bruised, achy, and still drunk, and called it a night. The grand launch of Twitter had been a flop.

On Monday morning Jack's head still hurt from the weekend as everyone sat around in the office talking about the disastrous evening. "So how many new users did we get?" Biz asked, after hearing about Ray's computer being ruined, about the failed bartending, and about Jack's head being stitched up.

"Let me check," Jack said, twirling around in his chair and logging on to the servers, his fingers dancing on the keyboard.

After a few moments he twirled back around as Ray, Jeremy, and Biz stood there smiling.

"Less than a hundred," Jack said, a defeated look on his face. "Less than a hundred new users."

Chaos Again

The sound of the fire crackled just outside the tent Biz and Jason Goldman, the astrophysics major who had dropped out of college and joined Blogger in 2002, were sharing as they lay in their sleeping bags giggling like teenagers. They had been up for hours chatting and telling jokes as everyone else lay sleeping in their tents nearby. Then Goldman interrupted Biz and asked a question that had been on his mind for weeks. "What's the deal with Twitter?" Goldman said. "I really want to work there."

Biz fell silent for a moment.

It was a Saturday evening and Ev and Sara had organized another camping trip to Big Sur amid the giant redwood trees on the central coast of California.

Goldman, just like Biz a year earlier, yearned to work with Ev again. It wasn't just that they enjoyed being around their friend but also that Ev was an entirely different kind of boss to work for, always giving people creative freedom to explore ideas. At Google, where they had both worked, ideas were put on spreadsheets and crunched with numbers to see if they were really worth exploring.

This wasn't the first time Goldman had expressed interest in working at Twitter. He had made his request in May during a last-minute trip to Las Vegas with Ev and a group of friends that had included enough partying to see the sun rise over the Nevada desert. He had asked Ev and Biz a couple of times at social affairs in San Francisco. Now he was trying again in a tent.

"Twitter is kind of Jack's thing right now," Biz said, "but you should talk to Ev in the morning and ask him."

The following day they awoke late and Ev and Goldman stood stirring scrambled tofu (Ev was a staunch vegan) on the camping stove. Biz was lying on a bright multicolored beanbag that they had stolen from Google's office. Goldman tried his question again. But the response wasn't what Ev wanted to hear. "You'll have to come in and spend some time with Jack and we'll see," he said.

So Goldman did just that and started wooing Jack, stopping by the Twitter offices to talk his way into the company. But Jack said he wasn't in a position to hire anyone either. "It's really up to Ev," he told him. "You'll have to talk to him."

As Goldman soon learned, this runaround was typical for Twitter. When an engineer asked someone a question or when there was an SMS contract to be signed or when someone like Goldman was trying to get a job, the decision-making process was like a carnival.

After Noah had finally and officially left the company, the power vacuum had not been resolved as Ev had hoped; rather, it had spun into another orbit. No one to make a decision. No one to revoke the few bad decisions that had been made.

Having successfully returned the Odeo investors' five million dollars from his Google earnings, Ev's mind was elsewhere, focusing on Obvious Corporation and sifting through his ideas. He was still involved in Twitter and was the sole investor, having allocated one million dollars of his own money to nurture the company, though he was trying to leave Jack and Biz to run the operation. But it wasn't much of an enterprise yet. The site was growing slowly, with only a few thousand sign-ups. Goldman, like everyone who already worked at Twitter, was enamored with the idea as soon as he heard it and wanted to work there.

Eventually, after months of negotiations, Ev agreed to hire Goldman, albeit with a caveat: He would be part time at Obvious and part time at Twitter, a hybrid Twitter employee without a completely defined role.

Goldman had been in a similar situation with Ev before, five years earlier in 2002, when he first joined Blogger as a part-time employee before it was sold to Google.

Goldman's job at Blogger had been a mishmash of stuff. In addition to answering support e-mails complaining about the outlandish content on Blogger, he'd fixed the dripping sink, searched for a new office, managed the accounting, and helped Ev with the paperwork for the Google acquisition.

Five years later, in February 2007, on his first day at Twitter, it was apparent this job description would be almost exactly the same: a little bit of everything. And again, a lot of confusion.

Although Jack had taken a lead at Twitter, it was clear that no one was actually in charge. Companies often take on the traits of their founders and first employees, so Twitter, which was nurtured out of Odeo, a seedling from Noah's chaotic brain, was still operating as an anarchist-hacker collective with no rules.

Many of the employees did what they wanted, where they wanted— that was, if they wanted to do anything related to their daily job at all. Rather than fix the servers, people built their own little trinkets and apps that fed into Twitter. Jack had no luck taming them. There was also a tremendous amount of rivalry between him and his coworkers as, just a few months earlier, when Odeo still existed, Jack had been working below all of them.

Goldman was immediately caught up in the *Lord of the Flies*–like power vacuum. Technically he reported to Jack while on Twitter, but he was also reporting to Ev on Obvious and was possibly Jack's superior, as Obvious technically owned Twitter.

Still, just as in his early days at Blogger, Goldman dove into his new mishmash job and tried to institute a sense of order amid the chaos.

One of his first tasks was to work with Jack to help make Twitter friendlier for newcomers to understand. The service allowed people to perform actions through text messages with the ability to do things like "follow" or "unfollow" others. But there were other verbs that were puzzling to people on the site and needed to be culled. So the cutting began: "Worship" ensured that people received every single update from someone they followed. (Gone.) "Sleep" allowed people to pause updates they received. (Too unclear.) And a long list of other options were nixed.

There were, of course, much bigger problems than the question of which verbs to use on Twitter. Since the site had been built as a prototype in two weeks using a relatively new programming language called Ruby on Rails, it was rife with shortcuts and code problems. It was as if someone had rushed to build a skyscraper and in the time crunch had chosen to put together the structure with cardboard, glue, and tape, rather than nails, wood, and concrete. Worse, people were now moving into the building before construction crews could replace the flimsy materials with real ones.

And then there was the biggest problem of them all: trying to explain to people what Twitter actually was. Everyone had a different answer. "It's a social network." "It replaces text messages." "It's the new e-mail." "It's microblogging." "It's to update your status."

As a result, most newcomers didn't understand what to do when they first arrived on the site. People would sign up and send their first tweet, which often looked like one of the following missives: "How do I use this?" "What the fuck is this thing?" "Twitter is stupid." "This is dumb."

The confusion led to one of the first topics that Jack and Ev saw differently. Jack saw Twitter as a place to say "what I'm doing." Ev saw it as more like a mini blogging product. Both of them thought the way people had used it during a mini earthquake the previous summer held clues to what Twitter could be.

It was just after eight o'clock one night in late August 2006 when Jack's phone vibrated on his office desk. He reached over and saw a text message from Twitter, sent by Ev, and started to read, "Did anyone just feel that eart—" but before he came to the end of the message, he felt his chair shake a little. He looked up and away from his phone and saw the plant on his desk waving at him, its leaves swaying in the air like someone calling to a friend.

"Whooooa," Jack said as his desk briefly quivered like setting Jell-O. "Did you feel that?" he asked as he turned to a few others in the office.

Before they could answer, his phone vibrated again. He looked down and continued to read Ev's original message, "Did anyone just feel that earthquake?" Then the next tweet from someone else: "Wondering if I just felt an earthquake."

As a pop of adrenaline kicked in, Jack quickly typed, "Just felt that earthquake. No one else here did." At the moment he hit "send," a string of other messages started streaming into his phone like letters falling through a mail slot to the floor. "Agh earthquake," wrote one friend. "Yep. Felt the quake," wrote another. Then a handful of other earthquake tweets. "I felt the earthquake but Livy didn't believe me until the twitters started rolling in," wrote Biz. Finally, another person announced that it was a "4.72 magnitude jolt."

The quake didn't cause any damage, except for some frayed nerves and a few crooked pictures now hanging on the walls. But for the small group of people who had experienced the event on Twitter, it felt strangely different.

On the day of that small earthquake only a few hundred people were using the service. Of the fifteen thousand tweets sent across the network up to that point, almost all had still been focused on the original concept: "What's your status?" a question that often invited a narcissistic response.

Sharing the quake on Twitter had been a moment that was about the status of something bigger than each individual. Although the people on the site were all in completely different locations, time and space had briefly compressed. It was as if someone had pulled the end of a hanging thread on a sweater, forcing the fabric to scrunch up closer together. Or as Noah had originally foreseen, months before anyone else, Twitter had been used to "help people feel less alone."

For Ev it was another clue in a theory he was developing about Twitter's role as a way to share news, not just status—Twitter as a communication network, not just a social network. He told Jack about the concept of Twitter as a news network, but Jack disagreed, instead seeing the earthquake tweets as an example of the *speed* of Twitter. He focused on his phone vibrating a few brief seconds before his desk had become a puppet without a puppeteer.

Jack had continued to see Twitter as a way to talk about what was happening to *him*. Ev was starting to see it as a view into what was happening in the world.

While these little newslike events went mostly unnoticed by the public, philosophically Jack and Ev were developing different viewpoints as to what Twitter was. And what it had the potential to be.

And the Winner Is . . .

It was early evening on Sunday, March 11, 2007, as Ze Frank, a comedian and actor, looked out at the sea of heads bowed over the soft glow of phones. He continued talking as he paced across the open stage. His boyish blond hair bounced with each step in unison with the orange balloons in the background behind him. He was trying to add anticipation as he spoke, announcing the list of contestants for best start-up in the blog category at South by Southwest, the annual technology conference in Austin, Texas, that is the closest thing nerds have to the Oscars.

"SuperfluousBanter," he said, among a list of other finalists, then after a slight pause, ". . . and Twitter!" The packed auditorium began whistling and clapping, a very different reception from the launch of Twitter at the Love Parade five months earlier.

Jack turned to look at the people around him, almost in disbelief, and smiled as everyone cheered. Ev scanned the room too, taking a sip of the red wine in the short plastic cup in his hand, and then leaned over to Jack, whispering to him that if Twitter won, he should give the acceptance speech. Jack was thrilled, but having barely spoken as a child, he wasn't confident about talking in front of large crowds. He turned to Biz to share the good, or bad, news. "What should I say?" Jack asked him.

Biz stared off into space for a second and then said, "I got it." He grabbed a pencil and a piece of paper and scribbled down a short speech that he then handed to Jack.

Noah, now the outcast of Twitter, was seated next to the group and held a video camera, taping what was about to happen. He whistled and whooped as the word "Twitter" echoed throughout the room.

Noah had come to South by Southwest to explore other start-up ideas he was thinking of building alone and had bumped into his former coworkers and best friends outside the theater. After chatting about the mundane and about the extraordinary rate at which people had been signing up for Twitter at the conference, Ev had made a peace offering.

"Hey, Noah, would you like to sit with us?" Ev had asked.

It had been a rough few months for Noah, as he had recently written in a very personal blog post explaining that 2006 had been the "hardest year" of his life. "i lost more than i knew i could. i lost my two best friends. changed my definition of self," he wrote on his Web site. "i left my company, and everything i spent years creating. i learned about stress. about trust. about sadness. . . . i cried more tears than i ever have."

Now, as he was picking himself back up, Ev was holding out a hand. "Sure, that'd be great," Noah had said to him. "I'd like that."

As they sat in the audience together listening to Ze Frank, the Twitter guys were all excited, but they were also completely exhausted from the past few days.

Ev had been to South by Southwest several times before, and he knew the way people crowded in the hallways between conference sessions to chatter with friends. So months earlier, he had suggested an idea. Why don't we "put a flat panel with a cool Twitter screen in the main hallway where people hang out," Ev had written in an e-mail to Jack and Biz in the weeks leading up to the conference. "On that, put the twitters from people who are at the conference (and, of course, instructions on signing up)." He noted that it would be "highly compelling to see all these updates, with pictures, from people all around you."

Biz and Jack had been immediately sold on the idea and corralled the troops to get to work. The team at Twitter was still very small—just a handful of engineers and designers—but Blaine and Jeremy had started on the servers. Ray, who had done something similar for the disastrous Twitter Love Parade unveiling, had built a Flash animation that could be set up on fifty-one-inch plasma displays. A few days before the conference began, Biz and Jack had flown out to set up the screens throughout the halls. In the background of each display a large beige Twitter logo hung in the air surrounded by instructions telling people how to tweet what they were doing.

Attendees loved seeing their names, faces, and commentaries stream across the screens for all to view. It didn't take long for the plasma displays to became digital billboards, with people huddled around to see which talk or panel to attend as pithy updates scrolled down.

The Apple iPhone would not go on sale for another three months, so the act of peering down at a cell phone for hours on end wasn't part of the social vernacular yet—even at a technology conference. Most people, like Jack, had a Motorola Razr, which was a slim phone that flipped open to offer an extensive menu of features: sending text messages or making phone calls.

Since Twitter worked via text message, people with all types of cell phones could use the service and it started to spread quickly among the conference attendees.

As people sat in panel discussions, rather than look up at those speaking, they instead peered longingly at their phones, staring patiently while they waited for an update, hoping to find some snippet of information more important than real life.

As usage of the site started to spread, investors who were at the conference in search of the Next Big Thing soon found out about Twitter. One young investor, Charlie O'Donnell, a shorter man with a head as bald as Mr. Clean's, was standing on an escalator on Friday afternoon talking to a friend and couldn't believe what he was witnessing.

"This is fucking crazy," Charlie said as he wandered through the conference halls peering from side to side at everyone glued to their phones, constantly pecking for new updates. "Everyone here is on Twitter," he said.

"I've gotta tell Fred," Charlie added as he pulled out his phone to e-mail his old boss, Fred Wilson, who was a partner at Union Square Ventures, a well-known investment firm in New York City.

"Do you twitter?" he asked Fred in the e-mail. "You should check it out. . . . I didn't get it at first, but now that there's a group going to sxsw, I get it," Charlie wrote. "I'd never text all the people I'm texting now . . . but it's a really seamless way to text groups and individuals at the same time."

Fred wasn't convinced, telling Charlie that such a service would never work and that other companies that had tried to make Twitter-like products had all failed.

Yet by Monday morning, Twitter was gaining such popularity at the conference, and thus receiving so much attention on the tech blogs, that Fred changed his tune. As he sat sipping coffee, his short, dark hair still scruffy in the early morning, he went to Twitter.com and registered his name. "trying twitter," he wrote, sending his first tweet.

Fred was forty-five years old at the time, already a legend in the investing circles after having sold GeoCities to Yahoo! for $3.57 billion in stock in 1999. He had also gained a reputation for making adept predictions about new Internet services or themes. Now here he was, watching a stream of tweets fill his screen. Some of the messages talked about the conference, others mentioned Austin, and of course people complained about their hangovers from the night before.

At South by Southwest, one of the main pastimes of attendees is a treasure hunt for the biggest buckets of free liquor. After a few days, Twitter had become the equivalent of a decoder ring in a cereal box to find such a bounty. On several occasions, Jack, Biz, Ev, and Goldman were sitting in a packed bar, sipping beers and reeling from the day, when all of a sudden people's cell phones would start dinging with text messages. Like clones, people would look down at their tiny two-inch screens, read a tweet about a new party, then one by one grab their coats and trickle out of the bar. Off to the next alcohol-soaked gathering with Twitter guiding their way.

Soon bloggers at the conference were referring to the mass exodus from one place to the next as "flocking."

Back in San Francisco, Jeremy, Blaine, Ray, and the other engineers spent the weekend hunkered down at the offices, tinkering and tweaking the servers to ensure that the site stayed alive during the critical few days of the conference. When massive spikes of usage and conversation happened on Twitter, their hearts palpitated with anxiety, hoping the Web site could live through the influx of updates.

After the launch at the Love Parade—now a distant memory they would rarely speak about again—Twitter had been growing at a healthy pace, partially because of the chatter about the service, but mostly because Ev's well-known name was attached to it. That week in Austin, the sign-ups made the last few months look like Twitter had been growing in slow motion.

As Ze Frank stood on the stage preparing to announce the winner for the best new start-up, the servers were about to get battered again.

"And the winner is . . . ," Ze Frank said into the microphone as he looked down at a piece of paper, the audience quieting for a brief moment as he prepared to tell them all what they already knew.

"Twitter!"

Noah began whistling and clapping as he heard the announcement. But his happiness was diluted in a matter of seconds as Jack, Biz, Goldman, and Ev rose from their seats, squeezing past Noah as if he were just another conference attendee and then wading through the ocean of applause and up the staircase to the stage. Jack's brown cowboy boots hit the floor as he rushed toward the microphone. Biz stood to his right holding the award in his hands. Ev and Goldman stood back, giving the spotlight to Jack as he delivered the pithy speech that Biz had written.

"I would like to thank everyone in 140 characters or less," Jack said to the crowd as he leaned forward into the microphone ". . . and I just did." He waved, then said, "Thank you," as the group walked off the stage to thunderous applause.

By the time they returned to their seats, Noah was gone.

Jack, Biz, Goldman, and Ev were gleeful after the announcement. They wandered the halls of the conference, holding up the rectangular glass prize they had been given, posing for photos and shaking people's hands as they made their way to an after-party.

Jack was wearing a blue scarf that swirled around his neck and over his black long-sleeve T-shirt. When he arrived at the party, he was glowing and elated, like a prom queen with a crown atop her head. People continually walked up and congratulated him. Just two days earlier, he had arrived as a nobody. Now he was a mini celebrity.

Noah was dismayed as he wandered the halls for a short time after the awards, but he quickly decided that rather than harbor resentment at not being invited to join his former coworkers on stage, he would be happy for his friends' new success. Off he went, trudging toward the after-party, and he soon caught a glimpse of the Twitter crew from the corner of the room.

As he approached Jack, Noah reached out to shake hands, his mouth opening to offer congratulations. Yet when he was just a few feet away from his friend, Biz swooped in and placed his arm around Jack as he spun them both around and in another direction to pose for a photo. Noah was left standing there in a room full of people, his arm at a forty-five-degree angle, as if he were shaking hands with an invisible man. Jack, Biz, and Ev then slipped off into a side room as more people asked to take their photos. Noah, devastated by what had just happened, left the party.

After the festivities started to die down, Jack tweeted that the small group of founders were making their way to a diner to decompress. As they sat inside, the neon MAGNOLIA CAFE sign glistening in the rain, snacking on chips and salsa and sipping from tall glasses of beer and water, they reeled from the excitement of winning. "At magnolia's, sopping wet," Ev tweeted. Then shortly afterward Biz added, "Chowing down late night at magnolia with the guys."

But it wasn't all the guys.

Just a few blocks away, Noah wandered alone in the rain as his former friends and cofounders toasted to the award they had just won without him.

The First CEO

T he engineers were staring into their computer screens, their headphones wrapped around their heads, as Jack, Ev, Biz, and Goldman wandered toward the back of the office and into the rear room that had once been Noah's office.

No one paid them any attention; it looked just like any other meeting as they shuffled inside, each grabbing a mismatched rolling chair. Goldman slid the glass door closed behind him, giving it an extra push to make sure no one could overhear the conversation they were about to have.

In the few months since South by Southwest, Twitter had quickly passed one hundred thousand people who had signed up for the site. There was still no revenue, or even talk of a business model, but figuring that out would be the job of the CEO.

After weeks of private discussions—some over coffees or beers, others via e-mail—they were finally going to decide who would be running Twitter, what each person's title would be, and how they would split up the stock. Until this moment, the company had belonged solely to Ev, who had financed it with his personal money after buying out Noah and the previous investors almost six months earlier.

It had been a confusing and stressful few weeks for the top half of the Twitter mast. Though they were less concerned about their monetary stakes, their titles, and in turn their egos, were paramount.

In the early days of start-ups, titles are usually handed out without much thought or resonance. Who will be a vice president, chief technology officer, or director of X, Y, and Z is often discussed in a land of make-believe. Given that 90 percent of start-ups don't make it past their toddler years, such decisions rarely matter in the long run. At Twitter it was no different.

Although it was unlike Biz to politic for anything, he had been pushing for a more important title at Twitter for months, hoping to avoid the fate that had befallen him at his previous jobs. When he'd joined Blogger it had already been acquired by Google—no fancy titles for him there. When he'd landed on Odeo's shores, important titles had already been divided up there too. Throughout his career he had always been in the right place at the wrong time. To ensure he didn't fall into the same trap at Twitter, he had begun campaigning with an e-mail he'd sent to Ev and Jack a few weeks earlier.

"Maybe this is inappropriate, but if I don't ask, I'll never know!" Biz wrote in the message after debating over a long weekend about what to say. "What do you envision my title to be? Is there a chance I could be called co-founder?" He knew that if the company grew, the title of cofounder would garner him more respect, both internally and externally. Unlike titles like CEO, CFO, or COO, to which specific roles are attached, the title of cofounder also meant Biz could do what he wanted, moving around the company with a lot of power but without too much responsibility.

At the time, it had been assumed that Ev would be CEO of Twitter and Jack would be president or director of technology. But Biz's role had always been unclear.

"I don't know the answer to this yet. It is not an unreasonable request," Ev wrote back to Biz, also noting that he wasn't sold on the idea. "But it might not be best, for a number of reasons." (For one thing, he worried that if he made Biz a cofounder, then Blaine, Ray, or Jeremy would want the same grandiose title.)

The room in the rear of the office had now been nicknamed the Purse Factory by some employees after Sara, Ev's fiancée, had moved into the office a few months earlier with the goal of making women's purses there. A few scraps of fabric hung about. Some tailor scissors. A sewing machine. And although it was rarely used to make women's handbags, this had become the impromptu office for important meetings.

"I've decided I'm not going to be CEO," Ev told Jack, Biz, and Goldman as he leaned back in his chair. He explained that although he wanted to be involved with Twitter, offering his guidance and vision for the product, he wanted to focus on Obvious Corporation and continue to build new Web start-ups from within his idea incubator.

This wasn't what Goldman wanted to hear. He was hoping that Ev would run Twitter and that Jack would report up to the CEO, not be the CEO. A few days earlier, at a private lunch with Biz, Goldman had tried to convince Ev not to make Jack CEO, telling him he "didn't think he was capable of running the company." And although he agreed, Ev believed Jack could be molded.

"So who is going to be CEO?" Biz asked.

They all looked in Jack's direction. There was no question that Jack had taken on leadership of Twitter after Noah had been pushed out, but there were questions as to whether he could pull off building a real company. Especially one that was growing as fast as a bacteria in a petri dish.

Jack had already shown he could make deft decisions, including an e-mail he had sent in late January. "We have 4, and only 4, priorities: performance, usability, development efficiencies, and costs," he wrote. Then, offering a plan to take Twitter from a buggy Web site to a smooth operation, he added that the company needed to fix the servers, sort out confusing design issues on the site, and hire new engineers.

Jack had also made one of the most important decisions for Twitter to date: limiting the length of tweets. "Currently the number of characters you are allowed in your update is dependent on the length of your name," he had written to his colleagues. "We're going to standardize this at 140 characters. Everyone gets the same amount of space to Twitter, no more confusion or guessing as you are typing." Until then, messages had been limited to 160 characters, which was the maximum length of a text message that could be sent from a cell phone. The move to 140 characters would allow Twitter to include someone's username in the text.

Jack's next move had been to transition to usernames everywhere on the site. Jack had written in the same e-mail, "If your name is bob2342, your friends are going to get "bob2342: walking the dog." He added: "This should clear up massive amounts of confusion and complaints." But this was the type of thing Goldman worried about from Jack. Using usernames, rather than real names, was a typical engineering decision. People in the real world didn't call themselves bob2342; they were simply Bob.

Still, Ev had been impressed with Jack's leadership. "Excellent writeup, Jack. I agree with everything, wholeheartedly," he'd written.

Back in the Purse Factory, Ev looked at Jack and asked him if he thought he could be the chief of Twitter. "We can do a CEO search and find an outsider who has experience running a company," Ev said. "That would make you something like chief technology officer."

"No, I can do it," Jack said. "I want to do it."

Goldman looked skeptical. Biz rocked on the legs of his chair. They sat silently for a few seconds thinking about it. Jack looked at them all with a sense of yearning.

"Okay. Here's the deal," Ev said, pausing again. He dictated that Jack would be CEO. Biz, Jack, and Ev would be cofounders. Goldman would be the vice president of product.

Biz and Jack immediately felt a sense of elation.

As Ev had personally financed Twitter with his own money to date, he told the group that he would retain a 70 percent stake in Twitter. Jack, as CEO, would be given 20 percent of the company. Biz and Goldman would receive around 3 percent each. The rest would be split up among current engineers and new hires.

Eventually, Ev explained, Twitter would need to seek venture funding from investors, which would dilute some of their stock, but as the company consisted of only a handful of engineers, that conversation could wait.

As the meeting wrapped up, they slid the glass door to the office open, and Jack walked out into the office as an official boss. He was beaming with pride and excitement. The CEO of Twitter.

At least for now.

The Hundred-Million-Dollar Offer

Blaine looked up from his desk, leaning back in his chair as Ev walked briskly by, heading toward the front door. "Hey, Ev," Blaine yelled, his long, pin-straight hair hanging down over his shoulders. "Don't take less than a hundred million dollars!" Ev smiled, nodded as if to say okay, and then closed the door to 164 South Park behind him.

It was mid-June 2007 and Jack, Biz, and Goldman were already outside on the curb as Ev emerged. Small pockets of fog lingered on the grass as they started to walk, turning right onto Third Street. Their destination was a mere 350 feet away. As their sneakers tickled the concrete sidewalk, Goldman broke the silence. "This'll be interesting, if nothing else, to see what our value is," he said. "We really don't have a sense of what we're actually worth."

Biz and Ev agreed. Jack was silent as he walked, deep in thought and excitement about his first acquisition meeting.

They could hear car tires thumping on the grates of the freeway up the block as they approached the large gray building on the corner of Third and Bryant streets: the home of Yahoo!'s offices. Although Yahoo!'s company headquarters were in Sunnyvale, forty miles south of San Francisco, the company had recently set up this satellite office, called Brickhouse, as an incubator for entrepreneurial Yahooers to develop entirely new start-ups. The Twitter employees had all been to the office before, often for some of the company's popular Web 2.0 parties. Usually mundane affairs—beer, wine, cheese, crackers, and lots of networking—the parties were meant to celebrate the resurgence of the Web after the cold winter of the early 2000s bubble pop. Most events were the same. People wandered around aimlessly, constantly peering down at the name tags stuck to everyone else's shirts, searching for a venture capitalist, a blogger, or one of the esoteric "famous" people who had sold their start-ups already (like Ev).

But this morning's meeting was different. There would be no cheese, beer, or name tags. Instead, Yahoo! wanted to buy Twitter. "They want to talk acquisition," Ev wrote in an e-mail to Jack and Goldman at the time. "Says that if our price is not hundreds-of-millions, but tens-of-millions 'even several tens-of-millions' [Yahoo!] doesn't think it'll be a problem." Although Twitter had no revenue and no projected business model at the time, Yahoo! envisioned this new start-up as an extension of its mobile offerings.

More than a year after it had begun as an experiment, Twitter had grown to nearly 250,000 active users. While the internal debates over who was in charge had been sorted out—at least for now—outsiders still often reached out to Ev, whom they knew and trusted from Blogger. It annoyed Jack, who was technically the CEO, to hear that someone wanted to buy the company through Ev, but he never let on.

When the request to meet with Yahoo! came in, Ev had been lining up meetings with five prospective venture capitalists and was preparing to put five hundred thousand dollars of his own money into Twitter to continue funding it until the company decided who would finance it. He had also talked to angel investors who came with lots of connections and could help Twitter grow. Among them was the legendary Ron Conway, a wheeler and dealer who came with a slew of connections in Silicon Valley and access to a team of private investigators, if needed.

Although lots of investors, including the big names like Fred Wilson, had started lining up with term sheets offering millions of dollars to finance the company, some investors immediately opted out, telling

Ev that they didn't see a business model in 140-character updates about people's lunches. All of these discussions were put on hold when Yahoo! called.

Brickhouse was a cavernous, loftlike space. Huge white columns randomly interrupted the floor like giant linebackers standing on a football field. At one end of the room, floor-to-ceiling windows looked out on the city; at the other, a wall had been meticulously covered with thousands of fluorescent Post-it notes, creating an image of a giant pixelated hand. Engineers lay about on beanbags programming on their laptops. It was a nerd's paradise.

As the Twitter team wandered in, Bradley Horowitz, who ran Brickhouse, greeted them with some other Yahoo! executives. "Hey, man!" Bradley, said as he patted Ev on the back, then shook his hand. "Great to see you."

Bradley wore his signature dark glasses, the frames as thick as his brows. The creases in his cheeks made him look more like an army general than a computer engineer. He lead them to the right, toward the conference room, where they shuffled inside, grabbing unassigned seats. As everyone got comfortable and introduced themselves, Ev began talking. He had learned how offers to buy start-ups work when he went through the process with Google and Blogger. It was more like trying to negotiate with a high-level escort than selling your company. In the end it almost always came down to the highest price.

Ev ran through the numbers, explaining that at the end of February, days before the company had set off for Austin, the Twitter Web site had been receiving about two hundred thousand new visitors a month. By the end of March, after the South by Southwest award, the number of people coming to the site had quadrupled, quickly zooming past one million visitors as April rolled in. He explained that there was no revenue at Twitter yet, but that would come later, he said, "possibly through advertising or some new kind of business model." For now, Ev was paying all the bills to keep the lights on.

Jack clasped his hands together on the table, barely saying a word. He was nervous but attempted to portray an air of confidence that didn't come across to the others in the room. He simply watched Ev walk Bradley around the Twitter garden. Then the discussion turned to what Twitter actually was.

"So it's a social network?" Bradley asked.

Silence filled the room.

Almost a year into the service, there was no consistent answer to the question. Even since March, after South by Southwest, the site had continued to take on a life of its own, not just for status updates but also for news. The technorati were clearly obsessed with the site, using it mostly to talk about themselves. But other people, and companies, were using it differently. Major news outlets—including the *New York Times*, Dow Jones, and the *Defamer* blog—had set up on the streets of Twitter, all sharing breaking, local, and gossipy news. There were now a fake Bill Clinton, Homer Simpson, and Darth Vader who posted jokey fake statuses. A few "real" celebrities had also joined. Janina Gavankar, an actress from *The L Word*, had been the first celebrity to start tweeting— although Biz had spent a few hours trying to figure out if she was real or an impostor. John Edwards, the presidential candidate, sent messages from his campaign trail. There were also "things" on Twitter. Fire departments had joined. Police scanners. Baseball games. Food trucks. Yet even with this flood of distinctive use cases, no one in the press really seemed to understand what Twitter was. Some in the media had taken to calling it "hipster narcissism," "self-absorption," "self-obsession," "egotistical," and more than a few people who had tried Twitter called it a "complete and utter fucking waste of time."

But the question made Jack pipe up for the first time and start speaking, referencing a blog post written by Fred Wilson in late April. "What exact role is Twitter going to play?" Fred had asked in the post, discussing its place in the future of the Web. "It will be the status broadcasting system of the Internet."

"I see Twitter as a utility," Jack said. "A broadcasting system for the Internet." Then he began to describe his vision for Twitter, noting that it was "like electricity." All of this confused Bradley, who looked around the room, perplexed by the idea of a social-media company as a utility.

As the meeting came to a close, they all shook hands, and Bradley walked everyone out. He thanked them for coming, then looked over at Ev and said, "We'll be in touch soon."

As they plodded back toward 164 South Park, Ev spoke up. "What did you guys think?" he asked. There was a certain air of excitement from the meeting.

"I like Brickhouse," Biz said as they wandered back. "It seems like it'd be a fun place to work."

"Me too," Goldman said.

"So what's the lowest price we sell for?" Goldman asked.

"A hundred million?" Ev hazarded. Biz and Goldman would each get about two to three million dollars if a sale went through at that price. Although such a number is like winning the lottery for most of the world's population, a million dollars in Valley terms is like finding a quarter between your couch cushions. Such a number would give Ev more money and leverage to continuing putting start-ups on the Obvious Corporation conveyor belt.

Given Twitter's growth and attention, though, Ev was thinking about pausing his idea incubator and focusing on the 140-character machine. Prior to the Yahoo! meeting, in an e-mail to Goldman and Biz, he had noted that he was prepared to "double-down on twitter," pushing Obvious Corporation to the side. That still left the question of what to do next: whether to take money from an outside investor or try to sell Twitter to Yahoo! or a similar suitor. Jack didn't have the confidence, or the power within the company, to make that type of decision, so he quietly looked to Ev for guidance.

Jack had the most to win from a sale. Although he was making seventy thousand dollars a year, he was still flat broke, living paycheck to paycheck, paying off credit card debt and student loans from a year of college at New York University before dropping out years earlier. A sale for one hundred million dollars would give him twenty million, a gargantuan sum that could change his life forever.

"Maybe we would take eighty million?" Jack asked. (This would be a sixteen-million-dollar win for Jack.)

"Eighty million is the absolute lowest," Goldman said as they pulled the door open, walking back into the offices.

They didn't have to wait long to find out the real number. In the late afternoon Ev got a call from Bradley. They spoke for a few minutes, then hung up.

"Hey," Ev said to Jack as he walked over to his desk. "Let's talk outside." Goldman followed them.

"So?" Goldman asked as they stood on the sidewalk. "What's the number?"

"Twelve," Ev said bluntly, his arms folded as he toed the edge of the sidewalk with his sneaker.

"What's twelve?" Goldman asked, now slightly confused. Jack started to giggle.

"They offered us twelve," Ev said, his voice pitched higher with slight disbelief.

"Twelve million dollars?" Goldman asked, his eyes widening slightly when he said the number aloud to himself.

"Yep," Ev said. "Twelve million dollars."

They weren't upset by the offer, as investors were begging to fund the company, but they did think it was comical that Yahoo! would offer such a low number.

"We should really take the deal," Jack said sarcastically as they all laughed.

The comical tone was interrupted as Ev told them what Bradley had said on the phone: that he believed Yahoo! could easily build the technology behind Twitter, that it was "simply just a messaging service" and "a few engineers could do the same thing in a week." He had concluded that if Twitter didn't sell, Yahoo! planned to build and release a competitor.

It was a typical relationship offering in the Valley: Either you fuck us, or we'll fuck you.

But hearing such an offer, followed by the fearful threat of attack by a much bigger company like Yahoo!, was also a relief. Now that they knew they weren't going to sell Twitter, they had a clear path. They could move forward and raise their first real round of venture capital, money they needed right away to expand the servers and hire engineers to help with the company's growth. Before the Yahoo! meeting, they had already decided that their first choice for investment would be Fred Wilson. This was partially because Ev and Jack believed Fred understood what Twitter could be. But more important, Fred didn't care about a business model and wouldn't pressure the founders of Twitter to come up with one—that, he told them, would come later.

As Goldman, Jack, and Ev walked back into the office, there was a rare esprit de corps among them. In a single day they had almost sold their company, then found out the suitor was now coming after them. Although they didn't know it yet, it was one of the few moments they would agree on a direction for Twitter. By the end of the coming summer, it would no longer be Twitter versus its competitors. It would be Twitter versus itself—Jack on one side, Ev on the other.

"Twelve million?" Goldman asked again as the door closed behind them.

"Yep," Ev said, laughing. "Twelve million dollars."

Is Twitter Down?

The blog post appeared on the Twitter Web site at 11:53 A.M. on Thursday, July 26.

"First, Twitter was a fun side project, then it was cared for lovingly at Obvious until it was time to form Twitter, Inc.," Jack wrote in the blog post. "Today, we're excited to announce an important moment for Twitter. We've raised funding from our friends in New York City at Union Square Ventures." Fred Wilson, a partner at Union Square, would be leading a five-million-dollar round of funding that would value Twitter at just over twenty million dollars.

Then in a separate blog post, Fred explained why his firm was investing in a company with no income. "The question everyone asks is 'What is the business model?' To be completely and totally honest, we don't yet know," Fred wrote on Union Square's Web site. "The capital we are investing will go to making Twitter a better, more reliable and robust service. That's what the focus needs to be right now." Revenue would have to come later.

Fred was right. There was no time to worry about business models while Twitter was in its current state: broken.

Each morning had been the same for the Twitter employees. A scene of Jeremy's wife finding him on the couch at home in the same position as the night before, his laptop still glowing a warm blue haze on his chest, a small waterfall of drool coursing down the side of his cheek, his fingers lying on the keyboard as if he had been shot in a break-in gone awry. Blaine was found in the same position at his apartment.

They had both been working through the night, trying to keep Twitter up and running—but often to no avail. The Web site was continually breaking and nothing could be done to stop the outages.

Because of the way the site had been built—hacked together over two weeks—the influx of people on Twitter was making it fall apart. It wasn't just one aspect of the service that was breaking; it was every aspect of it. Posts weren't showing up in the timeline. Accounts were disappearing. The site was off-line for hours or sometimes more than a day at a time. The servers were collapsing. And because everything was in such disarray, the employees were revolting. Twitter had been built as a small rowboat designed to carry a few people across a pond; now the same vessel was being used to carry the same number of passengers as a cruise ship across an ocean.

As a result, it was sinking.

The outages also had a domino effect, with the failure of one aspect of the site knocking down everything else. The third-party tools Twitter gave to developers were being harnessed by hundreds of companies and apps that used Twitter's content (Twitterrific, Twitteroo, Twitterholic, Tweetbar, Twittervision, and Twadget, to name a few). This influx of applications was straining resources away from the Web site. The site itself, which was still stuck together with the digital equivalent of plastic wrap and Scotch tape, would often bring down the servers. The servers would get clogged up with all the tweets waiting to be sent to the Web site and, bringing it back around to the beginning, the third-party tools would stop working. Almost daily, the entire operation would just come to a halt.

Although the site's problems should have slowed the flood of people signing up, they were only making it worse, adding bad press that would pique more curiosity about this Twitter thing—"If everyone else is signing up and breaking it, then surely I should see what this thing is about"—a pile-on of hundreds of thousands of people on one tiny little company.

When the site reached one of its daily snapping points, the biggest problem was that the engineers had no idea where the breakage had originated. To solve this problem—or at least try—Jeremy and Blaine built code into the servers that would notify them via text message and e-mail when the site was suffering from one of its many issues. Like a patient put on life support, tubes and wires and cords sticking out and beeping about his health, the new code was designed to help engineers determine where the patient had fallen ill. Then they could go in and operate. This worked for a short while, but as they soon found out, the road to chaos can be paved with good intentions.

In a matter of days the notifier was sounding a series of alarms that couldn't be turned off, and the engineering team was inundated with bulletins. Their phones woke them in the middle of the night—sometimes every few hours, other times every few seconds—vibrating, ringing, and buzzing on the nightstand, with Twitter begging for help, as it had flat-lined again. On several occasions, the problems were so severe that Jeremy and Blaine woke up to find more than a thousand text messages from Twitter servers complaining about a problem that had shuttered the site.

People who used Twitter were complaining as much as the servers. In one instance, a group of Twitter's faithful users decided to hold an online boycott. They proclaimed, on Twitter of course, that they would snub the service for twenty-four hours to show their disdain for the free site going off-line all the time. On the same day, after reading about the boycott, another group of Twitter supporters decided to send free pizzas to 164 South Park to show their love of the service.

But no amount of pizza could fix Twitter; it had been born broken.

As things worsened, Biz took to the company's blog to address the situation.

"Twitter. Is. Slow. We are painfully aware," he wrote on the site in a post appropriately titled, "The Tortoise and the Twitter." "The slowness is being caused by massive popularity which makes for a bittersweet type of situation. We thought we'd let you know what we're doing to make things more sweet than bitter."

Its slowness didn't stop Twitter's growth. People kept signing up. The press kept coming—some good, some bad. The site kept growing. Every two weeks the number of people joining Twitter doubled. And as the *Financial Times* noted in a story on the front page of its print paper, the "mini-blog is the talk of Silicon Valley." There was a *BusinessWeek* profile. Twitter was referenced in *Time* magazine as one of the top fifty new Web sites. "Broadcast where you are and what you're doing right here and right now by texting from your mobile phone," the article said. Mainstream newspapers, television stations, and nontech blogs were picking up the story. Even though the site was not ready for its moment on the stage, it was getting it.

Twitter employees were so busy trying to keep the site alive that they were stripping things out of the site, rather than adding new ones. As this all happened, some of the loyal tech nerds on the service decided to take the lack of new features into their own hands, and two new strange characters started to appear regularly in people's Twitter stream: the symbols @ and #.

In programming speak, @ was used by engineers to talk to other people on a server, so it was natural that it would transfer over to Twitter. The first use of the @ symbol was by a young Apple designer, Robert Andersen, who on November 2, 2006, replied to his brother by placing an @ before his name as they talked. The symbol started to slowly steep into the vernacular of Twitter. Before long, people were referencing one another not by their first names but by their Twitter @ names. The new communication method grew so popular on the site that in early May, Alex Payne, a Twitter programmer, added a new tab to the Twitter Web site that showed people's @-replies.

Then there was the hashtag, the pound symbol that until then had primarily been used on telephones while checking an answering machine. On Flickr, the photo-sharing site, people sometimes used the hashtag symbol to group similar images. In one instance, people had been using Flickr to share pictures of forest fires in San Diego,

California, and had started to organize the newsy pictures with a tag that read "#sandiegofire." Chris Messina, a designer who lived in the Valley and was friends with many of the Twitter employees, started using the same symbol on Twitter, and before long it was picked up by others on the site.

One day Chris decided to stop by the offices to pitch a more formal usage of this strange-looking hashtag icon. He wandered inside and on the stairs bumped into Ev and Biz, who were on their way out to grab lunch.

"I really think you should do something with hashtags on Twitter," Chris told them.

"Hashtags are for nerds," Biz replied. Ev added that they were "too harsh and no one is ever going to understand them."

Chris argued otherwise, pointing out that people were actively using them now and that they could connect conversations on Twitter with chatter taking place in the real world. But Ev and Biz weren't sold on the idea. Instead, they said they would "come up with something better later, something friendlier."

But it didn't matter what Ev, Biz, or anyone else who worked at Twitter thought or said. In an example of the site taking charge where the founders could not, people continued to use hashtags to organize everything, including group chats, conferences, and discussion of news events.

Internally, amid the growing outages on the site, Ev and Goldman continued to try to forge Jack into a better CEO—a struggle that proved to be even more difficult than keeping the Web site alive.

Ev, who had since taken on the role of chairman at Twitter, pressed Jack to supervise Blaine—who was often still anarchistic and thrived on the chaos—explaining how to give him financial incentives and set up regular check-in meetings. (It turns out even anarchists like a good pay raise.) Yet this backfired when Jack started talking down to employees. Or, as Ev noted in an e-mail discussing the problem, "Jack was acting like a cowboy."

Each step forward felt like two steps back. When Ev told Jack to send a Twitter-wide e-mail setting company goals, his first draft began with the subject line "3 things I want for Twitter." Jack then went on to begin each milestone with the off-putting "I want to be able to . . ." or "I want . . ." or "I. . . ." Goldman suggested "we" might be a more appropriate way to address the company. Sounding like a dictator wasn't the best way to talk to your employees.

Although Jack really wanted to learn how to manage, how to run a company, and how to be a good CEO, he often found himself at a loss for what to do next. Although he would never admit it, pretending that he knew exactly what he was doing and that his actions were all part of a bigger, more resolute plan, he was so far out of his league that he was often speechless. When things grew frustrating, rather than confront the problem with his employees, Jack would walk out the front door of the office and then spend an hour or more walking in circles around South Park, a petulant look on his face.

Some of his coworkers, including Biz and Crystal, believed that the company's problems weren't Jack's doing or undoing, that no one could keep Twitter afloat in these tumultuous seas, especially with the influx of new people joining each day. But Ev didn't care whose fault it was or wasn't. His personal money was invested in the company and his name, again, was on the line. It didn't matter if it was Jack's fault or the Easter Bunny's. Ev wanted to stop the site outages, fix the lack of management, and settle the overall chaos of the company. As 2007 wore on, Ev was growing increasingly impatient with the reality that these issues weren't being fixed and they were actually growing worse.

The Dressmaker

I t was late in the afternoon when Jack and Ev walked up the stairs to the conference room that had been nicknamed Odeo Heights. Their feet moved in sync, like two programmed robots, stair by stair, upward to the second floor. They opened the door to the dinky meeting room, pulled back the chairs across from each other, and sat, hands clasped.

Jeremy watched them ascend the staircase as they had done a hundred times before. As did Blaine. And a few others in the office too. But no one paid them much attention. Just a normal meeting between the CEO and chairman of the company. They had no idea—until much later, at least—that Jack would walk up those stairs as one person and walk down as somebody completely different. Two different Jack Dorseys.

Things often don't break; they bend. Relationships rarely just splinter apart; they slowly start to bow, curving in another direction, distorting, and eventually separating. The relationship between Ev and Jack had been doing just that for some time, bowing like wet wood, moving between good and bad, but right now, as they shuffled into their seats in the conference room, it was about to break in two forever.

Ev immediately dropped the gauntlet.

"You can either be a dressmaker or the CEO of Twitter," Ev said. "But you can't be both."

Although Jack worked hard, coming into the office well before any-one else arrived, he often left at around 6:00 P.M. to attend to one of his extracurricular activities. For a while he had taken drawing classes, sketching nudes in his notepad. He attended hot yoga classes, rushing off after work to contort his body into downward dog and sweat out the stresses of the day. He had also been taking classes at a local fashion school to learn how to sew, still contemplating a future career in fash-ion. He loved sewing and enthusiastically set out to learn how to make an A-line skirt for his first class assignment. The eventual goal was to make his own pair of dark jeans, maybe even end up working for his favorite jeans maker one day, Earnest Sewn in New York City.

Jack's social life had also grown exponentially, just as Twitter had. People had started to invite him to parties, lots of parties. He was taken to baseball games by affluent bigwigs like Ron Conway. Girls were pay-ing attention to him, including one, a twentysomething blonde named Justine, who had gained a reputation in tech for dating several well-known start-up founders.

Jack was also feeling his first glimpse of fame as a Z-list celebrity in San Francisco, being written about in the media in Twitter-related arti-cles and blog posts. For the first time in his life, the invisible boy from St. Louis was being recognized by tech enthusiasts at local coffee shops who showered him with their love of Twitter (when it worked). People who used Twitter were also starting to be given ranking based on the number of followers they had on the site. And who better to be the king of the nerds than user number one: Jack Dorsey.

But there was one person who was not Jack's biggest fan: Ev. He believed Jack didn't work hard enough. Wasn't in the office enough. Was distracted by his hobbies. Was too lackadaisical with his manage-ment style. Was . . . was . . . was.

When Ev was in the office, he demanded quiet. Jokes and chatter among coworkers were often met with a long "Shhhhhhhhh!" from Ev. Biz, the always-on jokester, often laughed off the shushing, but Jack took such requests personally.

Jack had been trying to befriend his employees, organizing movie nights and dinners on a regular basis. He had also started a new ritual called Tea Time: a weekly event for Twitter staff that was held on a Friday afternoon to discuss the company's latest news. Although people were supposed to drink tea at the discussion, they instead showed up with beer and other spirits.

But Ev didn't care about Tea Time or movie nights. He was concerned with the company. A company that was in trouble.

The continual site outages had started to take their toll on Twitter. For a few weeks sign-ups had started to slow slightly, and Ev had sent e-mails sounding alarms.

"You leave the office too early," Ev said. "You go off to your dress-making classes and yoga, and to socialize, and we have all these problems with the site and growth is slowing." Ev went on listing Jack's flaws. Jack was furious but didn't respond. He didn't know how to respond. He didn't know if he could respond. Could a CEO argue with a chairman?

It was unclear what Jack could and couldn't say to Ev, as their relationship and the power dynamic between them were full of twists and turns. They had started out as employer and employee, with Jack reporting to Ev, then became cofounders and friends as they started Twitter together. Then the roles of employer and employee had switched as Jack became the CEO and Ev, although the lead investor in the company and chairman of its board was technically an employee reporting to Jack. Now they were two people at odds with each other.

It hadn't always been this way. For a time they had become very close, bonding over Noah's exodus, over winning at South by Southwest, and over drinks—which always helped them both loosen up. In late 2006 Ev, Jack, and Sara had even gone skydiving together for Sara's birthday, thrusting themselves out of a perfectly good airplane and bonding over the experience of falling to earth at 125 miles per hour. They'd even gone camping. But as quickly as they had become friends, their camaraderie had fallen apart.

But more pressing than their opinions of how well the company was being run, Ev and Jack had fundamentally different views of what

Twitter was and how it should be used. Jack had always seen Twitter as a status updater, a way to say where *he* was and what *he* was doing. A place to display yourself, your ego. Ev, who was shy and had been shaped by his days building Blogger, saw it as a way to share where *other people* were and what *other people* were doing.

Ev saw it as a way to show what was happening around you: a place for your curiosity and information. This was the debate that had originated with the concept of Twitter as a news source after the earthquake months earlier.

"If there's a fire on the corner of the street and you Twitter about it, you're not talking about your status during that fire," Ev said during one of their unending discussions about the topic. "You're Twittering: There's a fire on the corner of Third Street and Market."

"No. You're talking about your status as you look at the fire," Jack replied. "You're updating *your* status to say: I'm watching a fire on the corner of Third Street and Market."

To many this might sound like semantics. Yet these were two completely different ways of using Twitter. Was it about me, or was it about you? Was it about ego, or was it about others? In reality, it was about both. One never would have worked without the other. A simple status updater in 140-character posts was too ephemeral and egotistical to be sustainable. A news updater in 140-character spurts was just a glorified newswire. Though they didn't realize it, the two together were what made Twitter different.

They also disagreed over the importance of mobile versus the Web. Jack was adamant about focusing on mobile development, devoting resources to building new SMS tools, allowing more countries to sign up for the service using text messages, and focusing energy on mobile applications. Ev was more focused on the Web and was constantly pushing the team to expand features on the Twitter Web site. He also worried that an emphasis on text messaging was going to bankrupt the company. Each month Twitter was being forced to pay cell-phone carriers tens of thousands of dollars in SMS bills. And each month the bills were higher than the last.

The only thing that Ev and Jack agreed on was that there was very little Ev and Jack actually agreed on.

Jack believed he had been growing and changing. He had even started to look more the part of a CEO, getting his hair cut, tucking his shirt in, and, in the boldest move yet, taking out his nose ring, the same nose ring he'd proudly worn under a Band-Aid years earlier rather than remove it at the behest of an employer. He'd wanted to lead Twitter enough to make that concession and others, but they weren't enough for Ev.

Jack's bond with another employee of Twitter had also deteriorated. Earlier in the summer Crystal's relationship with her boyfriend had fizzled. Although Jack now had lots of girls to choose from, he still yearned for his first Odeo crush. He had planned to ask Crystal out, to organize something special—maybe an old movie, a gesture that could move him from friend territory to kissing territory. But his courage had failed him when he lost her forever in Las Vegas.

He knew exactly when it had happened. It was the weekend of September 7, 2007. Twitter had struck a deal with the MTV Video Music Awards, where celebrity tweets, including those from rapper Timbaland and the band Daughtry, would be integrated into the channel's on-air programming during the awards show. To help with the festivities and ensure that the nontechie musicians knew how to tweet properly, most of the team flew off to Las Vegas to help. But Jack couldn't attend, as a prior commitment took him elsewhere. At the end of the long weekend, the employees came back with dreadful hangovers and lots of stories of partying with the stars. Crystal, though, came back from Las Vegas with a new boyfriend: Jason Goldman.

Jack was outraged. His one chance with Crystal had been stolen from him by one of Ev's best friends and one of the board members of Twitter. "Jack versus Ev" was now "Jack versus Ev and Goldman." And as Jack saw it, Crystal was on the wrong side.

Goldman wasn't deterred by Jack's anger about his new love affair. He was, after all, one of "Ev's boys," not Jack's. What's more, Crystal could date whom she wanted.

Jack's resentment toward Goldman over Crystal didn't compare, though, with the anger he was feeling toward Ev as he was told he could either be a dressmaker or the CEO of Twitter.

There was no cursing during the meeting between the two that day. No screaming or fists banging either. But with each critique slung across the table, Jack was seething.

When the meeting finally ended, they walked down the stairs. As Jack sat at his desk, fuming at the things Ev had said to him, Ev grabbed his things and walked out. Jack shook his head at the irony. After railing against him for leaving the office early, Ev had done just that.

And in that moment, the click of the beige front door, the departure of Ev, the relationship between Jack and Ev was no longer bending. It had just broken.

Rumors

T he rumors had been circling the Valley for weeks. Twitter was raising its next round of funding.

"Love it or hate it, Twitter, a service that embodies our narcissism, is one that we can't stop talking about," Om Malik wrote in a blog post on May 21, 2008. "That buzz is turning into a bidding frenzy for the company's next round of venture funding."

And a frenzy it was. Everyone wanted a piece of the company. In the outline that was sent around to investors at the time, Twitter laid out its stats: The company was now made up of fifteen employees. There were 1,273,220 registered users on the service. Those people were sending almost fifteen million status updates a month. The outline noted that updates were global, coming from all over the planet. But while the document showed rising numbers everywhere, there was one digit that hadn't changed since day one: Revenue = $0, the presentation said. They were still paying the bills with the first round of financing from Fred Wilson and other investors a year earlier, but that money was quickly running out.

The venture capitalists didn't care about the bills, which were flowing in. Each month's user growth was higher than the one before; the projections for the coming months, higher still. The charts accompanying the presentations looked like stairways to heaven.

Ev noted in his presentation that the company hoped to raise ten million dollars in capital at a rate that would put Twitter's valuation at fifty million dollars. But by early May, amid the frenzy and excitement of investors hoping to attach their name to Twitter, the valuation of the company had jumped to sixty million. Then it spiked to seventy million a few days later. In the end, when the news finally broke, the company was worth eighty million.

It didn't matter that Twitter still had no business model or even the faintest sign of one. Or that the site was broken. Everyone still wanted a piece of the fledgling company because it was gaining so much attention. Investors wanted their names associated with the Next Big Thing, and they believed they could help fix its problems.

From the outside looking in, it appeared that Twitter was just growing too quickly. The venture capitalists lining the streets, ready to hand over millions of dollars, believed that with the right check and the right investor guidance, the company would be able to hire new engineers and scoop up a few new servers, and all would be right in the world. Of course, what happened inside the company was often very different from how things were perceived on the outside.

Inside, it was complete disarray.

In April 2008 Jack fired Blaine in an attempt to show Ev his control of the company. Internally it was a typically ugly exit, with Blaine being sacked while he was on vacation. Yet externally the tech media believed it was just an oh-shucks-it's-time-to-move-on-and-we're-still-friends story. Then Jack fired Lee Mighdoll, another senior engineer who had been hired only a few months earlier. After Blaine was fired, the site's problems only worsened. Blaine had been the core programmer of Twitter, and without him Jack had no idea how to fix certain issues.

Since the site's inception, when Twitter went down, people were greeted by a picture of a cat doing something funny. "I is in your komputer," one notification proclaimed, a picture of a sleepy kitten curled up inside an old PC. As the company had grown up slightly, Biz decided the cat pictures were too jokey and went in search of something more serious. He soon came across an illustration on a stock-photography site by Yiying Lu, an artist and designer from Sydney, Australia, of a whale being lifted from the sea by some birds. This became the new image people saw when Twitter crashed. As the site was going off-line so much, it didn't take long for the whale to garner its own nickname: the Fail Whale.

There was also the bittersweet problem that celebrities were now using Twitter, bringing more followers and sign-ups with them. In a trend that would continue indefinitely, some of those celebrities would randomly show up at the office. The pilgrimage to the great blue bird. One morning, when a couple of engineers strolled into the office and walked into the kitchen to get their morning coffee, they found a member of the band blink-182, half-asleep and half-drunk, pouring a small bottle of gin into a bowl of Fruity Pebbles cereal, then chowing down on breakfast. At other times, the rapper MC Hammer would show up out of nowhere with his entourage and just hang out.

But the celebrities didn't get a true glimpse of Twitter either. They were ignorant of the disputes between Jack and Ev. Even the fundraising had been a cluster fuck—at least behind the scenes, where it had become another internal tug-of-war gone awry: Ev pulling on one end, Jack on the other, Biz trying his best not to get caught in the middle.

While Ev had been leading the funding talks, Jack felt excluded from the conversations. Wanting to prove to Ev that he could handle the task, Jack tried to negotiate with investors on his own. As a result, one minute a venture capitalist would get a call about a meeting from Ev, the chairman. The next, the phone would ring with Jack, the CEO on the line, hoping to set up the same meeting. To the venture investors, it just came across as a slight misunderstanding. To Jack it came across as being slighted.

One afternoon Jack got on the phone with one of the venture capitalists and negotiated a deal that would value Twitter at one hundred million dollars with the latest fund-raising. Proud of himself, he trudged off to tell Ev. But it was too late. Ev had already decided that he wanted to use another firm. The lead investor would be Spark Capital, and Bijan Sabet, a well-respected and kind partner at the Boston-based firm, would be joining the board of Twitter after it closed its eighteen-million-dollar round of investing in June 2008, which would value the company at eighty million dollars.

From Jack's perspective the deal that he had struck was a better one than Ev's, and he was once again irate that Ev was going above him to make decisions.

Though Jack didn't know it at the time, for Ev the funding round hadn't just been about the money or the valuation of the company. It had been about a bigger goal, fixing the company the best way Ev knew how: by taking more control of its daily operations.

Fuck Fuck Fuck . . .

Bijan's fingers moved on the keyboard in a repetitive motion. Back and forth he typed, one single word, like a parrot with Tourette's syndrome. "Fuck fuck fuck fuck fuck fuck fuck fuck fuck fuck fuck fuck fuck fuck fuck fuck fuck fuck." Then he hit "send," catapulting the words in an e-mail to Fred Wilson's in-box. Nothing else, just the word "fuck," eighteen times.

He didn't need to add anything to the message. No explanation was needed. Fred knew exactly what had just happened.

Bijan buried his head in his hands, closed his eyes, and repeated the word one last time to himself. "Fuck!"

In Twitter's eighteen-million-dollar round of financing in June 2008, Bijan's company, Spark Capital, had invested fourteen million, with Jeff Bezos of Amazon and Fred Wilson investing the majority of the other four million—along with several angel investors. The large sum put in by Bijan's company had secured him a seat on the board of Twitter, along with Fred Wilson. Over the next couple of months Bijan had started to become entrenched in the company, attending a few meetings, raising his hands for a few critical infrastructure votes. And now here he was, fucking it all up already.

He sat for a moment, pointlessly trying to reason whether he could somehow, by some means, any means, delete an e-mail he had accidentally sent to Jack a few minutes earlier. It was impossible, he knew. You can't resurrect the dead or delete an e-mail that has traveled eighty-five thousand miles per second across from Boston to San Francisco.

After a few seconds trying to calculate the incalculable, Bijan sat up and frantically began typing another e-mail.

To: Jack. "Please call me when you get this message," he wrote, noting that he wanted to clear up his previous e-mail. "Out of context this could be really confusing."

It had all started in July 2008, when Twitter purchased its first company, Summize, which used Twitter's third-party tools to allow people to search everyone's public tweets. People had taken to the feature as quickly as they had taken to Twitter itself. Before long, so many people were using Summize that Twitter found itself competing with the company for page views. Rather than snuff it out, Twitter decided to purchase Summize and its small team of highly competent engineers.

The sale had been relatively painless. The initial negotiation between Fred and John Borthwick, an investor who was on Summize's board, occurred while the two were standing next to each other at a bathroom urinal. "Why don't we just join these companies and call it a day?" John said as he peered over at Fred, a tinkling sound emanating from their respective urinals.

Fred agreed. After a couple of in-person meetings, a deal was struck (not in a men's room, thankfully).

July had already been a busy month as Twitter had also moved into new offices: a fancy, modern, loftlike space with lots of windows and room to grow. Among the fun features they had added to the office (a living-room setup with a couch and video games, a large red phone booth, and a fully stocked kitchen with cereal and other snacks), Jack had suggested putting in a Radiohead room. "It can play Radiohead twenty-four hours a day!" he said excitedly when suggesting the idea.

After the company had signed the paperwork with Summize and divvied up Twitter stock as part of the sale, Jack got on the phone with Greg Pass, the engineer who had been running the tech side of Summize.

"Hey, so we're thinking that, since we don't really have any real leadership here on the engineering team, that you can run all of it," Jack said.

Greg sat silent for a moment, processing what Jack had just said, immediately realizing that something must be amiss at Twitter, as he heard the CEO utter the words "no leadership" on the engineering team. "Um, okay," Greg said, but before he had a chance to ask what Jack meant, he was interrupted.

"And," Jack said, "how about you run the operations side too?"

The operations side of the company included managing the so-far-disastrous scaling of Twitter's servers. "Um, I don't have any experience running operations," Greg said.

"Well, there is no one here that can run it better than you," Jack replied matter-of-factly.

When they got off the phone, Greg was shocked. And he wasn't the only one. Jack sent an e-mail to the company announcing that there would be a management switch, that Greg was now director of operations, or "ops" for short, and overseeing all of engineering. (Jack planned to focus his time on product development.) When the message arrived in Ev's in-box, he was livid. "You're just going to put someone in charge of engineering and ops for the entire company and not discuss it with me or the board?" he said to Jack in pure frustration.

It was the "enough's enough" moment for Ev. But also for Fred and Bijan. And in several secret calls and meetings, they decided it was time to figure out what was going on inside Twitter.

Fred and Bijan, now the two investors on the Twitter board, flew out to San Francisco from New York and Boston on the red-eye. They set up meetings with Goldman, Biz, and Jeremy. For what? "Oh, just to talk. We want to get your thoughts on how things are at Twitter." It was partially true. But in reality, Fred and Bijan wanted Jack out. So did Ev. The main purpose of the meetings was to learn how such a move would go over with employees. Twitter's senior staffers didn't need much cajoling.

One by one, Goldman, Biz, and Jeremy were shuffled away from

Twitter's office and into coffee shops and gently interrogated. Then the most senior employees were told that Fred and Bijan, with the full support of Ev, were going to demote Jack, removing him as CEO. "What do you think?" they asked, even though the decision had essentially been made.

Bijan and Fred soon found out that Jack had been incompetent with the company's finances too. Although revenue was still at zero, expenses were quiet the opposite, with growing server fees, text-message bills, and payroll. Jack, who had been managing expenses on his laptop, had been doing the math incorrectly. When Ev learned about this, he asked a friend and seasoned entrepreneur, Bryan Mason, to meet with Jack and show him how to manage the company's books, but Bryan spent the entire meeting at a whiteboard with a marker explaining the basics of accounting.

When Bijan and Fred met with the engineers, they heard mostly worries about Jack. "Engineering and ops are a disaster," they consistently said. "He's a great guy. A great friend. A fun boss. But he's in over his head," another announced. "He's like the gardener who became the president." "I don't know who is in charge. Ev presents the product and vision for what's going on, and Jack just sits in the corner and takes notes."

The board members knew they had to find a new role for Jack or let him go immediately.

Everything was all set; it was all about to happen. Then the plan came to a screeching stop.

"I'll quit!" Biz said to Fred and Bijan as he folded his arms and sat back in his chair like a petulant child. "Should Jack be running Twitter? Probably not," Biz admitted, but he believed that forcing Jack out would tear Twitter in two. Although most employees would have helped pull Ev's side of the tug-of-war rope given the choice, and although Jack was completely out of his league as CEO, some Twitter employees, including Biz, still loved him. "I'm serious. If you fire Jack, I'll quit."

It was a bluff, but it worked. Fred and Bijan knew they couldn't lose

Biz, especially if they were pushing Jack out too. As Biz's job as co-founder had unfurled, he had started to serve two distinct roles at Twitter. First, he had become the public face of the company. Given Jack's and Ev's strange and often quiet public posture, Biz had stepped up his gregariousness and become the guy who joked with the press, enlivened employees, and often entertained the visiting celebrities.

He had also become the moral line at the company. In late November 2007, Twitter had been used as a prop on the TV show *CSI: Crime Scene Investigation*: Tweets were used as clues to track down the victim of a murder. It didn't take long for fiction to turn into reality, and the FBI and other law enforcement started knocking at Twitter's door demanding information on certain people who used the service. Biz and Ev, along with Crystal, had emphatically said no, adamant about protecting people's identities on Twitter rather than caving to some big guys with guns in suits.

While Bijan and Fred were whisking employees away, Jack suspected something was amiss—secret closed-door meetings, quiet phone calls from Ev in the conference room—but he had no idea about the severity of the situation.

What's more, Jack had no idea that Biz's threat to quit was Jack's second reprieve in recent weeks. Another pardon had taken place earlier in the month after a disastrous attempt by Jack to break bread with Ev, whom he barely spoke to anymore.

The two cofounders had agreed to meet for dinner to talk about the turmoil. Jack thought the purpose of the meal was to mend some broken bridges. He suspected Ev wasn't happy, but as neither of them was direct about his views and feelings, they had been skirting around the conversation.

They met at Bacar, a California fusion restaurant, in early August. The smell of burning wood drifted through the air as they both doused their uncomfortable feelings with a few large glasses of alcohol. After long stretches of silence that were punctuated by short bursts of small talk, they got down to business. "What's going on?" Jack asked Ev as they waited for their meal to be served. "You don't seem happy."

Ev explained that the company's problems—the blackouts, the lack of communication with him and the board, and the text-messaging bills that were approaching six figures—were all hurting the growth of Twitter. Ev noted that over the past few months the Twitter company blog had been one post after another explaining that the site was down—all of this, he said, was an embarrassment to Twitter.

"Do you want to be CEO?" Jack interrupted, point-blank. Ev was caught off guard by the question. "Do you?" Jack asked again, in a rare stern moment.

"Well, I've been thinking about things," Ev replied, taking a sip from his martini, then swerved and jumped back into a slew of other problems the company was going through: the lack of hiring, the costs, the chaotic culture.

Jack interrupted again. "You're not answering the question. You have to tell me if you want to be CEO. I don't want to leave this table without knowing your intent; I do not want to work under a cloud."

Ev paused briefly. He had not planned to tell Jack that evening about the board's plan to demote or remove Jack, but he was now being pressured to answer. He hadn't even told Goldman what was going on, fearing that such a conversation would be told to his girlfriend, Crystal, and eventually come back to Jack. Finally Ev took a deep breath and replied. "Yes. I want to be CEO. I have experience running a company, and that's what Twitter needs right now."

"Fine," Jack said, a look of anger and disgust on his face. "I want to move immediately on this. I want to tell the management team tomorrow."

After an extremely awkward dinner, Jack walked home panicking about what to do. When he opened the door to his apartment, he paced, his feet tapping the brown hardwood floor as he tried to clear his head. Then he dropped down onto his white couch, slipping his laptop out of his Filson bag and quickly rattling out an e-mail to the senior management team telling them there would be an emergency meeting the following morning. Then he sent another message, to Fred and Bijan, describing the conversation with Ev.

Jack then tried to go to sleep but found himself lying awake in bed, tossing and turning as he replayed the evening's conversation in his head. He suspected that this was all some elaborate ploy by Ev to take power and control of the company and that the moment Fred and Bijan read the news, they would stop the miscreant chairman.

The next morning in the office, everyone filtered into a conference room for this emergency meeting. As Jack and Ev stood a few feet from the conference-room door, about to walk inside, they both received a text message from Bijan saying that they should call him immediately, together. Do not do anything, Bijan said. "Call me now."

They walked out of the conference room, where the management team now sat utterly confused. And although they were about to get on the same conference call, Jack turned in one direction, entering the Radiohead room, and Ev walked into another separate conference room, both to call Bijan.

"Look, we've heard what's going on and we don't want you to do anything yet," Bijan said. "Just hold off for now."

While Jack listened, he paused for a moment as he heard Radiohead lyrics floating in the background in the tiny conference room, his iPhone pressed up to his ear trying to block out the faint music. He looked in the direction of the speaker, briefly registering the irony of the song "Karma Police" playing while he was embroiled in this confusing power battle with Ev.

Bijan continued, "Fred and I are gonna fly out there next week and meet with you both and the management team," he said.

The call ended, and Bijan hung up the phone, relieved that he had held off the switch from one CEO to another. Ev and Jack opened their respective conference-room doors simultaneously, paused briefly as they looked at each other as in a dramatic romantic-comedy scene, then walked briskly across the concrete floor in the same direction to sit awkwardly and silently across from each other.

In addition to creating the Radiohead room, Ev and Jack had agreed to sit in the same place in the new office. Their desks butted up against each other, back to back, like conjoined twins. As they shuffled into their seats after the call, their frustrated scowls were obscured by two large monitors that stood on the desks like sandbags piled high on a battlefield to hinder enemy fire.

Although the call with Bijan had stopped his execution, Jack now knew there were larger forces at work than just Ev. He sat, playing the things Bijan had said over in his head and trying desperately to figure out what was going on. Words like "yet" and "not now" spun in circles but didn't offer clues to the future.

It was a week later that Fred and Bijan flew out to Twitter HQ. The plan all along had been to fire or demote Jack and put Ev in as CEO. But when it came time to pull the trigger, Biz protected him, temporarily. So Bijan and Fred were left with no other option but to keep Jack in his current role. They sat him down and gave him an ultimatum. "You've got three months," they told him. "Three months to fix things and take control of the company."

Of course, they knew Jack couldn't fix anything in three months, or three years. He was incapable of running the company. It was like watching somebody try to build sand castles underwater.

The two investors flew back to New York and Boston and started organizing a way to remove Jack, sending e-mails back and forth discussing a possible new job for him at the company. It was then that Bijan made his heinous error.

First thing in the morning, his coffee cup still full next to his computer, and weary from a night without much sleep, Bijan accidentally pressed the "reply to all" button on his computer instead of replying just to Fred.

"I believe Jack would take a 'passive' chairman role," Bijan wrote. "It would then really be up to Ev to decide if he could live with Jack's new title." He hit "send" before he realized what he had done.

Seconds later, he looked up at the exchange and uttered a word he was about to write eighteen times in an e-mail that he then sent to Fred:

"Fuck fuck fuck fuck fuck fuck fuck fuck fuck fuck fuck fuck fuck fuck fuck fuck fuck fuck."

He then quickly rattled off the e-mail to Jack: "Please call me when you get this message. Out of context this could be really confusing."

But it was too late. Jack knew what was about to happen.

Building Sand Castles Underwater

Thehe summer of 2008 was coming to a close, the seasons changing as August rolled into September and Jack's three-month
reprieve began.

Although Jack had spoken to Bijan after the accidental e-mail, he
believed he could somehow save himself from being thrust out of the
company. So he immediately went into panic mode and held a meeting
with Twitter's leadership team to announce his battle plan.

"Before we start, I want to take a moment to address the events of
last week," Jack said. "For me, it was a wake-up call." He took responsibility for the problems at Twitter, admitting that there was a lack of
strong leadership. He also laid some of the blame on Ev and Goldman,
noting that he needed to execute his own vision for the company, not
theirs. And he admitted that Twitter needed to "think bigger," as Ev
had been saying since day one.

But Jack's idea of thinking big wasn't to fix Twitter's endless thirty-
hour-long outages. It wasn't to resolve the bank-robbery-size SMS bills.
It was, as Jack outlined in an e-mail to Fred and Bijan, to "be at the
forefront of this historic 2008 Presidential elections [*sic*]."

"As we've been pointing out consistently in the past, events, massively shared and immediate experiences, capture the essence and

engagement of what Twitter has to offer the world," Jack wrote to the board. "And the biggest shared event we can plan for already has traction with our users, is right under our noses, will deliver us to mainstream usage, and is rapidly approaching." Then, beating the rallying drum, he announced: "Twitter will be at the forefront of this historic 2008 Presidential elections [sic]. Whether we do anything or not, it's going to be huge for us. Imagine how big it could be if we fully embraced it as a company?"

As they read, none of the team members were in support of this idea. Fred: This won't solve our problems! Bijan: Oh, Jack. Ev: WTF! Goldman: What the hell is he thinking?

Blogger had been down this road before. Four years earlier Goldman had set out to the Democratic National Convention in Boston to try to persuade the media and attendees to blog. There he had seen firsthand that if people were going to use these new technologies, they did it of their own accord, not because a company willed them to.

Goldman remembered the 2004 election vividly. He had hopped on the phone with Noah, who was in California, and explained the scene in Boston, recording a podcast that described the apocalyptic setting with thousands of Boston police and protestors.

As the 2008 presidential election approached, people were no longer talking about podcasts or blogs. A new word had obliterated the vernacular of politics and media: "Twitter."

Outside, protesters were using the service to organize massive demonstrations against the police. Inside, a young senator from Illinois named Barack Obama was using Twitter to try to disrupt politics and grassroots campaigning and, he hoped, win the election. And the media, including the *Huffington Post*, had set up Twitter accounts to update live snippets from the 2008 conventions.

The reality was, Twitter didn't need to do anything to ensure that it kept growing. It was already on its way to becoming a "personal newswire," as Biz explained it.

Twitter continued to compress time, often reporting news more quickly than news outlets that had been in the business for more than a century. As more people joined the service, it moved even faster. During the 2008 conventions, the 1.4 million people who were actively using Twitter sent more than 365,000 tweets from both the Republican and Democratic conventions. Such numbers showed that the elections were important, Ev agreed, but they weren't more important than growing the tiny team of twenty-two employees and getting the site working properly.

Like rolling blackouts in a country already starved of electricity, the site had continued to go off-line daily. The Fail Whale took over the site almost hourly. Some outages lasted a few minutes, others more than a day. The fire hose, the name given to the stream of all the tweets coming through the service for third-party applications, would often turn off.

As Jack got to work designing a dedicated elections page, Ev said nothing, waiting for Jack to fail. And it didn't take long.

At the next board meeting, after going through the slides announcing the number of new sign-ups, Fred and Bijan asked Greg Pass, who was now running engineering and operations, to present a plan for how to fix Twitter's outages. It was an altogether impossible task, like asking a mechanic to figure out how to replace the engine of a moving car filled with 1.4 million passengers.

The sun shone brightly through the conference-room window when Greg walked in. He sat down slowly, methodically, like a doctor about to deliver bad news to a patient.

Greg began by explaining that he had built software to detect what was wrong with the site, to find out why it continued to go off-line. As he opened his laptop and began talking, Jack sat silently. Ev too. They had both been warned by Greg what he was about to say to Fred and Bijan.

"We have a bit of a problem," Greg began. While he had been running tests on the site, he had discovered that there was no backup of Twitter. "If the database goes down right now, we would lose everything," Greg said awkwardly. Every tweet, every user, everything. Gone.

"You're fucking kidding me," Fred said with almost comical disbe-lief. "Well, what the fuck are you doing in here?"

As Greg rushed out of the room to figure out how to back up Twit-ter, everyone looked in Jack's direction. And although he didn't know it at that moment, they all did: Successful election site or not, Jack Dor-sey's days as Twitter's CEO were numbered.

Calling My Parents

The week Jack Dorsey was fired from Twitter began much like any other. Monday started with the usual Jack routine. He got up and made his white bed. Showered. Dressed in his dark blue Earnest Sewn jeans and black cardigan. Grabbed his keys and bag and ran down the stairs.

At some point that morning, Jack checked his e-mail and was greeted by dozens of messages that had filled his in-box throughout the night. There was one message that stood out like police lights on a dark city street. It was from Bijan and Fred, and it had been sent at 7:41 A.M. on the East Coast. The subject line simply said: "Breakfast wed morning."

Why were Bijan and Fred asking to get breakfast on Wednesday morning? They weren't supposed to be in San Francisco that week. Did Ev know about this? Jack thought.

He opened the e-mail. "Can you meet with me and Fred before the board mtg," the message from Bijan read. "Why don't we meet for breakfast Wed morning at 7:45am at the Clift Hotel. Let me know if that works." Jack glanced up at the time, where the numerals showed that it was 7:15 A.M. Pacific Time. Fred and Bijan wanted to meet exactly forty-eight hours later.

Routine interrupted.

Anxiety welled up in his chest. He knew almost immediately that this wasn't a good sign.

As his mind raced with scenarios, he wrote a response. "That works. I'll see you there." He hit "send" and the e-mail made its way to Fred and Bijan.

He spent his commute on the Muni train preoccupied with the meeting. The metal wheels clicked and screeched against the tracks as he tried to replay past conversations with the board in his mind. He glared out of the window, asking himself why Fred and Bijan wanted to meet. He was like one of Agatha Christie's fictional detectives trying to decode a meeting two days from now, his only clue a forty-three-word e-mail.

When Jack arrived at work, he stepped off the elevator into the Twitter office and was greeted by the familiar smell of percolated coffee that filled the hallway. He headed straight for Ev's desk, hoping by some miracle, by some obscure chance, he would be sitting there ready to answer questions.

But Ev's desk was empty. Just his roller chair, alone. His Mac computer, sleeping.

As the afternoon drew on, Jack's anxiety still hadn't abated, so he decided to write Ev an e-mail asking for some answers. He hit "send," then waited. Waited for a reply. A phone call. A text message. For Ev to appear in front of his desk and explain what was going on.

Ev never responded.

———

Fred's hand scrunched around his face as he rubbed his eyes, trying to abate the tiredness that was consuming him. It was Tuesday morning and he was exhausted after the six-hour flight from New York. He was also starting to grow impatient, as the conversation seemed stalled.

Bijan started speaking again as Ev paced in his living room, his feet brushing against the white shag rug and the dark hardwood floor. In the background his bookcase, filled with marketing, management, and business titles, watched over them. Surely one of these books covered this topic: firing a CEO.

The three had been talking for some time, having a variation on previous conversations that had taken place over the past few months.

"What if he goes to Facebook?" Bijan had asked on more than one occasion. "We have to do something to make sure that doesn't happen. It'll look terrible for Twitter if the founder goes to Facebook."

"He's not gonna go to fucking Facebook." Fred laughed, rolling his eyes in Bijan's direction, his hand in its usual resting spot, his chin. "Look, I get that he's all starry-eyed by Zuck, but he's not gonna go work there."

"He could!" Bijan said and argued that the board should make Jack director of product or chairman or give him another senior role at Twitter after he was let go as CEO, to ensure that he didn't go off to a competitor.

But that wasn't an option either. Jack had been quite vehement when he had been given his three-month reprieve that if things didn't work out, he would not work for Ev.

As the morning wore on Ev cupped his phone in his hand and paced, looking at it every few minutes to see if one of his confidants, like Chris Sacca, an investor in Twitter and one of Ev's trusted friends, had called with some advice on the matter.

"I'm not giving him a fucking board seat," Ev snapped. "He doesn't know what the fuck he's doing."

Then there was a group discussion to just fire him and call it a day.

But as Ev noted, Biz and Crystal and the people who enjoyed working with Jack would be distraught. If Biz even knew about this discussion, he reminded them both, he'd be fuming and might threaten to quit. At all costs, Biz must stay at the company, Ev said. Losing two of the three cofounders would be a disaster.

The discussion went on for over an hour. Round and round the proverbial merry-go-round they went. And then, finally, a decision. A plan. An execution.

———

Wednesday arrived quickly. Jack awoke weary and anxious. He felt sapped as he stepped off the train in the Tenderloin. Plodding up the steps to exit the station, he kept his head down as he walked in the direction of the Clift Hotel. Although it was still early, homeless people were everywhere, spilling out of halfway houses. Hookers—a familiar scene of leftovers from the night before in the Tenderloin—stood about without a care in the world. As Jack approached the hotel, the doorman pulled back the large glass door and repeated his morning announcement to guests, "Good morning, sir."

Not for Jack, it wasn't.

Jack was reminded of the sounds and the smell of the hotel from the last time he had stayed there. A year earlier, when Twitter was just a hatchling, he had spent two nights at the Clift. A staycation in his own city. Wining and dining in the hotel. He had worked too, spending an evening writing the code that would connect people's names together using the now famous @ symbol.

As the door to the Clift swung open, he walked inside, looking around for Fred and Bijan.

———

At the moment Jack exited the Muni train, across the city, Goldman's phone vibrated in his pocket as he took a sip from his morning coffee. He looked at the screen and a bit of confusion set in. A text message from Ev said to meet at Ev and Sara's apartment on Fourth Street in an hour. Greg got the same message. Biz too. As did Abdur Chowdhury, who had joined Twitter during the Summize acquisition. Each thought the same thing: *A meeting. This early in the morning. At Ev's. Can't be good.*

They all arrived, separately, buzzing as the door clicked open, into the elevator, into Ev's house. Before long the group of Twitter executives were sitting at Ev's kitchen table, sipping coffee and waiting to find out why they were there so early in the morning.

October 2005. Noah captains the boat through the San Francisco Bay as Biz pretends to hold on for dear life. Ev, at right with sunglasses, laughs. Rabble is in the rear right.

October 2005. Jack, middle, listens as Noah and Ev, not pictured, talk at Sam's Bar in the Tiburon Marina. Ariel Poler, an investor in Odeo, is at right.

January 2006. Noah, at right, records a podcast with Biz, seated in the chair, and Ev, seated on the floor.

May 2006. The Odeo employees gather at Amici's in San Francisco to say good-bye to some who have been let go in the layoffs. From left to right: Blaine Cook, Adam Rugel, Courtney Brown, Jack Dorsey, Rabble, Ray McClure, Noah Glass, Sara Morishige, and Evan Williams.

September 2006. Jack and Noah pose for a photo at the Love Parade in San Francisco during the grand public unveiling of Twitter. Hours later, Jack would end up in the hospital.

March 2007. Jack gives a speech at the 2007 South by Southwest Awards. Left to right: Biz Stone, Jack Dorsey, Evan Williams, Jason Goldman, and Ze Frank.

June 2007. From left to right, Jack Dorsey, Biz Stone, Jason Goldman. and Evan Williams gather to celebrate Biz and Livia's wedding.

January 2009. Twitter wins best start-up founders at the Crunchies Awards ceremony.

April 2009. Twitter employees watch Ev on the *Oprah Winfrey Show*.

April 2009. Jack peers out of an army helicopter on his way to the American-occupied Green Zone in Iraq.

May 2009. Ev, Jack, and the singer M.I.A. and her husband pose for a photo at the *Time* 100 dinner.

November 2009. Dick Costolo joins Twitter as the company's first chief operating officer.

August 2009. Arnold Schwarzenegger, the governor of California, stops by the Twitter office for a town hall–style discussion with Ev and Biz.

January 2011. Snoop Dogg rapping at the Twitter office.

June 2010. Russian president Dmitry Medvedev visits Twitter right as the site goes down.

July 2011. Jack hosts a Twitter town hall with President Barack Obama.

February 2012. Dick Costolo addresses employees during Tea Time, the company's weekly all-hands meeting.

May 2012. Jack, in one his now-signature suits, talks to Dick, now CEO of Twitter.

"So Ev, you wanna tell us what's going on here?" Biz asked after everyone was settled. Goldman looked up, nudging his glasses with his finger to push them back up his nose. They all noticed that Ev was fidgety. Not a good sign. As some of them knew, fidgety meant someone was getting fired.

Ev looked down at the table as everyone looked back. His arms crossed, he took a deep breath and then began to talk.

———

Jack walked by the huge, blazing fireplace in the lobby of the Clift Hotel. He spotted Fred and Bijan sitting in the rear of the hotel's Velvet Room restaurant. They were in a round booth, their backs pressed against the dark brown leather. Seven ornate lightbulbs hung from the ceiling, encircling them both.

"Hey, Jack," Fred said, motioning to an open black chair at the end of the booth, "take a seat." Fred was already tearing apart the eggs on his plate. Coffee cups had been refilled more than once. It was clear there had been a meeting before this meeting. Bijan seemed more solemn, pursing his lips as he nodded in Jack's direction and almost whispering, "Hey, buddy."

Jack sat, his hands clenched under the table. In an almost-sad whisper he asked, "How's it going?"

Fred was about to start speaking—there would be no small talk here—when the waitress interrupted. "Coffee?" she asked with a smile. Jack's stomach, already churning like a washing machine, couldn't even handle chamomile tea, never mind coffee. "No, thanks. I'll have a yogurt, please."

Then, as she turned to walk away, Fred dropped the guillotine.

"So we're making Ev CEO," he said, his fork clenched in his hand. "You're going to get a passive chairman role and a silent board seat. We have some paperwork for you and a recommendation for a lawyer."

Jack felt like he had just been hit in the face with a baseball bat. "Say that again," he stuttered to Fred, thinking he had heard incorrectly.

Fred repeated himself almost verbatim: We're making Ev CEO.

You're getting a passive chairman role. You will have a silent board seat. Here's the paperwork. Call a lawyer.

Jack was told that the chairman title was more honorary than actually functional. His board seat wouldn't actually be a board seat at all. Instead it was "silent," which meant it would belong to Ev, who would maintain Jack's voting rights. Jack would now be the company mascot, unable to make any decisions about Twitter. Passive. Silent. Ev, in comparison, was the majority stakeholder in Twitter, with four times as much stock as Jack, and would now have two board seats.

———

At almost the exact same moment, Ev spoke from the same mental script to the Twitter executives gathered around his kitchen table. "Jack's out," he said.

"The board met. This is the final decision. They want me to be CEO, and Jack will become chairman," he continued. "The board is telling him right now. Today will be his last day."

They all looked back in shock as Ev continued talking, explaining why the board had made the decision.

———

Jack stared at Fred, not sure what to say, as Bijan started talking.

"You know, you're really good," Bijan said, his eyes calm as he looked at Jack. It was clear that his role was to be good cop to Fred's bad cop. "You're a founder of the company, and we really believe in your vision, so we want you to stick around."

Fred interrupted him. "It's effective immediately, Jack; it has to be." Jack realized this wasn't a hostage negotiation; this was it.

———

"What? When did that happen?" Biz said, annoyed. "*Come on*. What the fuck? What happened?"

Ev tried to calm him, saying it wasn't entirely his decision, that the board had been pressing for a new leader and it was either Ev or an out-side CEO. Ev had even gone on a search for a replacement, interviewing a few external candidates to run the company, but in the end Ev made the most sense. He reiterated that he had experience running a company, adding that it was going to be the job of the people sitting at that table to tell the employees and ensure that morale stayed solid through the swift transition.

———

Jack rocked back and forth slightly in his chair, looking down at his untouched yogurt.

"You've done amazing things for the company," Bijan said. "But the site still keeps going down, and the SMS bills, and we just . . . we just can't wait anymore."

"But what about the three months?" Jack interrupted, anger now taking over his voice. Most of their words were starting to sound muffled as he looked up at them. "We're going on all cylinders and the election is coming up and . . ."

Bijan and Fred continued to talk from their script, irrelevant of what Jack had to say. They explained that he wouldn't get all of his stock options, that he had not fully vested, so they would be taking some of them back. But because they liked him, he was getting more than he deserved.

"But what about my three months?" Jack repeated. "You said . . ."

"It's done, Jack," Fred said apologetically.

———

"You can't tell anyone yet," Ev told the group as a barrage of questions came in. Goldman immediately protested. He was going to tell Crystal, who was now his live-in girlfriend. "No, you can't!" Ev's voice was now becoming stern. "I get that she's your girlfriend, and that she's really close with Jack, but we can't have all the employees finding out about this before we tell them. It'll be fucking chaos."

"So I'm supposed to just lie to my girlfriend?" Goldman said with anger and sarcasm in his voice.

"Yes. You need to learn to separate business and relationships," Ev responded. It was one of the few moments that Goldman felt a dislike for Ev. As he was about to respond, Biz interrupted them both.

"Have you spoken to Jack?"

"No," Ev said, then repeated what he had said earlier. "The board is with him now."

———

Jack was panicked as he stood on the sidewalk in front of the Clift Hotel. He peered down, scanning the legal documents. Certain words leaped out at him. Numbers. Percentages. Dollar symbols. But they were all lower than they should be. He reached into his pocket and pulled out his phone, scrolling frantically for Greg Kidd's number.

Kidd was one of the few people Jack trusted in San Francisco. As of a few minutes ago, he might have become the only person he trusted in San Francisco. The two had worked together in the past, and although a business they had once started in partnership had ended with near bloodshed, Kidd had always been there for Jack.

In 2005, after Jack had spent a week at Burning Man, traipsing through Black Rock City and dancing inebriated until sunrise to techno music, he had shown up on Kidd's doorstep in Berkeley, jobless and essentially homeless. He had been a different Jack back then, sporting blue dreadlocks and grimy clothes. Still, Kidd had taken him in and let him stay in the guesthouse in the backyard. He also gave him a job as a nanny for his newborn baby. A blue-haired, dreadlocked nanny with a nose ring in Berkeley. He fit right in.

"Greg, they fired me," Jack said, his voice frantic. "They took away my stock and they fired me. They made Ev CEO and I . . ."

"Just relax for a second. Hold on," Kidd said, interrupting him. "What's going on?"

Jack explained the conversation, what Fred and Bijan had said, that he would technically no longer work for Twitter. After a few minutes listening, Kidd explained that there wasn't much Jack could do. "Ev owns the majority of the company; you don't," he said. "You should call that lawyer."

———

Ev closed the door behind him as they left the apartment. Goldman was clearly upset. Biz too. Greg and Abdur, who were more employees of the company than friends to Jack, seemed almost relieved.

They all walked to the office together.

———

Jack hung up the phone with Kidd and started walking quickly. He didn't know where to go. He couldn't go back to the office. He walked briskly down Geary Street, then took lefts and rights and had soon trudged more than a mile. He was frantic when he paused in front of One Embarcadero, a giant concrete building near the water's edge—the same place where Noah had ridden his bike when he had been cast out of the company two years earlier. Cast out by Jack, who had given Ev an ultimatum: "It's Noah or it's me."

Now it was Jack's turn. He stopped and sat on the cement steps as people with jobs brushed by in suits and heels, off to work for the day. Then, the emotions too much, his throat started to itch. He started to cry. His head in is arms, he sat on the steps, sobbing. Alone.

———

The door to the office opened and Ev walked in, Goldman, Biz, Abdur, and Greg in tow. Rebecca, Jack's assistant, immediately rushed over and asked where Jack was. After a brief pause, Biz spoke: "We had an off-site executive meeting today, and Jack will be out of the office for some other meetings," he said.

He then looked over at Ev and said, "Hey, you got a second?" They walked into a conference room near the kitchen, the door closing behind them.

"Look. I get this is the best thing for the company. I just wish I would have known first," Biz said. Ev listened, agreeing while trying to explain the situation he was in with the board and the legal aspects of the transition. They sat for a brief moment in silence. A deep sigh came from Biz, then he spoke: "I should probably go talk to Jack, huh?"

"Yeah. That's probably a good idea," Ev said. "He has to come into the office tomorrow to tell everyone, so we'll have to make sure he knows what to say."

Biz pulled his phone out of his pocket and sent Jack a text message.

Jack's phone had been going all morning. His assistant was trying to reach him. Text messages, e-mails, missed calls. He didn't respond. What could he say? "I'm not coming in today; I've been fired"?

Suddenly a message from Biz popped up, saying they should talk. They arranged to meet at Samovar Tea Lounge in the Yerba Buena Gardens, near the Twitter offices. The two had spent countless hours and lunches there, often talking about Twitter or other projects they wanted to work on together one day. Jack would sip his favorite tea, masala chai, and mostly just laugh as Biz would crack jokes.

There would be no jokes on this particular morning. No masala chai either.

The two sat outside on a wooden bench looking out at the city. The sky had opened up, and Biz squinted as he looked at Jack in the glaring brightness. He could see his eyes were puffy and red.

"So obviously you heard," Jack said.

"Yeah, Ev told us this morning," Biz said quietly. "We're not telling the rest of the company yet, though."

"What do you think I should do?"

"I think you should come in and talk to Ev and figure out what to say to everyone."

They talked about the discussion at the Clift Hotel, and Jack told Biz he knew Ev was behind it all. That this was a coup by Ev, not the board.

"You don't know that," Biz said.

Like a wind changing direction, Biz could feel Jack's tone and demeanor go from pain and sadness to anger and vindictiveness as he heard Jack say: "I'm going to go in and tell the whole company what happened! I'm going to tell them Ev fucked me and he threw me out of Twitter because he wanted to be in control. I'm going to tell them everything."

"No! You can't do that. This is about Twitter and all the people that work there," Biz said, sensing the panic in Jack's voice. "This isn't about you and Ev. It's bigger than that."

Biz suggested they go for a walk to cool off, hoping to calm Jack down. They strolled around the block a few times. After a while Biz needed to get back to the office, but they agreed that Jack would come in later that afternoon to talk to Ev.

––––––––

It was dark outside as Jack sat in the Twitter conference room waiting. He was drained from the day. Ted, the company's lawyer, had explained that everything had been done by the book. Ev was the majority shareholder. Jack was not.

Twenty minutes had already gone by as Jack sat there. He was growing angrier by the minute. Biz was at his desk nearby, writing the blog post that would go online the following day announcing Jack's departure from the company. "Meet Our CEO and Chairman, Again," the title of the post would read. It would praise Jack for his "artful minimalism and simplicity, combined with great vision and ambition." And it would say that Jack and Ev had decided to make the switch. That it was the best thing for the company. "We took a good look at our path forward and saw the need for a focused approach from a single leader," the blog post would say.

But it wasn't the focused single leader Jack wanted.

As Biz wrote an e-mail to the employees telling them to meet for an all-hands meeting the following morning, the door to the conference room where Jack had been waiting opened and Ev finally walked in.

"What the fuck!" Jack said, pronouncing the *k* as if this were the last word he would ever utter. Jack's adrenaline was pounding.

"I'm sorry. These things aren't always easy," Ev said calmly. He had fired a dozen people before, but never a CEO.

"No. They're not fucking easy when you go behind someone's back to have them thrown out of their own company," Jack said. "You had the opportunity to tell me exactly what you wanted, to tell me exactly what I was supposed to be doing, but instead you went behind my back!"

Ev was silent.

"And I don't think it's right, or fair, that you took my stock away," Jack said. "This is my company; you can't take my stock away."

"We're not taking your stock away; you haven't fully vested yet," Ev said. "You've only been a full-time employee for two years, and your stock hasn't fully vested, so no, we're not taking anything away. We're actually giving you more than you deserve."

Jack laughed maniacally. "You're giving me more than I deserve?! Please. You guys are fucking me and you know it."

Ev tried again to explain the vesting time frame, but Jack interrupted. "This is my company!" Jack slammed. "I've put so much more into it than you have."

After Jack railed for a while, Ev calmly responded: "This isn't your company. It's done."

———

The following morning, Friday, Twitter employees shuffled in and grabbed their spots in the lounge, unsure what the announcement might be. Some people sat on the gray sofas in the meeting area, which was designed to look like a living room. A huge flat-screen TV hung on the wall. Others pulled over white office chairs. The company was still small, with just under thirty employees and freelancers.

Ev was clearly fretful as he stood to the side with a worried-looking Biz. Ev was peering down, his feet shuffling back and forth on the concrete floor, fidgety, as if he were trying to kick away a piece of gum that wasn't actually there. People could immediately sense something was off.

A few minutes later Jack arrived, walking out in front of the employees to deliver his brief address. His hands were shaky, his heart pounding. It was clear to everyone he was nervous.

"The board has decided," he said, then paused. "And I agree." Another pause. "That I'm going to step down as CEO." The last pause. "Ev will take over."

The employees were stunned by what they had just heard. Jack went on to talk about how much he would miss everyone. And for the first time he told a story he would repeat for years, that he would still be around, as the "executive chairman," involved in a larger role at Twitter. He didn't explain that his chairman title was a sham and meant nothing. That he was completely out of a job at the company he had cofounded. That he had been fired.

When he was done, he walked away, past Ev, whose turn it was to walk to the center of the living-room area and greet employees. The two didn't make eye contact.

"I know that some of you have felt like the company has sometimes been run like a two-headed monster," Ev said, now fidgety and anxious too. "Like you didn't know who to go to with questions, or who was in charge." He went on to say that the decision was the best thing for the company, that he and Jack agreed. Biz spoke too, trying to quell any concerns employees had.

———

Secretly, some of the employees were elated. Although they wouldn't say anything to Jack, they knew he was in over his head and had been for a long time. And they believed Ev, who had managed and sold Blogger, would be able to provide better leadership for the shaky start-up.

But two people were clearly distraught: Jeremy and Crystal. Jack was in the kitchen with them as Ev wrapped up his sermon. Crystal was sobbing. After Noah had left a couple of years earlier, he had disappeared as a friend. She worried that the same would happen with Jack.

Jeremy, normally not one for tears, was choked up too—partially thankful Ev was taking over but deeply disappointed that Jack would no longer be working at the company. They all hugged, and Jack could feel tears welling up in his eyes, but he held them back. He couldn't cry in front of his employees. That is not what ex-CEOs do.

––––––

When Ev and Biz wrapped up their speeches, they told everyone a blog post would be going up on the site to announce the changes and instructed them not to speak to the press or tweet about it.

Ev walked over to the kitchen where Crystal and Jeremy were talking to Jack, motioning for Jeremy to come in his direction. "I need you to go and disable all of Rebecca's accounts," Ev ordered, as Jeremy stood with a shocked look on his face. "I need you to do it now. Disable her e-mail, login, computer," Ev repeated. "Everything." Then he told Rebecca she was fired too.

––––––

Jack looked over at Ev and Jeremy as they spoke outside the kitchen. "I'll be right back," Jack said to Crystal. "I have to make a couple of calls before the blog post goes up."

As Jack walked out of the kitchen, he looked up at the silver and white clock on the wall, which read 11:59 A.M. He reached into his pocket for his phone, opened up the Twitter application, and tweeted, "Calling my parents."

His mother started crying on the phone when she heard that he was stepping down. But Jack convinced his parents that it was his decision, that he agreed it was best for the company. Then he hung up.

Compared with the next call he had to make, talking to his parents had been easy.

He turned around to make sure no one was within earshot. Then he opened the address book on his phone, scrolled down past the people's names that began with the letter *J*, then past *K*, then *L*, and finally arrived at the number he was looking for: Mark Zuckerberg, CEO of Facebook. He peered over his shoulder again as Crystal and Ev and others stood talking by the kitchen, then looked back at his phone as he pressed the phone number next to Mark Zuckerberg's name.

IV.
#EV

The Third
Twitter Leader

J
ack sat glaring at Ev, not a word coming out of his mouth, his eyes
so steady and precise you'd have thought he was in the middle of
a staring contest. Except his opponent, Ev, was trying his best—as
difficult as it was—to ignore him.

"People hear about Twitter a lot but don't know what it is or why
they'd want to use it," Ev read aloud from his slide deck, periodically
glancing as Goldman, Bijan, and Fred, who tried to listen attentively,
though they, too, were distracted by Jack's silence. Still, Ev went on.

It was October 22, 2008, Ev's first board meeting as CEO—just three
weeks after Jack had been ousted. Ev was explaining that the 2008
elections Web site, which Jack had previously put all of his efforts
behind, was the wrong approach for Twitter.

"On average, it only generated thirty-five thousand page views a
day," Ev said, pointing to a jagged graph to back up his statement. Next
to the chart were sample tweets from the site that were more high-
school jokes than intellectual punditry: "Palin is a S.M.I.L.F.," one read,
as Ev noted that a S.M.I.L.F. was a "sexy mom I'd like to fuck."

Then Ev moved on to more important matters, patiently going
through the agenda: venture debt, finances, burn rates, hiring plans,
revenue (which was still at zero), spam, and how to reduce Twitter's
now infamous downtime. It was clear to everyone in the room that

there was now an experienced CEO running the company, one who had a plan to fix all of the above.

Although some employees had been sad to see Jack go as a friend, they were relieved they no longer had to report to him as a boss. In the months leading up to Jack's departure, employees had complained to senior staffers that Jack had acted like a "cowboy" when he was CEO, sometimes ordering people around and rarely trusting those who worked below him. When Ev stepped up to take charge of the company, he took a completely different approach to management, always trusting employees from the get-go, which gave them a sense of pride and, in turn, a loyalty to Ev and Twitter.

Jack's stare was interrupted when the following words came out of Ev's mouth: "Mark Zuckerberg" and "Facebook."

In the weeks leading up to Jack's firing, Facebook had been trying to buy Twitter. Mark had made it his personal mission to woo Jack into selling the little blue bird to Facebook. After Jack was let go, it was the two other Twitter cofounders who now needed romancing.

Biz and Ev had driven down to Facebook's campus a few days earlier to meet with Mark. Like most meetings involving the chief of Facebook, it had been almost unbearably uncomfortable.

When Ev and Biz arrived at Facebook's campus, they were given what seemed like an endless tour, then ushered into a small office space with Mark. The room was gray and relatively sparse, looking more like a Russian prison than part of the office of the hip social network. Given the limited seating options, Biz and Ev chose a tiny two-seater couch that butted up against the wall. Facebook's boyish CEO had rushed to take the only other seat in the room, an almost high chair that sat above them on a higher plane. Facebook and its CEO looking down on Twitter and its CEO.

"Should I close the door or leave it open?" Ev asked.

"Yes," Mark replied.

Ev looked at Biz, who shrugged. "Yes I should close it, or yes I should leave it open?" Ev asked.

"Yes," Mark said again.

Ev decided to play it safe, leaving the door half-open and half-closed. Mark started talking, pausing slightly as he spoke from a script in his head. Every word was calculated, every sentence plotted, every comma mapped out; he was like an army general meeting on the battlefield to discuss merging armies.

"What do you think your valuation is right now?" Mark asked as they both sat uncomfortably across from and below him, peering up at a boy who could, hypothetically speaking, quite happily buy them or murder them, all with the same exact expression on his face. "Throw out a number," Mark said.

Ev paused, looking at Biz, then fired off a shot. "Five hundred million."

Silence filled the room. Mark looked at them, unfazed. "That's a big number."

"That's what we believe we're worth," Ev said.

But Mark had already known that Twitter believed it was valued at five hundred million. Jack had told him so.

Although Biz and Ev didn't know it, Jack had also been meeting with Mark. Which was why Jack had called Mark right after he had been fired, to tell him what was going on and to set up a secret meeting that was not about the sale of Twitter to Facebook anymore—Jack had no control over that aspect of Twitter now.

No. Instead, Jack Dorsey, the cofounder of Twitter, was going to try and get a job at Facebook.

"Are you sure there's nothing we can do?" Mark had said on the phone to Jack when he had called the day he had been fired. "I bet there's something we can do to keep you as CEO." Jack had been a little stunned by Mark's remark, unsure what such a statement could possibly mean. "Er, no, I don't think there's anything we can do," Jack had replied nervously.

Mark wasn't happy. His attempt to seduce Jack had been going well, and he had been methodical, starting with a phone call between the two that was organized by Matt Cohler, a wheeler and dealer in the Valley and an early Facebook employee. Then there had been an in-person meeting between Jack and Mark. More wooing. More romancing.

And it had worked.

Days after their meeting, an e-mail from Mark had arrived in Jack's in-box with an ominous subject line that simply said "T." In the long message he had laid out point by point the reasons why Twitter and Facebook made sense for each other: that together they could change the world, connect people, make billions of dollars. Then, as Mark often did when he was trying to buy companies, he had noted that if the founders chose not to sell, Facebook would continue "to build products that moved further in their direction." A threat with a kiss: You join Facebook and we live happily ever after. Or you say no and we do everything in our power to destroy you. Another possibility to get fucked.

Jack hadn't needed threats. He had been sold. Yet as the deal had approached the finish line, as Jack had been ready to press his foot on the gas pedal, Ev had taken the keys out of the ignition, thrusting Jack out of the driver's seat, spinning the wheel, and turning the company in a completely different direction.

Although the prospect of selling Twitter for five hundred million dollars was appealing to everyone on the board—and a far cry from the twelve million Yahoo! had offered just a year and a half earlier—and although Ev was worried Facebook would try, by any means, to destroy Twitter, he didn't believe in Facebook's mission.

"It seems to me, there are three reasons to sell a company," Ev wrote in an e-mail to the board outlining why they should decline Facebook's offer. 1. The price is good enough or a value that the company will be in the future. ("We've often said Twitter is a billion dollar company. I think it's many, many times that," Ev wrote.) 2. There's an imminent and very real threat from a competitor. (Nothing is going to "pose a credible threat of taking Twitter to zero.") 3. You have a choice to go and work for someone great. ("I don't use [Facebook]. And I have many concerns about their people and how they do business.")

Ev saw Blogger, Odeo, and now Twitter as serving a much more important purpose than just becoming big businesses. These start-ups he had helped build were all designed to give people across the planet an equal voice, to help those without power stand up to those who abused power. Twitter, he believed, which could work via text message on any phone or using a Web browser, could be the ultimate tool for that. He presumed that Facebook was more concerned with being a corporate money machine.

Jack wasn't completely convinced by Ev's decision not to sell to Facebook and replied to the message, "If the numbers are right, there's a success story in either path."

But it didn't matter what Jack said. He had no voting rights anymore. He was an invisible chairman, sitting in Ev's board seat, his title a conciliatory prize from Ev to help Jack save face when he was let go.

After a private call with the board on October 30, the people who did have power agreed that there was no interest in selling to Facebook. Later that evening Ev called Mark, telling him he was "honored by the offer" to buy the company, but "Twitter wanted to remain independent."

Although the call ended amicably, Mark did not like to lose, and he switched his battle plan from trying to buy Twitter to trying to hire Jack. He reasoned that such a move could show a lack of confidence in Twitter—its cofounder moving in with its biggest competitor. If such a move were to happen, publicly it could have been seen as revenge upon the people who had ousted him, or a battle of Jack's and Ev's product ideas. So the conversation between the two progressed. Mark asked Jack to meet with Chris Cox, who ran product at Facebook, at the local Peet's Coffee in Palo Alto. They chatted for a while, Jack sharing ideas about social networks.

A few days went by and Jack got on the phone again with Mark.

"So what do you think?" Mark said. "I think you'd be a great fit for the company."

"What would my role be?" Jack asked. "I'd want to run product there."

But they both knew that wasn't an option. That role was taken by Chris Cox. All of the other senior roles Jack would fit into were already filled too. "Why don't you just come here and we'll figure out a position for you?" Mark said.

Jack sat there, the phone pressed to his ear, thinking about Mark's offer. Although no one in the media knew that Jack had been fired from Twitter—the narrative had been sold as "Twitter's CEO and chairman switch roles"—the story that was out there had been picked up by the mainstream press, and Jack knew that if he was going to make the jump to Facebook, that news would similarly be splayed across the headlines. Such attention would be a double-edged sword. Sure, it would be payback toward Ev, Fred, and Bijan for pushing him out of the company, an embarrassment to them that the cofounder of Twitter had jumped to its biggest competitor. But he knew it would also be a stamp on his image. If the headlines read, JACK DORSEY, TWITTER COFOUNDER, JOINS FACEBOOK AS EXECUTIVE VICE PRESIDENT OF PRODUCT, it would be a win for Jack. But if the headlines read, JACK DORSEY, TWITTER COFOUNDER, JOINS FACEBOOK WITHOUT A FANCY JOB TITLE, then it would be ten steps back in his career.

"Let's just keep talking and see if we can find the right position for me," Jack told Mark. "I've got to think about this, and if I'm going to come there, I want to do it right."

Fight or Flight

As 2009 rolled into view, Jack set off in search of what to do next. Now that the possibility of working at Facebook had been put on hold indefinitely, he had no idea what lay ahead. But he was sure about one thing: He was determined not to follow in the footsteps of the cofounder who had left Twitter before him.

Since his ousting, Noah had fallen off the face of the earth, no longer showing up at parties, conferences, or bars—and no one seemed to have noticed.

Before disappearing, and before Jack was fired, Noah had e-mailed Jack twice to ask if they could meet to talk. But Jack had never responded. At the time, he'd had more important things to do.

Then, in late 2008, Noah decided to try Ev. Although they were once inseparable friends, they had not spoken since South by Southwest a year earlier. Ev agreed to meet with him at the new Twitter offices on Bryant Street. When Noah stepped out of the elevators and through the new front door, he entered a different company. Dozens of engineers buzzed around, fancy stickers were tacked to the walls, and wide glass windows lit the large, loftlike space as the soft hum of cars trundled by outside.

On that particular morning so many people were in meetings that there were no conference rooms available, so Ev and Noah sat in the open living-room area on two gray couches, the same place Jack had stood a few weeks earlier and announced his exodus to his employees. No one stopped by to greet Noah, as most of the employees didn't know who he was. After some small talk, Noah dove right in. "I feel like I'm being written out of history," he told Ev. "I had a lot to do with the creation of Twitter, and I'd like to be included in the story."

Noah had repeatedly felt slighted by events that had taken place, and he felt he needed to talk to his cofounders. Noah had tried to divert his attention elsewhere over the past two years and had attempted to birth other start-ups. Yet most of his ideas, though brilliant, were shuttered by the past. It wasn't a lack of skills or creativity or money—he'd made a couple hundred thousand dollars from the sale of Odeo to Ev— that became roadblocks. It was that he felt betrayed by his friends and coworkers. As the relationship between Jack and Ev had severed, Ev started to feel bad for what had transpired with Noah, though he still didn't tell him Jack had been the main catalyst for Noah's firing. Ev had offered to give Noah a small portion of stock from his personal equity share of the company—a gesture that helped soften the blow but didn't change Noah's sadness.

Ev had often been generous with his money. In the early days of Twitter, Jeremy's house in West Oakland had been robbed; thieves tore down the front door and took his family's computers, important documents, and his four- and seven-year-old boys' pink piggy banks filled with almost two hundred dollars in change. When Ev found out, he quietly pulled Jeremy aside in the office, handed him his personal credit card, and told him to replace everything that had been stolen, without expectation of receiving anything back.

Ev had done the same for Biz when he was running out of money, writing a check for fifty thousand dollars to help cover his bills and mortgage payments.

But money wasn't enough to help Noah. By the time Noah sat on the couch to talk to Ev, Twitter had practically become particles in the air that everyone was breathing, which for Noah was particularly bittersweet. It was as if he had helped invent the sky, choosing the color palette that would hover above everyone, and then, banished by its other inventors, was unable to escape from it.

In Silicon Valley, where people have an incredibly difficult time talking about anything other than technology, Noah felt like he was being stalked by his past with every turn and conversation. The little blue Twitter logo lingered on the chalkboards of bars, on the menus of restaurants, on food trucks, in conversations. Like everyone else in the area, he couldn't get away from it. "Are you on Twitter?" new friends would ask, unaware of his role in the creation of it.

"Look, I know you were a big part of the early story," Ev said to Noah on the couch, "but it's a completely different company now." After a brief chat about the past, Noah left the office that day, the door to the busy and flourishing Twitter offices closing behind him. And then he was gone.

He packed his life into boxes, sent one last tweet from San Francisco—"Ha! I just bought a giant semi truck. Trying to figure out how to drive the fucker. Got a place in Venice beach. Moving this weekend :-)"—and drove south to Los Angeles, the windows down as a different air flowed into his car. On the radio he heard some of the same music from the trip he had made a couple of years earlier with his former best friend, Jack, on their way to Coachella. But on this trip he was lonely. He tried to find solace in Twitter, sending a few messages about his journey, but that only made him feel worse. No one replied to his tweets. His original vision of a product that would allow him to talk to his friends didn't matter if he had no friends to talk to.

When he pulled up to the sunny land of Los Angeles, he soon settled into a lofty warehouse space near Venice Beach and tried to start a new life.

For a time he started to feel a happiness he hadn't felt in a while, but it was short-lived. Stories about Twitter had started to crop up on the business and technology pages of news outlets and into every crevice of culture. Even the sports section had been covering Twitter.

On a Wednesday morning in November 2008, an article in the *New York Times* announced that Shaquille O'Neal, the seven-foot-one behemoth of a basketball player, had joined the service.

Although Twitter had savored fake accounts since its inception, these lampoons were now starting to draw the attention of the real celebrities. A fake Shaquille O'Neal had graced Twitter for some time. That account was now going to be replaced by the real Shaq, who was going to bring his celebrity friends with him. And where the celebrities went, their fans followed. The same fans who now lived on Venice Beach, in Los Angeles. Noah's new neighbors.

Soon, just as in San Francisco, the blue bird appeared. "Hey, have you ever heard of Twitter?" people asked Noah in bars along the Venice boardwalk. "Whoa, why do you have so many followers?" they said in coffee shops on Abbot Kinney Boulevard.

Twitter's prominence in the headlines reached a pinnacle during an event dubbed "Miracle on the Hudson," when an Airbus A320 with 155 passengers on board took off from New York's LaGuardia Airport and was struck by a flock of birds. It landed safely in the Hudson River. A picture of the passengers escaping from the downed plane landed on Twitter, taken by a tourist on a ferry who had snapped a photo with his phone. And then it was all over the Web, magazines, and the nightly news.

Twitter. Twitter. Twitter. Twitter. Twitter.

Noah couldn't escape and he tried to retreat more. He turned off his phone, his computer, anything connected to the Internet, hoping that distance and time would heal his wounds.

At the end of 2008, Jack was starting to go through the same thing as Noah. But he chose to deal with it in a completely different way. Shortly after he was fired from Twitter, Jack, like Noah, was despondent. Like Noah, he traipsed through San Francisco, miserable and seething with resentment. And like Noah, he went on a walkabout to try to figure out what to do next. But that was where their paths diverged.

Although Jack had lost some of his equity when he was pushed out, the board had agreed to give him a two-hundred-thousand-dollar severance salary for a year after he was fired. He had always been care-less with money, taking it in with one hand and handing it out with the other, so he set off to live life and wait for the right opportunity to pres-ent itself. He fell in love with a ballet dancer in San Francisco, a relation-ship that soon ended. Then he visited his friends and family in St. Louis before traveling to New York to get his regular haircut and favorite cap-puccino and wander through the Earnest Sewn jeans store.

And then, finally, Jack found what he was looking for. On a return trip to St. Louis, he met up with his old friend Jim McKelvey, and they started to discuss ideas for a new business they could start together. Jim blew glass for a living and made elaborate glass art sculptures (along with pipes) that he sold to stores and collectors. He told Jack that one afternoon he had missed out on the sale of a large glass sculpture because his customer didn't have enough cash. They started to discuss a product that would allow people to make such a purchase using a cell phone and a credit card and got to work on an idea they would first call Squirrel, then rename Square.

Jack had another side project too: revenge. Unlike Noah, who was doing his best to forget and forgive the betrayal by his friends, Jack ran in the opposite direction, unable to flush the resentment he felt toward Ev, the board, and now Biz too, out of his mind.

Jack began obsessing over every news article, blog post, and status update about Twitter. Each time he read an article where Jack Dorsey wasn't acknowledged as the creator of Twitter, his blood temperature rose a degree. Each time a celebrity tweeted that they were visiting Twitter's offices, and Jack wasn't there to meet them, his wounds deepened.

Ego affected them all: Noah, Jack, Ev, and Biz. They were all driven by it. For Noah ego became a tool for reflection, for trying to understand whom he had wronged in the past and how he could be a better person in the future. For Jack it had the opposite effect, causing him to obsess over who had wronged *him* in the past and how he could return to the spotlight in the future. And what better way to achieve this goal than to eclipse other people's egos?

Although Jack didn't have a say in the daily operations of the company, he chose to accept any press requests that came into his personal Twitter e-mail address, which he was allowed to keep as a silent board member.

He started to meet with reporters and bloggers, and sometimes narrated a story about the invention of Twitter that excluded everyone else's role from the history of the company. No mention of Noah, Biz, Jeremy, Crystal, Blaine, Florian, Jeremy, or Tim. No mention of the other people in the room when Twitter was created or their role in the brainstorming sessions at breakfasts, lunches, dinners, and the hack days. And certainly no mention of Ev.

While Jack had the germ of the idea, of people sharing their status, without Odeo the idea would have remained just that—an idea. It was Noah's determination to save Odeo that brought Jack's status concept to a group of people who brainstormed during the hack days and could execute it. Without Noah's vision of a service that could connect people who felt alone, and a name that people would remember, Twitter would never exist. It was Ev who insisted on making Twitter about "what's happening," and without Ev's financial support and Silicon Valley fame, Twitter would never have grown as rapidly as it did. And without Biz's ethical stance on protecting and standing up for people who used the service, Twitter would be a very different company.

Most of all, without the dozens of dedicated Twitter employees building and developing new ideas and keeping the site alive, the start-up might have failed like so many others.

But Jack told a very different story. He had started to develop a creation myth.

The Marathon Man

A few months had passed since Jack had attended his first board meeting as silent chairman. But each session was still the same, as he sat deliberately glaring at Ev.

For Ev it was slightly different. He had become efficient at ignoring Jack's stare, as had Fred, Bijan, and Goldman.

But there was a new person in the room who was confused by the spectacle. Peter Fenton, or Fenton as he was called, was the newest member of the Twitter board and its latest investor. He had arrived at his first board meeting in early 2009 with the excitement of a child on Christmas morning. Becoming an investor in Twitter had been one of the biggest challenges of his career so far, and here he was, finally a part of the company. It took about ten minutes for Fenton to realize there were no presents under the tree and something was seriously amiss at Twitter.

He had been obsessing about the company for months. In January 2009 he caught wind that Twitter was about to raise its third round of financing. But the investment company Fenton worked for, Benchmark Capital, wasn't going to be part of this funding.

Fenton was thirty-six years old at the time and already worth tens of millions of dollars. He looked like a marine, with short light hair and a rigidly straight posture. As was the case for most venture capitalists in the Valley, it wasn't about the money for him; it was about winning.

Fenton had to be the best at everything he did: marathons, venture capital, learning to fly helicopters.

To ensure he was involved in Twitter's next round of investing, he pulled strings, pushed people, wined and dined Ev and Biz at Fenton's home in the affluent area of San Francisco nicknamed Billionaire's Row, and eventually, through sheer determination, became the lead investor in the company's new round of financing, depositing twenty-one million dollars that would value Twitter at more than two hundred fifty million dollars.

On February 13, 2009, Biz announced the new funding in a blog post that said, "Twitter is growing at a phenomenal rate. Active users have increased 900% in a year." Missing from the post were the revenue numbers, which had increased by 0 percent since the company began. Still sitting at $0.

Ev had fully taken charge of Twitter at this point, and although there were still just under thirty full-time employees (and a handful of freelancers) at the company, he had started to fend off the endless outages and other problems that had plagued Twitter in the past. Monetization was about to start moving up on the priority list. In January, Ev had hired Kevin Thau as Twitter's director of mobile business development, with the task of developing partnerships and finally making money. Ev had also forged a collaboration with Current TV, the television company run by Al Gore, which would display tweets over live video during Barack Obama's presidential inauguration.

While Ev was trying to fix the internals of the blue bird, Biz, who was the most gregarious employee at the company, had become the official public face of Twitter. He had started traveling around the country spreading the Twitter gospel at conferences, going on talk shows, including *The Colbert Report*, and doing hundreds of magazine and newspaper interviews. But there was also now a new unofficial public face of Twitter.

Jack had started work on Square, his mobile payments company, and settled into a new sparse and sleek apartment in Mint Plaza, just off

Fifth Street. Though small, his new home was minimalist and appealed to Jack's sterile sense. The floors were as flat and shiny as an ice-skating rink. The walls, blank.

To the ire of Ev and Biz, Jack had continued to take interviews with anyone who requested to talk to him: newspapers, blogs, television outlets. Worse, Jack was beginning to sell the world on a story that he was still involved in Twitter in a day-to-day role, talking about new features the site had launched as if he were associated with their development, even though he didn't even have a desk at the company's offices.

Rather than argue with Jack about his media blitz, Ev tried to solve the problem by including Jack in events. In early January 2009, Biz, Ev, and Jack had shared the stage at the Crunchies, an annual competition and awards ceremony for tech companies. Given Twitter's unfathomable rise in popularity at the time, the three cofounders had won the award for "Best Startup Founders." They took turns walking to the microphone and addressing the audience. Biz, who spoke first, thanked Jack and Ev for being an inspiration to him. Ev, second up, thanked Jack and Biz, who stood behind him on the stage. "This has really been a team effort and this should really be for the entire team," Ev said with the award in his hand, always trying to give credit where it was due. "We have twenty-six people back at Twitter HQ who work their asses off." Jack, last up, solemnly thanked the millions of people who used the service. "You're changing the world 140 characters at a time," Jack said in a monotone voice. Then they all walked offstage.

Before becoming an investor, like most of the people in the audience at the Crunchies, Fenton had believed Jack had more of a day-to-day role at Twitter. Yet after the board meeting concluded, a sickening tension lingering in the room, Fenton was in mild shock.

Back at his office he picked up the phone and called Bijan. "What the fuck was that all about?" he asked.

"You mean you didn't know?" Bijan said.

"Know what?"

Bijan dove in, telling Fenton everything: that Jack had been kicked out of the company, and why. That Ev had taken over, and why. And that, in case he hadn't noticed, the two cofounders had a deep-seated dislike for each other.

"I feel like I just walked into the conference room and there's blood all over the wall," Fenton said after hearing the story. He put the phone down and called Jack, asking him to meet for dinner. Jack suggested Chez Papa, near his apartment.

As they sat in the darkened restaurant amid the chatter of patrons, Jack told Fenton his side of the story: that Ev pushed him out for power and control and that Twitter had been Jack's idea. And he complained about the new direction of the company.

Ev had been busy since Jack left, making lots of changes to the site and the service. He had wasted no time discontinuing many of the text-messaging partnerships that Jack had set up during his tenure as CEO (the same partnerships that had been siphoning hundreds of thousands of dollars a month out of Twitter's bank account). Jack, who believed Twitter should work predominantly over SMS, complained to Fenton about this too. Ev this. Ev that.

Fenton was incensed. His mouth was agape. Impassioned, he slammed his hand on the table and made Jack a promise he planned to keep. "I will not rest until you're back in that company," Fenton said, as he spiraled into a passionate tirade.

For the first time in months Jack felt a sense of elation as he had finally recruited someone to his side. "You are the founder of this company," Fenton said, his hand trumpeting the table. "I will not rest until you're back at Twitter!"

Dinner with Al

Ev and Biz looked at each other and shrugged as they were directed through the St. Regis Hotel. They walked past the rectangular modern fireplace, then left, then right, through the doors, down a hallway, finally coming upon a semiprivate elevator, where they were directed inside.

"Okay, I got this," Biz said as the elevator doors closed behind the two of them. "We are going for dinner with the former vice president of the United States." He was clearly excited.

Ev smirked as they rose through the hotel to its upper floors. They were dressed in their usual outfits: jeans, sweaters, jackets, and sneakers. The elevator finally came to stop and they emerged into a relatively dark hallway with deep beige walls and a plain maroon carpet. Dim lighting gave the hall the ambience of a hip nightclub.

"I guess this is it," Biz said, tapping lightly on the door of a suite. They stood waiting for a few seconds, unsure what to do next, then heard footsteps approaching and a deep southern voice bellow from inside.

"Hey, guys! Come on in," Al Gore said as the door swung open and he waved them inside the extravagant apartment he owned atop one of the most luxurious hotels in San Francisco. "Welcome!"

"Hey, Al!" Biz said, slapping his hand into a shake, even though he had barely spoken to the former vice president before. Ev, a little more austere in his manner, shook Gore's hand and greeted him more formally. "Hello, Mr. Gore. It's nice to see you."

It was March 2009 and Gore was running Current TV, the television network he had purchased after his semifailed presidential bid, and he had invited Ev and Biz to dinner at his San Francisco home to discuss "how Twitter and Current TV could work together."

As Ev and Biz took in the large, ornate space, Gore introduced them to the two other people in the room, one of whom was Joel Hyatt, Current TV's cofounder.

"Let me get you boys a drink," Gore bellowed as he directed them inside. "We have everything. Whiskey, beer, wine, champagne?" he asked, then paused, peering back at them, his eyes popping open a little. "Shots?!" he said, followed by a deep vice-presidential laughter.

Biz had never been taken by celebrities. A-, B-, C-, and Z-listers were of equal importance, and in most instances, to Biz the rich and famous were far less impressive than someone who got up each day and toiled in a blue-collar job.

But Al Gore was different. Biz had been bursting with excitement to spend time with him. Like Biz, Gore had a great passion for the environment and animals. And they had one other thing in common: They both disliked George W. Bush.

The relationship between Current TV and Twitter had started to tighten in 2008, when they had joined forces to create an experimental version of the presidential debates. The idea, called "Hack the Debate," allowed people to tweet opinions about the presidential candidates that Current TV would then layer on top of live television. Although the missives people were sharing on Twitter were being referenced by mainstream news outlets, including CNN and MSNBC, Current TV had envisioned an entirely new way of creating interactive live television, almost merging the two mediums.

After the debates had concluded, and Barack Obama had tweeted about winning the 2008 presidential election, Gore immediately saw how compelling the combination had been: people making fun of Sarah

Palin in real time, debunking false statements by both candidates, rooting for their home team. Current TV was determined to develop a stronger bond with the future of media: Twitter.

Like most high-level politicians, Gore had more charisma and charm than a Hollywood star. He told jokes and shared dramatic stories about his time as vice president. He talked about how he had wrangled Current from a French conglomerate by pulling lots of strings and calling in lots of favors.

"We had to hold some metaphorical guns to some metaphorical heads," Gore said with a chuckle. Then Joel, his business partner, chimed in. "Al, the heads were real!" Followed by a roar of laughter.

More wine was poured. Then more. Before they knew it, Ev and Biz were getting sloppy drunk with the former vice president of the United States. Biz beamed at Gore and spoke to him as if they were old drinking buddies in a shabby Boston pub. "Al" this and "Al" that, followed by more jokes. He was smitten. Ev was having fun too, but upon noticing Biz's excitement, he decided to head off what was surely coming next from Gore and his executives.

"Just so you know," Ev said, interrupting the group, "Biz gets very excited and may very well come up with a plan about how we can all work together, but I want to preface that this is just him being excited." Then, sobering up for a brief moment, he added: "We're not necessarily agreeing to anything."

At this point in Twitter's life, Ev had been through dozens of acquisition attempts by celebrities who had asked to meet "just to talk" and then pitched him on a once-in-a-lifetime opportunity to partner up, all for the low-low price of an ownership stake in Twitter.

Celebrities wanted equity in Twitter in exchange for using the service. It had happened before with Ashton Kutcher, the actor turned entrepreneur, who had invited Ev and Biz down to his house in LA to "talk." There, by the pool at Kutcher's house, with his wife, Demi Moore, sitting close by, Kutcher had pitched them on ownership of the company. Sean "Puffy" Combs, the rapper, had also tried to negotiate an ownership deal with Ev.

Each time, Ev had politely responded, telling the rich and famous, who were never told no, "No." It happened with CEOs too. At a dinner at Bill Gates's multimillion-dollar house in Seattle, Steve Ballmer, the chief of Microsoft, told Ev if he ever wanted to sell the company, Microsoft would be very interested. Ev politely declined Ballmer.

For Ev it was never about the money or the celebrities. It always went back to Ev's vision of building something that gave people from nowhere—like, say, Clarks, Nebraska—the same equal voice as those from somewhere.

Now it was Al Gore's turn to try to get some of the blue bird's feathers.

"Listen, boys," Gore said, as he began presenting some ideas, including the concept that they team up to create a company called Twitter TV. It would be a sort of merger of the two companies. Gore said that Twitter and Current TV could build the future of television, that together they would take Twitter beyond just being a layer on top of TV and create an entirely new interactive experience in the living room.

Gore was very convincing. The arrangement would likely give him a large ownership stake in Twitter. Ev opened his mouth to politely turn down the offer, but Biz drunkenly interrupted.

"Al. Al. I think you're totally right," Biz slurred. "But if you're right—and I believe you are—why would we lock ourselves in with just you? Why wouldn't we do what you're asking with every TV channel out there?"

Gore paused for a moment before making an impassioned argument. It was persuasive, but not compelling enough for Ev and Biz. Ev politely said that they would give it some thought. Take it back to the company. Sleep on it.

As the dinner wrapped up, Gore wasn't giving up. He emerged from the kitchen with a bottle of Patrón tequila and a handful of shot glasses. "They tell me this is the good stuff," he said with loud laughter. Shots were poured, and soon they were swishing vice-presidential Patrón back with the wine. Ev said it was probably time to go. "Thanks so much for dinner and everything," he told Gore. "We'll be in touch soon."

Ev and Biz walked to the elevator, rode down to the lobby, and sat in the hotel bar, sipping more drinks and trying to decompress from the meeting.

"Holy shit!" Biz said as he almost fell out of his chair, wasted. "We just got drunk with the guy who was almost the fucking president!"

But it didn't take long for them to realize their answer was once again going to be no. They were determined to keep Twitter independent.

"We gotta stop doing these meetings with famous people," Ev said. "They keep trying to buy us!"

Oprah

Ev was resting on the beige satin cushioned bench at the edge of the bed in the Trump International Hotel & Tower when the lights flickered back on. The Chicago River glimmered below, reflecting the Second City like an underground fireworks show.

A series of thunderstorms had stretched across the Midwest, knocking out power and delaying flights—including Ev and Sara's—so the two had arrived in Chicago much later than they had hoped. Then, while checking into their hotel, the power had gone out.

Sara was pregnant with their first child and in a fit of hunger had raided the minibar in search of food. Now packets of peanuts, chips, and candy were strewn about the entire room as she began unpacking their suitcases.

It was Thursday, April 16, 2009, and one of the most bizarre weeks yet for Twitter still hadn't come to a close.

As soon as the power had come back on, Ev leaned over and picked up the remote control for the hotel television. He quickly turned to CNN and listened for a moment before he started shaking his head with a shocked laugh. Anderson Cooper was staring into the camera, as if he were talking only to Ev and Sara, not to the millions of other people watching the twenty-four-hour news network, and he said repeatedly,

"We need you to go to Twitter.com and follow CNN." Sara paused and looked over at Ev as she unpacked his brown shirt for the following day.

"What the hell is happening?" Ev said as he looked back at his wife with amazement. "What world are we living in here?"

They paused for a moment, taking in the reality of the situation: Here they were, in the Trump Hotel in Chicago, watching CNN race Ashton Kutcher to be the first account to get to one million followers on Twitter, and in a few short hours Ev would be going on *The Oprah Winfrey Show* to help Oprah, one of the most famous and influential women in the world, send her first tweet.

It might not have seemed like reality, but it was, and it was all set to take place over the next twelve hours.

Ev's anxiety had started with the flap of a single butterfly wing a few days earlier. Twitter had received a relatively standard e-mail from *The Oprah Winfrey Show* with a simple request: Could the company set up a quick call to chat about mentioning Twitter on the show?

Kutcher and CNN were very publicly racing each other to the one-million-follower mark, and as a result, Oprah had started asking more about what this Twitter thing was. Ev and a small group of employees gathered in a conference room, huddled around the speakerphone to hear from Oprah's producers.

"We're going to have Oprah send her first tweet on the show," the voice crackled out of the speakerphone. Everyone in the room looked around, smiling. "And we're thinking of making Twitter the feature segment of the show," the voice said. The smiles around the Twitter office started to fade slightly.

Twitter was once again unquenchable, each day slurping up tens of thousands of new users, all of whom were helping to feed an unstoppable organism. As a result, the site's servers were being pushed to their limits again. The engineering team was exhausted, with some employees working twenty or more hours a day to keep the site alive. Twitter could barely handle a mere mention on the massively popular *Oprah Winfrey Show*, which garnered anywhere between 26 million and 42 million viewers a week. For better or worse, Oprah represented the mainstream of the mainstream, and her fans could quickly turn into a tsunami of sign-ups that Twitter simply couldn't handle.

The voice on the speakerphone continued: "We're going to have Ashton Kutcher on the show to talk about his race with CNN." More worry crept over people's faces in the Twitter conference room. "And Oprah wants to do this segment for our Friday-morning show, which is live and our biggest audience." That was only two days away. "It would be really helpful if someone from Twitter could come out here and work with our people, just in case something goes wrong," Oprah's producers continued. "Would that be possible?"

"Of course," Ev said as he leaned closer to the phone. "We can send one of our engineers out there."

"Great," the voice on the line said, then paused and asked Ev, "Wait, who are you and what is your job?"

Ev leaned back into the phone and nonchalantly answered, "I'm the cofounder and CEO."

"Well, can you come out, then?" the producer asked.

He paused, looking around the room as he shrugged his shoulders. "Sure," he said. "Is it possible for me to get a ticket for my wife, Sara, to come so we can both sit in the audience?"

The producers said it was as the call ended and Ev looked around at the faces in the room.

"What are we going to do?" an assistant asked Ev.

"There's not much we can do. We have to make sure the site stays up," he replied with a smile. "I mean, it's fucking Oprah!"

Wednesday quickly turned into a series of internal meetings about how to make sure Twitter didn't collapse under the weight of Oprah's stardom. To ensure everything worked live on national television, Twitter engineers decide to create the Oprah Server: a computer server completely dedicated to Oprah, her own special Twitter, which would guarantee that even if the site went down during the live-television extravaganza, Oprah's account would not.

Ev's assistant immediately sprang into action, booking flights and hotels. The itinerary noted that Ev would fly out on Thursday at lunchtime and go to the show on Friday morning. Although he would sit in the audience, he would be there to help Oprah's producers if they had questions as the queen of daytime television strolled through the valley of social media.

The plan was starting to come together. And then, on Thursday morning just after seven o'clock, as Ev and Sara were getting ready for the flight to Chicago, packing clothes, Ev's cell phone rang with a Chicago number. "Ev speaking," he said, unsure who was calling so early.

"Hello, Evan," said a woman who introduced herself as one of the producers from *The Oprah Winfrey Show* he had spoken with earlier in the week. "We've had a bit of a change of plan," she said. "We've decided we want you on the show with Oprah tomorrow." The butterfly wing had just turned into a hurricane.

The producer explained that Ev would be interviewed by Oprah—in front of seven million viewers—and that Ashton Kutcher would be patched in via Skype videoconference from California. This would all follow Oprah sending her first tweet on live television.

Ev hung up the phone, his face white.

"Who was that?" Sara asked.

"Holy shit, I'm going to be on *Oprah* tomorrow," he said, petrified and excited. After e-mailing the team to tell them about the change of plan, he tweeted, "Tomorrow just became a very big day. (Sorry for the teaser—more later.)"

As the *Oprah* preparations were being put in place, Twitter was still scrambling to handle the sign-ups from Ashton Kutcher's race with CNN. Each time they secured more servers, the traffic spiked. And it was only about to get worse.

Larry King posted a video online taunting Kutcher. "Are you putting me on? Are you kidding?" King said to the camera. "Do you think you can take on an entire network?" This led to more sign-ups. Kutcher recruited his famous friends, like Shaquille O'Neal and P. Diddy, to help spread the word. Still more sign-ups. And now here they were, as Ev and Sara watched from Chicago, just minutes away from determining the first Twitter account to reach a million followers.

At Twitter's offices in San Francisco, engineers monitored the site as people kept signing up, following either Kutcher or CNN. On top of that, Anonymous, the troublemaking hacker collective, had written programs creating fake accounts to try to beat both Kutcher and CNN to one million followers—creating even more traffic.

Then, at 11:12 A.M. Chicago time, the verdict came in. As Anderson Cooper almost begged viewers to follow CNN's account, Ashton Kutcher was sitting in his office at home wearing a white cowboy hat, surrounded by friends and other celebrities as he stared into his computer, watching his follower count swell.

"This is bigger than the *American Idol* finale!" his wife, Demi Moore, said as she peered over Kutcher's shoulder. "Fifteen people to go!" he cried out, then seconds later there was an eruption of cheers as he officially passed CNN. Kutcher screamed with excitement as he popped a bottle of champagne and the half-dozen people in the room started pouring bubbles into cups. P. Diddy, who was on speakerphone, screamed, "Congratulations! Save me a glass, baby!" CNN admitted defeat as Kutcher tweeted: "Victory is ours!!!!!!!!"

On Friday morning Ev awoke feeling groggy from sleeping only a couple of hours. Ashton and anxiety had kept him from any real rest.

As soon as they arrived at the *Oprah* studio, a few hours from broadcast, everything became a blur. Makeup, producers running around, voice-level tests, televisions, audience members filing in. As he walked out onto the set to sit in the audience and later get called up to the stage to join Oprah, Ev asked to quickly use the restroom and tripped, falling flat on his face as he ran off in the direction of the toilet.

Ev didn't have much time to recover from his fall. Before he knew it, he was called up to sit next to Oprah, who wore a pink blazer, as giant, boxy cameras pointed at him from every angle. Hundreds of women sat in bleachers surrounding him, and Sara smiled at him from the audience. Then a voice announced, "And, we're on in five, four, three . . ."

"Hi, it's Friday Live and I'm on Twitter for the first time," Oprah said cheerfully. Ev's adrenaline was swirling as the cameras began to dance around the set like practiced ballerinas.

Oprah gave her speech about Twitter, described her conversation with her doorman that morning about the site, and then jumped in, asking a very nervous Ev a series of questions.

"How'd it come to light?" Oprah asked.

"My cofounders, Biz and Jack, are supergeniuses," Ev said. He explained to Oprah the difference between blogging and Twitter and said that the site made it possible to disseminate information in seconds. It's so fast, he said, that city fire and police departments are using it to publicize time-sensitive information. As Ev spoke, Oprah could see he was nervous. Ever the pro, she reached across the table and grabbed his hand, which helped calm his nerves.

Yet Ev's adrenaline was about to spike again. He had been warned more than a dozen times by Oprah's staff that the queen of television was completely inept with technology. To ensure she couldn't mess up her first tweet, the staff had set up a laptop with colored stickers that Oprah was instructed to press after typing her first 140-character missive. It was paint by numbers for a clumsy computer user.

The live-television plan had been meticulously set in place. Oprah would write a tweet, then send it; the show would cut to commercial. As advertisements filled the screen, Oprah was then instructed to "press the button on the keyboard with a yellow sticker" which would load tweets from all her friends, including George Stephanopoulos, Ellen DeGeneres, Shaquille O'Neal, Demi Moore, and others, who had all been told by producers to reply to Oprah, welcoming her to the site.

But instead Oprah pressed the caps-lock button first, then began typing: "HI TWITTERS. THANK YOU FOR A WARM WELCOME. FEELING REALLY 21ST CENTURY." Then, rather than hit "send" on Twitter, she accidentally pressed the key with the yellow piece of tape on it. This reset the screen and erased her first tweet. Cut to commercial. Oprah hadn't actually tweeted. Ev saw this and his throat tightened; he quickly pushed Oprah aside and grabbed the keyboard, frantically typing the same exact tweet in all caps and hitting "send," his heart pounding as he heard the cameraman yell: "And we're back in five, four, three . . ."

At one point in the show Kutcher appeared on the screen, sitting in the same office he had been in a few hours earlier when he beat CNN to a million followers. "Congratulations!" Oprah said to him. "This is a commentary on the state of media," Kutcher said to Oprah and the audience. "I believe that we're at a place now with social media where one person's voice can be as powerful as a media network. That is the power of the social Web." He went on to explain that Twitter allowed him to control the type of images and videos that were shared about him online, specifically beating the paparazzi: He could now usurp the *Us Weeklys* of the world by posting pictures he had preapproved before the tabloids could.

As the show went on, Oprah's viewers started signing up for the site in droves. From Chicago to Clearwater, Modesto to Miami, Seattle to Statesboro, more people joined Twitter on that day than on any single day in the site's history—nearly half a million people in the first twenty-four hours—and although the servers were battered, they managed to survive.

After the show concluded, Ev and Sara went to the *Oprah* store to purchase bibs for Miles, a baby boy they were expecting Sara to give birth to in the next couple of months.

Later Ev wrote an e-mail to the staff with the title "Holy cow." He continued: "Just going to bed here in Chicago. Am going to get about 4 hrs sleep," effusing about how proud he was of the thirty-five-person staff that had kept the site alive through the influx of users. "What a week for Twitter! Thanks for everyone's hard work."

Ev was glowing with pride. But not everyone was happy.

Although Kutcher had pronounced that anyone could be as powerful as a media company, there was one person whose tweets had faded into insignificance, one person who had happened upon the *Oprah* show and seen his former friend and coworker, Ev, on live television.

Noah.

Noah had watched in disbelief as he realized he'd been completely erased from the Twitter story. He tweeted: "Watching him on TV, I wondered how I became so invisible, so absent mise-en-scene. No fingerprints at all."

In the past, history was always written by the victors. But in the age of Twitter, history is written by everyone. The victors become the ones with the loudest voices who get to tell *their* version of history.

Ev hadn't been intentionally writing Noah out of the story. He had always been intent on trying to give credit where it was due in the creation of Twitter, thanking employees at award ceremonies like the Crunchies and talking about Jack and Biz's role in interviews. Ev honestly believed Twitter was a different company from the days when Noah had helped form it.

But Jack had never been forthright about the amount of collaboration that had gone on between him and Noah as they were hatching Twitter together.

As Jack watched *Oprah*, he was apoplectic that Jack wasn't the one appearing on the show. He would later voice a now familiar concern to Biz, "I'm being written out of history!"

"No, you're not," Biz told Jack. "Ev talked about you on the show. He called us geniuses!"

But it didn't matter what Ev said. Or Biz. Jack felt he was being erased. And unlike Noah, who had faded into obscurity after being kicked out of the company, Jack had bigger plans.

Spiraling into Iraq

The C-130 transport plane roared on the Tarmac, its propellers ferociously slicing through the arid Middle Eastern air. Even from where he stood, several hundred feet away, Jack could see the plane was a behemoth. Next to the other aircraft on the runway it looked like a giant blue whale resting among a pool of goldfish.

Army trucks and jeeps sporadically surrounded the plane and were, in turn, surrounded by American soldiers huddled in their fatigues, guns and large green duffel bags by their sides. The scene looked strangely like toys left on the bedroom floor of an imaginative boy.

Jack watched through dark sunglasses as the bright sun penetrated the massive windows of the lounge area in the Queen Alia International Airport in Amman, Jordan. Waiting to board the plane gave him a nervousness he hadn't felt in a while, and it diverted his attention from Ev's appearance on *The Oprah Winfrey Show* just three days earlier. Now he was obsessing about something else: Iraq, where he would be in a few hours.

As he tried to calm his nerves, there was a tap on his shoulder. Turning, he saw Jared Cohen, the State Department liaison who was responsible for the trip Jack was about to embark on.

"Did you see the article on the front page of the *Wall Street Journal* today?" Cohen asked him.

"No, what article?"

"It's about Twitter," Cohen said, already walking away to talk to someone else. "Look it up. It's called 'The Twitter Revolution.'" Jack pulled his iPhone out of his pocket and searched for the story, landing on the *Wall Street Journal* Web site a few seconds later.

Cohen looked like an actor in a low-budget spy movie, which was fitting considering he worked for the U.S. State Department. He had dark, messy hair and smooth skin. Even though he was large and lean, his suits always seemed to hang off his shoulders a little more than they should. His tie, always undone just a hair and pulled slightly in one direction, imparted a sense of constant busyness. And busy he was.

Cohen had joined "State," as it was called by insiders, under Condoleezza Rice in late 2006. He was just twenty-five years old at the time but came with a résumé more impressive than those of most people twice his age. He had highfalutin degrees from Stanford and Oxford universities; he was fluent in Swahili and Arabic; and he had written two books: one on genocide in Rwanda, the other on silent revolutions and Muslim youth in Iran and Syria.

When Hillary Clinton had become the Obama administration's new secretary of state, she had given Cohen—and his boss, Alec Ross, another young State official—the authority to promote diplomacy with the new technologies available to everyday citizens. In other words, they had a License to Social Media.

One of Ross's and Cohen's boldest ideas was to take an entourage of highly influential tech denizens, including people from Google, YouTube, Meetup, Howcast, AT&T, and, of course, Twitter, to war-torn Iraq. The hope was that they could offer input on how to rebuild the decaying country with technology and cell phones rather than bricks and cement.

Cohen had explained the objective during the group's stopover in Amman. They'd be meeting with both the president and the prime minister of Iraq. He had reminded them to wear suits for the flight to Iraq so the group could go directly to some meetings when they landed.

Now here they were, five hundred miles from entering a war zone.

Ev had been invited on the trip, but he was too busy to attend, as were Biz and Goldman. At first they had planned to decline the invitation, but they reasoned that Jack could go if he wanted to; what harm could he cause in Iraq? And now here he was, standing in the airport in Jordan, nearing the end of reading the *Wall Street Journal* article. Cohen soon announced that it was time to board the plane.

They crossed the hot Tarmac and received protective army gear at a staging area. They then shuffled into the C-130, immediately noticing there were no windows. Everyone was strapped securely into red mesh seats, army helmets fixed on their heads, bulletproof flak jackets wrapped around their torsos. Jack, sitting close to Cohen and Scott Heiferman, the founder of Meetup, looked to the rear of the plane, where army personnel sat holding machine guns, clearly heading to Iraq for different reasons.

For the tech delegation it was a difficult scene to comprehend. The dark, round hull of the military plane exposed its metal innards—except for an American flag that hung from the ceiling, proudly proclaiming which team its passengers were on. The heat inside the plane made the scene even more unnerving. There would be no peanuts on this flight.

A ripple of fear and excitement undulated across the group as the plane began the long, steady climb to twenty-eight thousand feet. As Jack sat dripping sweat, he wasn't thinking about the fact that he would soon be meeting with the Iraqi president. Instead he was obsessing about the last line of the *Wall Street Journal* article he had read on the ground in Jordan.

The piece had been a profile of Twitter and, as the subtitle suggested, "the brains behind the Web's hottest networking tool." But it wasn't the title or subtitle of the article that vexed him. Or the illustration of Biz and Ev, sans Jack. Or the mere mention of Jack's involvement in Twitter. It was, instead, the last line that sent a now-familiar anger through his veins.

Ev had told the *Wall Street Journal* reporter that there was a possibility that Twitter would soon go public, but "probably without [Ev], as he has little interest in running a public company." No, Ev was interested in working on another idea, he told the reporter. "He's been pondering a way to revolutionize email."

Jack repeated the last line in his head over and over during the flight. "Revolutionize email!" Why had Ev had kicked him out of the company if he didn't even want to run it?

As the plane started to slow he noticed people around him take their helmets off and start sitting on them like tiny footstools. One by one, others did this. "What's going on?" Jack yelled over the rumble of the engines to the State Department employee sitting next to him.

"We're landing!" the man screamed back. "We sometimes take small-arms fire as we land, and you don't want to take a bullet up your ass." Jack frantically removed his metal helmet and slid it below him to protect his balls. As he did, the plane started to turn rapidly.

Landing a C-130 at war-torn Baghdad International Airport is not like a simple passenger-plane arrival at JFK. There are no FASTEN SEAT-BELT signs or stewards demanding that you turn off your iPad. In Iraq planes have much bigger concerns; specifically, not being shot down by rocket launchers. The trick pilots use is to land in a corkscrew, spiraling down toward the runway like water circling a drain. (Or, as a pilot who landed there explained it so eloquently, "You drop faster than Paris Hilton's panties.")

As they taxied on the ground, the rear-ramp door of the plane cracked open and a slit of orange sky burst inside. Behind it the desert heat rushed in like a backdraft in a house fire, hitting them one by one with a blanket of scorched air. As Jack looked out, he could see dozens of helicopters speckling the horizon like tiny black ants crawling across the sky.

It looks like the scene out of Forrest Gump, Jack thought to himself.

They soon discovered that Cohen's request that they wear suits on the plane had been a terrible idea. Their flak jackets, which were made of rugged ballistic nylon, had spent the past two hours rubbing up against their blazers, which had torn the suits to shreds like sandpaper on tofu.

When the plane finally rolled to a stop, they were directed out of the rear and introduced to Tony, a bulky ex-marine with broad shoulders and alert eyes, who would be overseeing their security for the next week. He explained to the group what to do if they were kidnapped or held hostage.

After a few minutes they were shuffled to a group of helicopter gunships that would transport them to the Green Zone, the American-controlled area of Baghdad. Although not immune to missile strikes, they were told, it was the safest place in Iraq—at least for Americans.

The chopper leaned forward as its propellers carried them through the thick Iraqi air. Jack sat in the back and peered out the open side of the helicopter as marines seated next to him pointed their guns at the ground below. "This is the most dangerous road in the world," one marine yelled to Jack. "There are IEDs everywhere." (IEDs were "improvised explosive devices" planted by insurgents to kill Americans.)

"Interesting," Jack said nervously, pulling his head back inside and taking a deep breath. He looked at the others in his helicopter and smiled slightly. Scott was snapping pictures with a digital camera, Cohen was on his BlackBerry, and Steven Levy, a reporter, was writing in his notepad.

Beyond Cohen's ability to talk his way into almost any situation, he also had another very impressive skill: an knack for bringing the press along on his excursions. Levy, a columnist for *Wired*, had been invited to come along as this particular delegation's embedded reporter.

"The idea is to use the brains of this small collective to give ideas to Iraqi government officials, companies and users that will help it rebuild," Levy wrote on *Wired*'s Web site when he arrived in Baghdad. "Who knows that stuff better than a contingent of internet goombahs heavy on the Google juice and includes the guy who thought up Twitter?"

The following days became a blur of meetings, press interviews, and photo ops.

They were shuttled around in black bulletproof Suburbans to meetings with Iraqi officials of all ranks and levels of importance. Helicopters flew above, tracking their every move with guns hanging from the sides, like guardian angels keeping watch as they drove through the Iraqi streets.

"Taking off my helmet and flak jacket," Jack tweeted at one point. The group had decided to use the hashtag "#iraqtech" for the trip. Though Ev, Biz, and Jack had at first been uninspired by hashtags, calling them "too nerdy," they had now become an integral part of the service and were being used to organize everything from discussions of TV shows to riots.

"So much concrete. It's everywhere." Jack tweeted as they drove out of the Green Zone. Jack spent a lot of the time thinking about Ev's and Biz's media appearances over the past months, which made Jack seethe that he wasn't giving these interviews.

But that was all about to change.

One of the group's first meetings was with the National Investment Commission, an economic arm of the Iraqi government. Then it was off to meet with senior government officials.

Each meeting began with awkward explanations of what the delegation's respective jobs were. "I started a company called Twitter." "Tweeter?" "No, Twi-t-ter." "Ahhh, yes, Tweeter." They all genuinely wanted to help the Iraqis, offering suggestions about how technology could be used to help rebuild the country and its shattered economy.

During one meeting, as the group sat drinking from ornate cups in the home of Barham Salim, deputy prime minister of Iraq, Jack tried to convince officials that they should join Twitter. "The people of Iraq and the media will follow you," Jack told Salim. "A technology like Twitter can bring access and transparency to government." As they sat sipping wine, surrounded by guards, the deputy prime minister assured Jack, "I will sign up tomorrow."

"President Obama uses it all the time," Jack said, eloquently explaining how Twitter had played a role in Obama's election. Like a traveling salesman, he managed to sign up a few American Blackwater security guards who were assigned to protect the delegation.

When the entourage finally met with the Iraqi president, Jalal

Talabani, word had made it to the Western world about the delegation of tech wonders traipsing through Baghdad explaining how Twitter and YouTube worked. Media outlets, including CNN, the *Los Angeles Times*, the *New York Times*, and Al Jazeera, along with dozens of others, began covering the entourage like paparazzi following Britney Spears at a shopping mall.

The slew of reporters now following the delegation continually asked Jared if they could talk to "the Twitter founder" who was on the trip. Jack, happy to maneuver the spotlight away from Biz and Ev, gladly obliged.

On the last evening of the trip they all sat outside at a long mess table at the American army base. Their laptops open, sipping from warm cans of Budweiser, they reflected on the week, where they had gone from nerds to consultants trying to help a scorched government enter the twenty-first century. But one of them, Jack, had also turned into an international superstar. A photo of Jack talking to reporters was splashed across newspapers, blogs, and magazines around the world.

Ev, Biz, and Goldman's plan to allow Jack to come along and keep him out of the way had completely backfired. FOUNDER OF TWITTER SENT TO SAVE IRAQ, read the headline of in a British newspaper, with a picture of Jack Dorsey below.

On the last morning they were whisked back to the airport and stood on the dented rubble-strewn Tarmac, waiting for the C-130 that would hurtle them out of Iraq and back to America. While they waited, Jack reached for his phone to check Twitter. As helicopters thumped in the air above and fighter jets tore holes through the calm sky, Jack saw that the deputy prime minister had actually kept his word.

"Sorry, my first tweet not pleasant," Barham Salim said in his first 140-character proclamation. "Dust storm in Baghdad today & yet another suicide bomb. Awful reminder that it is not yet all fine here."

The *Time* 101

Flashes of white light exploded in the air like miniature fireworks in front of Jack, Biz, and Ev. *Pop. Pop. Pop.*

"Over here!" "Look this way!" photographers yelled as their cameras rattled like muted gunfire. Friendly fire: *Click. Click. Click.* "This way!" they yelled. "Look over here!"

The Twitter founders paused every few feet—*pop, click, pop*—then walked forward as they continued on the red carpet as if they were on a conveyor belt. Coiled white earpieces crawled up the necks of Secret Service agents who stood watch over the scene.

"Hi, Jack Dorsey," a young woman said as she approached with a clipboard in her hand. "Hello, Evan Williams," another woman gleefully cried without ever having met him before. "You must be Sara," she added to Ev's wife. "Mr. and Mrs. Stone," another said, matter-of-factly. "I'll be escorting you inside," they all heard separately. The shouts of the paparazzi could be heard trailing into the background as they walked forward. "Liv! Liv Tyler!" "Kate!" "Whoopi, over here!"

They were shuffled along red carpets with red backdrops, through metal detectors, past the second security gate. Along another carpet for some television interviews. "Hey, it's the Twitter guys!" they heard as microphones and TV cameras hovered inches from their faces. Questions were asked. Jokes made. Then they were shuffled along a few more feet to the next microphone. The next camera. The next set of questions and jokes. At the end of the media gauntlet they found themselves at a final booth where they were given a card noting their designated table for dinner. "Before you go inside, there's one more thing I need to give you," their handler said. "You'll need to wear this lapel pin so guests know you're one of the *Time* 100 Most Influential People in the World." Shiny gold and red badges of honor were tacked to their suits.

Inside, white gloves floated in the air transporting trays of champagne that swept smoothly around the room like magic carpets, immune to the turbulence of the power that swirled around them. World leaders, musicians, actors, billionaire CEOs, media moguls, Nobel laureates, First Ladies, Second Ladies, all mingling, quietly and properly clinking glasses and looking around at the who's who of the who's who.

Amid them stood Jack, Biz, and Ev. How far they had come: A couple years earlier they had been somebodies among nobodies, visible only to the tech nerds in San Francisco. A couple of years before that they'd been just nobodies: Jack with blue dreadlocks, wheeling a stroller around Berkeley, a hacker nanny sleeping on couches. Biz, who was afraid to fly on airplanes, juggling credit cards to pay the rent with fifty thousand dollars in debt. Ev living in a six-hundred-dollar-a-month garage atop someone's home, riding a borrowed bicycle to work across dirt roads to a tiny cubicle, where he sat silently each day. All lonely and alone, searching for something. And here it was—or so they thought.

Some people are destined for greatness; others fall up a hill to get there.

Jack surveyed the room, realizing that he should let the world know where he was. "Having champagne at the Time 100 Gala," he tweeted.

"Oh, you're Whoopi Goldberg," Biz said upon meeting the award-winning actress. "I loved you in *Star Trek*," he said excitedly. She wasn't amused. Behind him Stella McCartney, the world-famous fashion designer, stood huddled with her entourage, including Liv Tyler and Kate Hudson, each with their own fancy cocktail in hand. Laughter ricocheted around the space under the soft hum of conversation.

Although the room was filled with celebrities, many of them were talking about three people: the Twitter guys.

John Legend told the a camera crew, "I do Twitter. I just joined the bandwagon a few weeks ago. I'm up to 230,000 followers, which is not bad so far."

"Oh, wow, there's M.I.A.," Jack said to Biz with the excitement of a child seeing a favorite cartoon character in real life. He briskly walked in her direction, the champagne in his glass sloshing like a giant storm in a tiny ocean.

M.I.A., a famous rapper from West London, had signed up for Twitter only a few months earlier but had instantly fallen into the deep end of the 140-character swimming pool. Standing there in a black dress and jean jacket, she told Jack that she loved Twitter because it allowed her to engage with fans and say whatever she wanted. As they stood there talking, Ev walked up and introduced himself. "And you're with Twitter too?" M.I.A. asked Ev.

"Yes."

"Great, what do you do?"

"I'm the CEO," he said.

M.I.A.'s attention instantly shifted to Ev. Jack was annoyed that Ev had stolen the conversation and that he was able to introduce himself as Twitter's CEO. "Can you get together so I can take your photo, please?" someone asked. As Jack stood scowling, a photograph was taken of the group. M.I.A.'s husband leaned in. She scrunched closer, tilting her head. Ev turned and smiled, his black bow tie pointing up at an angle. But not Jack. He pursed his lips slightly, his brow tightening. *Pop. Click.* A moment caught forever.

They were soon shuffled inside the main ballroom at Lincoln Center for dinner. Biz and Livy found their assigned seats at table 10. They chatted with Lauren Bush, the former first cousin, and Jon Favreau, the personal speechwriter for the president of the United States.

As Jack found his way to his seat on the upper level, he scanned the room, looking for Ev. He caught a glimpse of Michelle Obama, then spotted Lorne Michaels, producer of *Saturday Night Live,* who looked like a forlorn teenager as he played with his phone and ignored everyone around him. Close by, Glenn Beck, the conservative Fox host, was snapping pictures with his smart phone while he chatted with Arianna Huffington, the liberal blogger. Behind them Jimmy Fallon gave a small laugh at a joke.

Then Jack saw him. Ev, seated at table 2, literally the best seat in the house, in front of the stage where Michelle Obama stood. Ev was seated with Joy Behar, cohost of *The View,* and Moot, who had won the title of World's Most Influential Person after his Web site, 4Chan, had rigged the *Time* vote.

Jack took a large gulp from his glass of champagne. Even at the *Time* 100 Most Influential People in the World gala, there is a pecking order. And in 2009, at the top end of that chart there was Evan Williams, the CEO of Twitter.

The upper level seemed to house less important guests, like Christine Teigen, John Legend, and Lou Reed. (Oprah was back there too, though only because she had to leave early.) As Jack seethed, his thoughts were interrupted by a tap on his shoulder. "And who are you?" an older women asked, as her hand, which was covered in ornate rings, stretched out to greet him.

"I'm Jack Dorsey, the founder of Twitter."

"Oh, are you coming on the show tomorrow?" the woman said, then introducing herself "I'm Barbara Walters." She was wearing a black dress with a mesh top that exposed her shoulders. Large sparkly earrings hung from her ears like chandeliers in a French palace.

"No," Jack said. "What show?"

Walters explained that the following morning, after the *Time* 100 gala, the Twitter cofounders were scheduled to go on the *The View,* the show she cohosted with Joy Behar and Whoopi Goldberg.

Jack was immediately perturbed and started to deliver his version of the events that had taken place over the past year, as if he were being interviewed by Walters in a special on her own show.

He told her that a few weeks earlier, he had heard that the latest issue of *Time* magazine, which was consumed by twenty-five million readers, would announce the one hundred most influential people in the world. Ninety-eighty of those influentials would be political leaders, physicists, Nobel laureates, economists, musicians, and the kings and queens of the A-list celebrity jungle. The other two spots on the list had been reserved for Evan Williams and Biz Stone of Twitter. Jack Dorsey was not included.

When Jack had found out, he'd sent Biz an infuriated note demanding to be included on the list. Biz explained that it was out of his hands. The editors of *Time* magazine hadn't seen Jack as an employee of the company and therefore hadn't thought it made sense to include him on the list. Biz had known how delicate the situation was and had tried to get Jack added, but to no avail. E-mails among Jack, Biz, Ev, and *Time*'s editors had shot in every direction. But *Time* had reiterated its position, reasoning that Jack was not involved in the daily operations of Twitter. Eventually, after some tense negotiations, Biz had managed to get Jack invited to the dinner, but technically he was not considered one of the *Time* 100. So the dinner had become the *Time* 101. Although no one knew this except the editors, the Twitter guys, and now Barbara Walters.

Walters listened to all of this like a mother whose child has just come home after fighting with his best friend. "We're going to take care of this," Barbara told Jack, explaining that Ev was scheduled to be interviewed by her the following day and that she would talk to him about the turmoil. But Jack wasn't finished yet. The world's most famous interviewer, who usually listens to presidents, kings, and princesses, heard Jack continue to complain about Ev and Biz.

When Jack had first grabbed a copy of the magazine, he had quickly flipped to the page that said "The Twitter Guys" and started reading. *Time* had asked celebrities to write each of the three-hundred-word blurbs announcing the influentials, and Ashton Kutcher had been chosen to showcase Twitter.

"Years from now," Kutcher wrote, "when historians reflect on the time we are currently living in, the names Biz Stone and Evan Williams will be referenced side by side with the likes of Samuel Morse, Alexan-der Graham Bell, Guglielmo Marconi, Philo Farnsworth, Bill Gates and Steve Jobs." Jack was mentioned in the article later, in passing, as one of the cocreators of Twitter, and was "(not pictured)" in the accompany-ing photo. Instead, it was an image of Ev and Biz staring at each other with a few fake birds suspended on a tree branch above them.

To Jack it didn't matter that Kutcher was lauding Twitter as the "front door to the Internet." Or that *Time* called Twitter "a stage for humanity and connection." Or that more than two trillion tweets had now been sent across the site since his first update. What mattered was that Jack Dorsey wasn't mentioned more in the *Time* article. He wasn't compared with the inventor of the telephone or the creator of Morse code or the genius behind the television.

Biz and Ev had called Jack into Twitter's office to talk through the confusion that had arisen surrounding the *Time* 100. Jack was starting to complain vocally to people involved with Twitter about the press supercell that had formed around the company and the lack of attention on him.

It was rare for Ev to grow visibly annoyed with anyone. Even as the company he was running grew, he still despised confrontation and tried to avoid it at any cost. But he also had a breaking point, and Jack, who had been in a one-man media frenzy, was starting to infuriate Ev. The board had concerns as well, and began noticing that Jack often gave commentary on topics he didn't know much about, including internal developments he was not apprised of, as he technically didn't work for Twitter. Biz was starting to grow frustrated too, as Jack would often tell people in these interviews that he was the "inventor" of Twitter; the sole creator of an idea that actually had many creators.

Twitter's offices were being expanded when Jack arrived for the meeting. The trio decided to talk in private—away from the prying eyes of employees with Twitter accounts—and they walked into one of the conference rooms, which was now under construction.

As they sat at a long square table, Ev told Jack he had to "chill out" with the deluge of media he was doing. "It's bad for the company," Ev said. "It's sending the wrong message." Biz sat between them, watching like a spectator at a tennis match. Then Ev told Jack to amend his Twitter bio, which stated that Jack was the founder and inventor of Twitter.

"But I invented Twitter," Jack said.

"No, you didn't invent Twitter," Ev replied. "I didn't invent Twitter either. Neither did Biz. People don't invent things on the Internet. They simply expand on an idea that already exists." Biz nodded in agreement with what Ev had just said, and also offered a similar commentary.

Ev told Jack that he had not worked at the company for more than seven months and that what Jack had envisioned Twitter to be— a status-updating service—was not what Twitter had become. He reminded him that the Jack Vision of the company had always been about status, about "What are you doing?" whereas Ev's vision had been more akin to blogging, about "What's happening?" To Jack it was about telling stories about yourself—about Jack. To Ev, Twitter was about telling stories about other people.

Twitter had continued to evolve in a way that none of them could have predicted. The early discussions about the service being used to share a person's status had started to become eclipsed by Twitter's role as a twenty-four-hour news service and a network to share what media outlets were reporting. Or, more important, for people to report what they were seeing in real life. The press pass and the the title of "journalist" had been replaced by a smart phone and a Twitter account.

But Jack couldn't see past his feelings to grasp Ev's reasoning. He believed he had been pushed out in a coup over power and influence. If he wanted to tell people he invented Twitter, he would. And the bigger it became, the more he hungered to be back on the throne as its rightful owner.

Seated at dinner with the one hundred most influential people in the world, Jack couldn't get past the fact that Ev was being introduced as the CEO of Twitter, not Jack. That Ev was sitting at table 2, not Jack.

That Ev was a few feet from the First Lady of the United States of America, who was speaking into a microphone on the stage, talking about innovation and entrepreneurship as she looked directly at Ev, not Jack.

Ev.

Not Jack.

Iranian Revolution

Secretary of State Hillary Clinton waited patiently for Alec Ross, her senior adviser on innovation, to finish drawing in his notepad. She was sitting on a robin's-egg-blue silk couch in her outer office at the State Department. A large crystal chandelier hung motionless from the ceiling, overlooking the group of government officials below. Ornate white molding framed every aspect of the room: doors, windows, and the faux-candle lights that protruded from the walls.

After drawing a number of shapes on the page, Ross stopped his pen's erratic motion and paused to take in his masterpiece. He gave himself a slight nod of approval, smirked, then handed the page to Secretary Clinton.

If someone had barged into the room at that moment, they might have believed the group was in the middle of a game of Pictionary with the highest-ranking diplomat in the United States. But of course they weren't.

There was a momentary stillness in the room as Clinton studied the page. The scene could have been straight from an old painting hanging in the National Gallery of Art a few blocks away. Seeing such a scene without knowing the people in the room, one would would have had a hard time determining what era it was from. Although the group surrounding Clinton were all tech and innovation advisers, there were no cell phones out on the oval oak coffee table sitting like a fire pit in front of them. No laptops or iPads, either. Just a single coffee-table book and small, decorative beige bowl.

Every single gadget belonging to the group sat about forty feet away, sleeping behind the "crash doors" of the secretary of state's office. All forms of technology, with the exception of paper, are strictly forbidden inside any high-level Top Secret Sensitive Compartmentalized Information, or TS/SCI area, to ensure that no one can record a sensitive conversation or snap pictures of a top-secret document.

This was why Ross was drawing Twitter on a piece of paper, explaining to Secretary Clinton, in the abstract, how it worked.

"So people type what they want to say into a box," Ross explained, pointing to the top of the page as he scooted his chair forward on the large blue and peach oriental rug beneath him. "They can then send the tweet pressing this button," he said, pointing to the right of the page, "and then it's distributed to their followers, who can then reshare it with the people who follow them." He paused midsentence, realizing that he would now need to explain the concept of "following" to Clinton.

He looked over at the other State Department officials, including Anne-Marie Slaughter, director of policy planning at State, who had been summoned to a private meeting with Clinton to explain how Twitter worked.

As they continued explaining the importance of the service, Slaughter jumped in. "A seventeen-year-old with a smart phone can now do what it used to take an entire CNN crew to do," she said. "It's bringing transparency to opaque places."

Ross, who was thirty-eight years old at the time, had thick, brown, wavy hair and a boyish demeanor that made him look like a teenager. During his first year at State, he had been nicknamed the Obama Guy after he was hired from the Obama campaign, where just a year earlier he had helped the current president beat Hillary Clinton in the democratic primaries. One of the tools in his arsenal had been the same technology he was now explaining to her: Twitter.

"It's allowing us to see inside places like Syria and Iran, places where the media can't go," Ross said.

The meeting was taking place now because of something that had happened a few days earlier.

On June 12, 2009, Biz had noticed a few green Twitter avatars fall into his feed that looked slightly alien, like colored sprinkles landing on vanilla ice cream. Ev saw them too, then Goldman and other Twitter employees. But at the time, no one knew what they meant. That was, until Twitter engineers started noticing spikes in the amount of activity coming from Iran.

A few hours later news reports, some citing Twitter, began surfacing that Mahmoud Ahmadinejad, the Iranian president, had announced that he had won the majority vote in the Iranian presidential election. But accusations were being whispered around the country that Ahmadinejad had rigged the election. Hours after the vote was announced, Iran's opposition candidates took to Twitter and Facebook to voice their disapproval, and small pockets of protest began in the streets. By the following day, as information spread on Twitter, the protests had grown to dozens of major cities across Iran. Seas of people wearing green bandanas and waving green flags, which reflected the color of the losing opposition party, took to the streets demanding a recount.

Although Ahmadinejad dismissed the protests, equating them to "passions after a soccer match," he cut off text messaging, Facebook, Twitter, and a variety of other forms of communication in the country, hoping to quell the protests. But the tech-savvy Iranian youth began using work-around Web sites to one-up the government, continuing to get information out to the rest of the world with Twitter and other social tools.

"#iranelection," "#iran," "#stopahmadi," and a long list of other Iran-related hashtags became the top-trending topics on Twitter. People shared videos of protesters being beaten, attacked, and sometimes shot by Iranian government forces. Before long those sporadic green avatars started to meld together, and Twitter streams soon looked like the Chicago River on Saint Patrick's Day.

As real-time news percolated out of Iran, America was mounting its own protest on Twitter.

The hashtag "#CNNFail" quickly started to rise through Twitter. Instead of reporting on the violent protest in Iran, CNN had been reporting the "news" that seminude photos of Miss California had surfaced online. But as Ashton Kutcher had demonstrated two months earlier, with the rise of social-media sites like Twitter, CNN was increasingly becoming irrelevant.

In recent months, governments around the globe had started to monitor the site, making Twitter a panopticon that was now being watched from every corner of the planet. The White House, Ten Downing Street, the Kremlin; scholars, activists, and dictators; the CIA, the FBI, and the State Department were all watching, collecting information about the protests in Iran, and using Twitter as one of their tools to get a better understanding of what was happening on the ground there.

So in mid-June, when a junior State Department employee called an "Iran watcher," whose job it was to compile memorandums about the goings-on in the country, noticed that Twitter was going to be down for "scheduled maintenance," that fact was included in a report.

When Jared Cohen, just back from Iraq, noticed the addendum that Twitter would be off-line, he e-mailed Jack. On the trip to the Middle East, Jack confided in Cohen that there was trouble at Twitter between the cofounders, but Cohen believed Jack could help persuade Biz and Ev to hold off the maintenance.

Cohen explained that there was a large protest planned in Iran at the same time the site was scheduled to go down for maintenance. He asked if they could postpone the upkeep. "This could literally make the difference in terms of what happens in that country," Cohen wrote in the e-mail.

As Jack passed the message along to Biz, another e-mail, which included Cohen, came through from the State Department, adding pressure to the moment: "There is quite literally a Twitter Revolution going on in Iran right now!"

It wasn't the first e-mail Biz had received on the matter. The company had been inundated with messages from dozens of people who had noticed the scheduled maintenance outage and knew about or were involved with the Iranian revolts. Biz, Ev, and Goldman called a meeting to figure out what to do. Although the site's scheduled maintenance was critical, and failing to do it in the coming days could potentially decimate Twitter's servers, the consensus was to delay the site closure. Biz grabbed Goldman to help him write the blog post announcing the decision.

"We're clearly not smart enough to understand Iranian politics," Biz said to Goldman as they sat in a quiet conference room together trying to figure out what to write. "We don't know who the good guys are or who the bad guys are." Biz paused and then joked: "Wait, are there any good guys?" Goldman laughed.

For a moment they both sat there silently in the conference room, trying to digest what was happening, what they were doing: writing a blog post to notify the world that a maintenance upgrade for Twitter, a technology they had both helped pioneer, a technology that just three years earlier people had used to say when they were going to the toilet or to figure out where to get free beer at a party, was now being used in the streets of Tehran to try to overthrow a government.

It was a testament to the resilience of humanity. Give a man a tree and he will make it into a boat; give him a leaf and he will curve it into a cup and drink water from it; give him a rock and he will make a weapon to protect himself and his family. Give a man a small box and a limit of 140 characters to type into it, and he will adapt it to fight an oppressive dictatorship in the Middle East.

Biz interrupted the silence, noting that he wanted to ensure that Twitter remained completely impartial in the Iranian revolution. "I want to be sure that Twitter is not in the story," he said as they began writing again. "We are not standing with, or against, the protesters. We just love this use of Twitter."

At 4:15 P.M., Biz published to the company Web site the blog post announcing that the downtime had been rescheduled. "A critical network upgrade must be performed to ensure continued operation of Twitter," the post said. "However, our network partners . . . recognize the role Twitter is currently playing as an important communication tool in Iran. Tonight's planned maintenance has been rescheduled to tomorrow between 2-3p PST (1:30a in Iran)."

He added, trying to distill Twitter's involvement: "Our partners are taking a huge risk not just for Twitter but also the other services they support worldwide—we commend them for being flexible in what is essentially an inflexible situation."

Biz's plan backfired. The story went global, with Twitter and its involvement appearing on the front page of newspapers around the globe.

Mark Landler, the *New York Times* diplomatic correspondent who broke the story, noted that although "the Obama administration says it has tried to avoid words or deeds that could be portrayed as American meddling in Iran's presidential election," it looked like it just *had* meddled.

"On Monday afternoon, a 27-year-old State Department official, Jared Cohen, e-mailed the social-networking site Twitter with an unusual request: delay scheduled maintenance of its global network," wrote Landler, who had heard about the delay through sources at State, "which would have cut off service while Iranians were using Twitter to swap information and inform the outside world about the mushrooming protests around Tehran."

And the media storm continued.

"I wouldn't know a Twitter from a tweeter," Secretary Clinton had said at a news conference as the protests had begun. "The United States believes passionately and strongly in the basic principle of free expression," Clinton said as she stood at a podium surrounded by dozens of TV cameras and news reporters. "And it is the case that one of the means of expression, the use of Twitter, is a very important one, not only to the Iranian people but now increasingly to people around the world, and most particularly young people."

After the *New York Times* article, people behind the scenes were not happy: the White House, the State Department, and, of course, Twitter.

At the State Department, Cohen's name was being tossed around with the word "fired." When he showed up for a prescheduled meeting with his counterparts at the White House, he looked as if he were suffering from a rogue flu. "What the fuck did you do?" a friend who worked at the White House asked him. "And you look like shit."

Cohen returned to the State Department and was told to wait at his desk until his fate was decided. Clinton argued to the president's senior staffers, who wanted Cohen and anyone involved in the Twitter incident publicly fired, that they were just doing their jobs and this was all part of the changing cultural fabric, with Twitter woven right into the middle of it. The next day, during a morning meeting, Clinton walked up to where Cohen was sitting, dropped the *New York Times* on his table, and sternly pointed to the article. "This is great," she said, her finger thudding against the newspaper. "This exactly what we should be doing."

But one person who didn't have a full-time job was not being treated so kindly. Jack. The *New York Times* article had mentioned Jack's name as the person who had agreed to pause the site's downtime, even though he wasn't an employee at Twitter. Although it wasn't Jack's fault that he was perceived as taking credit this time, it didn't matter to Ev, Biz, and Goldman, who were dismayed when they read his name in the article.

Biz and Ev had spent days turning down press interviews about the situation in Iran, telling media outlets that they didn't think it was "appropriate" for Twitter to get involved in such a volatile political situation, especially one where protesters were being attacked by their government.

Now it seemed Twitter had been seen as picking a side in an international war of words. It had been seen on one side of a moral and diplomatic fence—exactly the last place it wanted to be.

The Accidental Billionaire

I bet he tries to buy us," Goldman said to Alexander Macgillivray, who had recently joined the company as its general counsel. Ev looked at them both as he took another bite of his sandwich at Charlie's Restaurant in Palo Alto.

"No way," said Macgillivray, who was nicknamed Amac, which sounded like someone saying "Hey! Mac!" when they called him. "Not after what he just did; there's no way they'll try to buy us."

"I agree with Amac," Ev said. "Come on, that would be totally awkward."

"No. He will," Goldman said. "What do you want to bet, Amac? Come on. Let's bet."

Goldman, Ev, and Amac had a relationship that stretched back to 2003, when Google had purchased Blogger. At the time, Amac had been a deputy general counsel at Google, and he had become the new blogging team's go-to lawyer at the company. At Twitter he had been thrown in headfirst.

"I'm not a big gambler," the boyish-looking thirty-six-year-old replied to Goldman as Ev laughed at the two of them.

"Okay, then a handshake?" Goldman responded, reaching across the table.

"Fine," Amac replied, looking back at Goldman through his round wire-rimmed glasses. "A handshake, but there's no way he's going to try and buy us."

"We should go," Ev said, looking at his watch.

A few minutes later they were back in Amac's decrepit 1985 brown Honda Civic. Ev, sitting in the front seat, was dictating directions from his phone. Goldman stared out the back window. "This guy's worth seven billion dollars?" Goldman said sarcastically as they drove past the nondescript house. They soon found a parking spot a few houses away.

As they walked up to the house, it seemed tiny. The exterior color looked like a flat beige from a distance, but up close it was apparent that areas of the walls had been touched up with different mismatched shades, some darker, some lighter. The front yard, which was about the size of a studio apartment, was scattered with browning patches of grass. A few spindly plants swayed in the light breeze. They meandered around the unassuming black Acura parked in the driveway and walked up to the front door. Ev knocked, then turned to Amac and Goldman, who stood with curious looks on their faces. A few seconds passed and they heard the door handle turn. Mark Zuckerberg appeared.

"Oh. Hey, guys," Mark said as he opened the door, standing there in jeans, a T-shirt, and his signature blue Adidas flip-flops. "Hey, guys," he said again, as if he hadn't already said it once. "Come on in."

Mark spoke in sound bites. "We're still waiting on a couple of people to show up. Let me show you around," he said as he led them down the hallway of the home he shared with his girlfriend, Priscilla Chan. "Thanks again for coming down here. I appreciate you meeting at my house. You know, I didn't want anyone to see us on campus. And to think something is going on." He laughed as he looked at Ev.

Ev returned an awkward smile. "Understandable." He wasn't in much of a laughing mood.

A few days earlier, relations between Twitter and Facebook had turned from cordial to sour. Now here they were, trying to resolve something that was likely unresolvable. At 3:00 P.M. on Wednesday, June 23, 2010—a couple of weeks earlier—Josh Elman, an engineer at Twitter, had unveiled a new Twitter tool, called "Find and Follow," which allowed people to find and follow their Facebook friends on Twitter. But barely seconds after the new feature was publicized, it stopped working.

Elman, a clever, round-faced engineer who always seemed to be squinting through his glasses, had joined Twitter after working for Facebook for nearly two years, so he knew immediately what had happened. "We've got a problem," Elman told Ev and Goldman as he rushed toward Ev's office.

"Are you sure they shut us down?" Ev asked after hearing the news. "And it's not a bug?"

"Nope, they shut us down," Elman replied confidently. "Our app is still live on Facebook, but they've disabled the friends-dot-get call and it keeps returning a zero," he said in programmer speak. In other words, Facebook had changed the locks on its door, at least for Twitter, blocking access to the site's friends lists, even though thousands of other sites were allowed to access the same Rolodex.

The tech press had already started picking up the new feature and was quickly adding that it was broken, pointing fingers directly at Twitter. So to defend itself, the company spent the next few hours engaged in a very public spat with Facebook.

"We believe this is an issue on Facebook's end," Twitter declared on its company Web site, publicly slapping Facebook in the face. Facebook responded, telling the press that, awww shucks, it's just a silly technical problem, and "we are working with Twitter [to] resolve the issue."

But of course this was "total fucking bullshit," as Goldman said when he saw Facebook's response. Twitter executives had known Facebook was going to be upset by the new feature, but they'd had no idea the company would euthanize the feature the moment it emerged into the world. Earlier in the week, during a Twitter management meeting, executives had decided to show Facebook what it planned to release. Some people in the room had argued for an "ask for forgiveness not permission" philosophy. But Goldman decided to reach out to Bret Taylor, Facebook's chief technology officer, whom he had worked with at Google years earlier.

"We really don't want you to launch this," Taylor had told Goldman on the phone. "You're a big company, and we want to develop a better relationship with you."

"Okay, that's fine. We're happy to develop a better relationship, but we still want to launch this feature," Goldman had replied, noting that Twitter was using fully public feeds that Facebook made available for anyone to use. "We're just giving you a heads-up of what we're releasing," Goldman had said. This response had annoyed Taylor, and the call had quickly become heated as it reached a stalemate.

Mark and the rest of the Facebook management team had been in Barcelona at the time, attending a conference. When Taylor had called Mark to explain the situation, Facebook's CEO had given clear instructions to shut Twitter down the second it tried to launch.

And that was where it had ended. At least, until they arrived at Mark's house.

"So. This is our study," Mark said as he walked them through his tiny home, pointing to a room with blue walls. Two wooden desks sat, chairless, on the right side of the room, and a single leather ottoman in the left corner. "I had some designers from Facebook come in and paint the place," Mark added proudly as he directed them into the sparse yellow kitchen. The black marble countertops were practically empty.

"Did you just move in here?" Goldman asked.

Mark stopped walking and looked Goldman in the eye. "No," he replied, confused. Goldman didn't know how to follow up his question, so he stared back for a moment. Luckily, the awkward moment was interrupted by a knock on the door. The rest of the Facebook team had arrived.

Ev was fully aware of how uncomfortable the meeting would be. He had been in a similar situation when Facebook had tried to buy Twitter a year and a half earlier.

Everyone shuffled into the living room, where there were not enough seats for all the people in attendance.

Although Mark had been publicly disregarding the 140-character competitor, once telling a group of close friends that Twitter was "such a mess it's as if they drove a clown car into a gold mine and fell in," he was actually worried about the company. In a recent interview with the blog *Inside Facebook*, Mark had admitted, "I looked at their [growth] rate and thought if this continues for 12 months or 18 months, then in a year they're going to be bigger than us." But then he downplayed his worry. "It just turned out that their growth rate was kind of unnatural," he said. "They got a lot of media attention, and it grew very quickly for a little period of time." But that wasn't actually correct. Twitter was still growing at speeds it had never seen before. You don't end up on *Oprah*, featured in *Time* magazine, in front-page stories in the *New York Times* and *Wall Street Journal*, featured in the World Cup, and fueling revolutions and then find that people suddenly stop signing up. Each week Twitter continued to break records.

After Facebook had shut down Twitter's latest feature, Mark had reached out to Ev and suggested the two meet "to figure out how we can work together better."

As everyone shuffled into the living room, Mark sat down first, and like a kid's game of musical chairs, everyone else quickly grabbed the seat closest to where they were standing. This proved to be awkward, as Mark and Ev were now sitting right next to each other. The meeting was very cordial, as Mark, Taylor, Dan Rose (Facebook's head of business development), and a Facebook lawyer delivered a pitch for how Twitter and Facebook could find ways to work together. They used words like "opportunity," "constructive," and "partnership." Every few seconds Mark awkwardly turned his head to look directly at Ev, who was a mere few inches away.

Mark explained that people coming to Facebook to view other people's profile pages made up a majority of the site's traffic. Facebook's newsfeed, or timeline, was being used only as a springboard to get people to look at profile pages, he explained.

"We have the exact opposite experience," Ev said, noting that the Twitter timeline made up 90 percent of the site's traffic, people's profile pages just 10 percent.

"I know," said Mark, who always did his homework. "That's why I think you guys are doing great stuff. It would be amazing if we could . . ." He paused. "If we could do something with you guys as a partner. But there might be things that made sense if they were more closely aligned." Goldman immediately tilted his head and looked at Amac, wondering if Facebook had just offered to buy Twitter. But in the court of Amac, that would not count.

Then Rose interrupted, "And of course, if you guys ever want to just sell the company, we would be interested in buying it."

At that point Ev had received more offers to buy Twitter than he could count. Yahoo!, Google, Facebook, Microsoft, a former vice president, celebrities, and rappers had all made overtures toward Twitter, and each time Ev had said no.

But it wasn't the money that made him turn down Facebook's proposal. It was that Twitter and Facebook were two completely different companies, with different goals and, as Ev saw it, vastly different morals. Twitter's ideals had been cemented when Ev started Blogger almost a decade earlier, forming his resolute belief that blogging, and now Twitter, should offer people a microphone that allowed them to say whatever came to mind. It was the same reason Ev had hired Amac, who had become a staunch proponent of free and open speech on the Internet while at Google. The same reason Goldman worked there. The same reason Biz was so important to Twitter's moral fabric. They all believed that these technologies, first and foremost, should be a mouthpiece for everyday people.

In the past, when government officials had come knocking on Twitter's door demanding information about people on the service for any number of reasons, Ev, Biz, Goldman, and Crystal, who managed Twitter's support team, had always said no, "not without a warrant." Such a stance would become the conviction of Twitter over the years. And it would be the DNA that made it a different kind of company in Silicon Valley. Twitter, with Amac at its legal helm, would eventually fight a court order to extract Occupy Wall Street protesters' tweets during protests. It would stand up to the Justice Department in a witch hunt for WikiLeaks supporters online. And in stark contrast to Facebook,

Twitter would eventually allow newcomers to opt out of being tracked through the service.

Facebook had a completely different approach to free speech and tracking, often infringing people's privacy and sometimes removing content that violated its strict terms of service. Facebook also demanded people use their real names and dates of birth on the site. Twitter, on the other hand, was as open as a public swimming pool. That was the way Ev liked it. Push-button publishing for the people, now in 140 characters.

As Ev still owned the largest majority of the company, he would become a billionaire in a sale to Facebook or any other big suitor. But it wasn't about the money for Ev, it was about protecting the sanctity of Twitter and giving a voice to the people who used it.

"I appreciate the offer," Ev responded to Mark in his living room, using a polite tone to show respect. "But I don't think anything is going to change for us for now."

They agreed to keep talking, and the meeting wrapped up with a few handshakes. "We'll be in touch."

As they walked outside, past the planters, past the browning grass, away from the tiny house of the accidental billionaire, Goldman looked at Amac and quietly whispered, "See, I told you!"

The Coach and the Comedian

Every aspect of the company was growing. The number of sign-ups, the number of people visiting the site each minute, and every other Twitter-related metric continued to double, triple, and quadruple. In 2007 people had been sending 5,000 tweets a day. By 2008 the company had been processing 300,000 tweets each day. As 2009 rolled on, that number grew by 1,400 percent to 35 million tweets sent each day.

But the number of employees at the company had grown slowly and was still in the double-digit range. Although the board had been pressing Ev to hire a new CTO, COO, and CFO, among other high-level jobs, Ev couldn't decide which candidates were the right ones. In typical Ev fashion, he preferred to pick from a litter of friends, people he trusted who wouldn't try to undermine him or hurry his slow decision making.

This was something Ev had promised himself he would never do again—take too long to make a decision.

Back in 1996, when he was twenty-four years old, Ev had moved back to the family farm after the company he had started in Lincoln, Nebraska, had flopped. "We're giving up the office," he told his employees and friends one afternoon. "Everyone just go home." Then, penniless and crushed, he packed up his life and drove the eighty-five miles back to Clarks.

The company, which was called Plexus—a name he had randomly found in the dictionary that meant "a network of nerves or vessels in the body"—had been run by Ev and his brother and, before they shut the doors, had employed ten part-time staffers, most of whom were Ev's friends.

Ev had pitched his father, Monte, on the idea a year earlier: "The Web is going to be huge," he'd explained. Plexus could be the biggest Web shop in all of Nebraska. Monte trusted his nonconformist son and agreed to bankroll the business. After nearly a year, his father's money was completely gone; some of his friendships, destroyed; his relationship with his brother, splintered.

After the company flopped, Ev sat at the table where he had once toiled over algebra and history homework and played back the past year in his mind. He took a deep breath, put his pen to paper, and started to make a list.

One, two, three, four, five . . . He paused as he rounded the corner past ten. Before long, he made it all the way to thirty-four.

The list was a collection of all of the ideas he had come up with while running Plexus. But this wasn't a good list. Instead it was a collection of thirty-four abandoned hatchlings, thirty-four concurrent projects he had started and never finished. He knew the company hadn't failed because it didn't have enough work. Quite the opposite. It had cracked because each week Ev would come in and announce to his friends and employees that he had a new idea, a new project, a new focus. When Plexus had finally focused on a single project, Ev couldn't make a final decision about when to release it. He had been like a geologist searching for oil and changing the drill site before his workers had even cleared the ground to start digging.

Eventually the projects had piled up and fallen under their own weight. The feeling of guilt from squandering his father's money— savings that had been slowly collected by toiling in fields and irrigating crops—added to the defeat.

In that moment, looking at the list, he made two promises to himself: First, he would repay his father. Second, if he ever had an opportunity to run another company, he would never lose focus like that again; he would always make a firm decision and stick to it.

The former would eventually happen, and Ev paid his dad back with interest and much more. The latter wasn't as easy to solve. Coming up with ideas was what made Ev Ev.

Ev was doing his best to avoid this at Twitter in 2009 and focused on helping the company navigate the unrelenting attention it had been receiving for its role in everything from America to Iran, Oprah to Obama, businesses to protests. He was also overseeing the latest round of funding, which would put Twitter in an entirely new league.

Although Ev had originally set out to raise fifty million dollars in venture money for the company's fourth round, there was so much interest in Twitter that he would end up raising one hundred million dollars, with New York–based Insight Venture Partners leading the round, which valued the company, for the first time, at one billion dollars. But Twitter's revenue was still stuck at that same number from three years earlier: zero. Now, as with Plexus, Ev's hesitation when making final decisions was starting to slow Twitter's business growth.

Earlier in 2009, at Fenton's urging, the board had encouraged Ev to adopt a CEO mentor to help him manage these decisions better. Fenton had pitched the idea of bringing in Bill Campbell, a legendary CEO coach, who had mentored Steve Jobs and a long list of other titans. But to his surprise, both Ev and Campbell said no. "Twitter? Not interested," Campbell told Fenton, "I don't need a CEO coach," asserted Ev.

But Fenton wasn't the type of person who understood the word "no."

He called Campbell every few days and shared news snippets about the company with him.

One weekend Campbell set out on a fishing trip with some bigwig friends. Among the people on the boat was a friend's technology-savvy son. And instead of reeling in trout, the friend's boy spent the entire trip using Twitter. Campbell returned to Silicon Valley realizing that there was more to the Twitter story than he had first thought, and he told Fenton he would take Ev on.

"Campbell is the real deal," Fenton explained to Ev, trying to convince him to meet with the mentor. "He's coached Eric Schmidt, Larry and Sergey, and Steve Jobs. He's a fucking legend." Ev finally agreed to the meeting.

Campbell was an institution in Silicon Valley. A former Ivy League football player, he was nicknamed the Coach by those who knew him. Although he was in his late sixties, he still carried around a bulky physique. His hairstyle, which hadn't changed in decades, parted on the left and drifted across his scalp like choppy white water.

As the first meeting approached, Ev, now thirty-seven years old, was excited about what he might be able to learn from the man, the legend, the Coach.

He sat on a couch in Campbell's office, one hand firmly gripping his notepad and the other grasping a pen, ready to jot down Campbell's advice. Fenton watched the two of them with excitement. Campbell leaned back in his chair and began his role: coaching. He ranted, raved, and yelled, throwing out one-liners as if he were telling Ev to rush a ball into an end zone. And he cursed. Like a hammer striking metal, the word "fuck" was used in place of the period at the end of each sentence. Fuck this . . . Fuck that . . . Fuck. Fuck. Fuck.

When it was Ev's turn to talk, he asked his first question: "What's the worst thing I can do as CEO to fuck the company up?"

Without skipping a beat, Campbell responded: "Hire your fucking friends!" He went into a ten-minute tirade about friends and business and how they don't mix. Ev scribbled in his notepad.

Ev was smitten with Campbell. They shook hands and agreed to start meeting once a week. Fenton was elated. "This is going to be great!" Campbell said as he slapped Ev on the back. "Just fucking great!"

One of the reasons Fenton and the board had been pushing for Ev to see a CEO mentor was Ev's insistence on hiring his friends at Twitter. Ev didn't see this as a problem. Most of his friends were the few people he could relate to about technology, and they had often fit perfectly into the companies he had started over the years. He also saw his success as a lot of hard work and a little bit of luck, and he wanted to give the people he knew the opportunity to be a part of it. He had hired his sister, a chef, to run the kitchens at Twitter. His wife, Sara, had been hired to help design the new Twitter offices. Numerous friends from Google were employed working on engineering and design at Twitter.

Ev also reasoned that his friends would never betray him.

While Ev was willing to hear Campbell's advice, he still had one last buddy to hire, his good friend Dick Costolo, whom he had met at Google a few years earlier.

In 2009 Dick was forty-five years old and lived in Chicago with his wife, Lorin, and their two young children. Although he wasn't as young and hip as most tech founders, he was well known in the tech scene and had become close friends with Ev.

Dick had grown up near Detroit and studied computer science at the University of Michigan. During the first semester of his senior year, he decided to take an acting class to fill one of his open classes, figuring that acting wouldn't require much additional homework. This way, Dick reasoned, he could spend his evenings focused on his computer science assignments. Yet after the first thespian session he was hooked, and he signed up for another acting class the second semester.

Before he knew it, he started ignoring his computer science assignments and instead spent his evenings on a small stage near campus performing stand-up comedy. Although he graduated with a number of job offers from big tech companies, Dick instead chose to pursue his new and improved dream of becoming a world-famous actor, comedian, or both. He packed his bags and set out to Chicago to join the Second City sketch-comedy and improv troupe in hopes of eventually making it on *Saturday Night Live* or getting his own TV show.

It didn't work out that way.

Although Dick was a talented comedian, he found himself doing improv shows at night and working in a Crate & Barrel, wrapping flatware and selling place settings, during the day to pay the bills. Eventually this wore thin, and in the early 1990s he decided it was time to put his computer science degree to work and took a job at Andersen Consulting to subsidize his comedy career.

On numerous occasions he walked into work and explained to his bosses that there was this new thing they should all be paying attention to called the World Wide Web. But his superiors laughed it off, thinking it was just another Dick Costolo joke.

He eventually grew tired of the corporate atmosphere and quit. Rather than return to comedy, he corralled a small group of coworkers, and they started their own consulting firm, called Burning Door Networked Media, which specialized in building and managing Web-based projects. Before long he was creating and selling companies, three in all, and making millions of dollars in the process. One of the companies that put him on the map was Spyonit, a service that notified people when a Web site they were interested in had been changed. Finally, in 2007, Dick hit the jackpot when he sold a company called FeedBurner, which helped bloggers syndicate their blog posts, to Google for more than one hundred million dollars. Along the way he met Ev, and the two became close friends.

In 2009, after running into Dick at a party in San Francisco, Ev asked if he would be interested in managing the Twitter employees while Ev went on two weeks' paternity leave with his first child. The conversation quickly escalated to Ev asking if Dick would be interested in a full-time job as chief operating officer of Twitter. Until then no one had held the role, but Fenton and the rest of the board had been pressing Ev to hire someone.

At first Bijan and Fenton were not interested in hiring Dick, noting that he was just another friend of Ev's. "I hate to be a stick in the mud," Fenton wrote in an e-mail, but hiring the wrong COO could "create a level of chaos when it's not clean." Bijan agreed, questioning whether they should go outside to fill the role rather than hire another of Ev's friends.

Still, Ev didn't give up. "We've been friends for a couple years, and I think he'd be a great complement to myself and the team," Ev told the board in an e-mail. "I have a high degree of trust with Dick that I wouldn't have bringing in an outsider, no matter what their experience."

For Dick the prospect of being Twitter's COO was a redux of the opportunities he had missed by pursuing his improv career instead of taking a job at a big tech firm after college. Twitter was changing the world, and Dick wanted to be a part of it. Here was his chance to be back on the stage, a global stage.

After he underwent extensive interviews with Biz, Goldman, Bijan, Fred, and Fenton, the Twitter board agreed to hire him, although Ev didn't leave them much of a choice. In contrast to his inability to make smaller decisions, when Ev made up his mind about something big, it was going to happen. As he had been the time he had driven to Florida to get a job with the advertising guru, Ev was determined: Twitter would hire Dick.

In early September 2009, the day before Dick arrived for his first day at Twitter, he thumbed his first tweet as an employee of the company. It was a joke that made people laugh, including Ev. But it would later haunt Dick.

"First full day as Twitter COO tomorrow," he wrote. "Task #1: undermine CEO, consolidate power."

Jack's Gone Rogue

We need to talk," Biz said to Ev. "Jack's gone rogue."

"What do you mean, he's 'gone rogue'?" Ev asked, laughing.

Biz turned his laptop around and slid it across the table so Ev could see.

"Jesus," Ev said, shaking his head with disbelief as he started reading. "Again?"

As 2010 began, here was another article about Jack, touting him as the founder, inventor, architect, and creator behind Twitter, another article that made Jack seem like the only employee at the company, even though there were now nearly a hundred people toiling away on the site. Jack not among them. It had been growing worse by the day. Since Jack had been pushed out, he had taken on almost any press asked of him. Blogs, newspapers, TV, magazines, public talks. Yes, yes, yes, and yes. He would do them all.

Even Biz, who rarely got upset, was starting to grow more impatient with Jack's media junkets. Not only was he taking on press, but he was also failing to mention anyone else's involvement in the creation of Twitter. What's more, Biz was increasingly upset that Jack was giving interviews about moral issues related to Twitter. Biz had always been clear that Twitter employees and executives should not take on interviews where Twitter was being cast as the catalyst in a social issue. Discussing how Twitter was being used as a tool for war, politics, or major news events was strictly off limits for anyone who worked for or with the company. "I don't want it to seem like we're taking a side in anything," Biz often said.

Jack believed this rule didn't apply to him, and when he did talk about these issues, he often got them wrong. During a taped interview with the famous artist and protester Ai Weiwei about digital activism in China, Jack was asked about Twitter's stance on trying to open the service in China. With no knowledge of Chinese politics, he fumbled, and appeared unaware that Twitter had been blocked in the communist country.

At the time, Ev asked Sean Garrett, who had been hired as the director of communications to help with the unrelenting Twitter media onslaught, to talk to Jack and give him some media tips. "If he's going to go out and do this press, he should at least know what he's talking about," Ev said.

Publicly, Jack couldn't explain some of the decisions that were taking place inside the company, and even if he could, he often didn't agree with them. He was convinced that Ev was too focused on the Web and not paying enough attention to the mobile aspect of the service. And he completely disagreed with a major alteration Ev made in early November 2009—one of the biggest to the Web site since Jack's departure.

Ev had finally changed the question in the Twitter box, from Jack's "What are you doing?" (which he'd always seen as a question about ego) to "What's happening?" which he believed gave Twitter more of a blog-like feel. It was a win by Ev in the debates between the two founders in the early days, with Jack's saying that Twitter was about your status, Ev's touting it as being about the status of the events taking place around you.

"Twitter was originally conceived as a mobile status update service—an easy way to keep in touch with people in your life by sending and receiving short, frequent answers to one question, 'What are you doing?'" Ev and Biz wrote in a blog post on Twitter's Web site. "Sure, someone in San Francisco may be answering 'What are you doing?' with 'Enjoying an excellent cup of coffee,' at this very moment. However, a bird's-eye view of Twitter reveals that it's not exclusively about these personal musings. Between those cups of coffee, people are witnessing accidents, organizing events, sharing links, breaking news."

They added: "'What are you doing?' isn't the right question anymore—starting today, we've shortened it by two characters. Twitter now asks, 'What's happening?' We don't expect this to change how any-one uses Twitter, but maybe it'll make it easier to explain to your dad." Jack, of course, did not agree with the change, and in interviews he continued to talk about "status" as the basis for a tweet.

Internally at Twitter it was obvious that Ev was in charge of the company. Externally, some people believed Jack was running it from his "chairman" role.

The media didn't know the difference, as news segments touting Jack as the brains behind the operation made clear. One, in late 2009 by CBS, was titled, "The Twitter Mastermind." The segment began with the CBS anchor talking about the company. "Wall Street recently put a value on the social network Twitter at one billion dollars, even though the company has yet to make a dime," the anchor said; then, as the screen flashed to a portrait of Jack, he noted: "Jack Dorsey was only twenty-nine years old when he invented Twitter, and now, at thirty-two, it's clear he's helped change the way we communicate."

The video, which included a walk-along interview with Jack, never mentioned Ev's, Biz's, or Noah's involvement. "Dorsey has become a superstar," the CBS host said. "He was honored last month at his home town of St. Louis, where he spoke at Webster University, he got the key to the city from the mayor, and threw out the first pitch at the St. Louis Cardinals game."

When Ev heard about the report, he just shook his head.

Each morning the Twitter employees would come into the office to find more press about Jack—articles, talks, and interviews from all over the planet. From the big, including the *Los Angeles Times*, *New York Times*, and *Wall Street Journal*, to tech-only outlets like *GigaOM*, *Tech-Crunch*, and *Mashable*, and then the esoteric, like *AskMen*, *Alive* magazine, as well as a number of speeches. Later Jack even gave a public talk at a New Jersey elementary school.

As Jack stacked up press like a Hollywood star on a movie junket, people who worked at Twitter were growing increasingly annoyed, and in some instances embarrassed.

The company's investors had started to become frustrated by the press too. There were a number of meetings held at Twitter's offices to discuss how to handle the situation. On more than one occasion, Ev debated removing Jack from the board entirely, but he thought the public-relations backlash and resulting tarnish to Jack's image would do more to damage Twitter than Jack was currently doing.

But it wasn't just Jack's press junkets that were gaining the ire of his cofounders and Twitter's investors. As he continued his development of his new company, Square, he was using his Twitter e-mail address to set up meetings with venture capitalists and the media, often saying he would be happy to discuss Twitter, when he actually intended to present his new company. When investors realized this, it started to get back to Ev, Biz, Fred, Bijan, and others at the company, and there were more meetings to decide what to do.

They were also frustrated that Jack had previously changed his Twitter bio to read "inventor" and "founder" of Twitter.

There had been decisions to fire off warning shots to Jack, telling him to stop pulling a bait and switch with his Twitter e-mail address, but as it continued, senior executives, especially Ev, decided enough was enough.

In an internal meeting, Ev, Dick, Amac (Twitter's general counsel), Sean Garrett, and others decided it was time to shut down Jack's Twitter e-mail address.

That afternoon Jack's phone rang. It was Amac, who explained that they were going to disable Jack's e-mail address because he was using it for things that could damage the image of the company. He walked Jack through a number of legal and business implications at play. Jack was enraged, calling Biz and others to try to stop the eradication of his e-mail. Then his phone rang again. This time it was Dick, who was not a fan of Jack's at the time. He explained that Jack going on all of these press tours and using his Twitter e-mail to set up meetings for his new company was becoming detrimental to Twitter's public image—and, possibly more important, detrimental to another aspect of Twitter that had finally and miraculously improved.

For the first time in the company's history, a number that had been at zero since day one had started to grow: revenue. In December 2009, Dick had been instrumental in striking a deal with Google and Bing to make the nearly forty million tweets being sent across the site each day viewable on their respective search engines. In exchange Google had agreed to pay $15 million to Twitter. Microsoft would hand over $10 million. Twitter would collect $25 million total.

Jack was furious that his e-mail address was being taken from him and demanded that they reactivate it at once.

It was too late; jack@twitter.com was gone. A bounce-back. And there was nothing Jack could do about it.

"They took my fucking e-mail address away!" he complained to Fenton, then his only ally on the board.

Fenton was furious too. "We're going to fix this, Jack," Fenton told him.

Once again, an attempt to mute Jack was about to backfire on Ev. Jack, together with Fenton, started to hatch a plan that would get much more than just Jack's e-mail address back. One that would see Jack return to Twitter.

Steve Jobs 2.0

To most people it was just like any other tweet sent late in the evening on September 9, 2009: "Listening to the Beatles."

The next one, in early December, also just flittered by. "Listening to the Beatles and working." Then three more tweets referencing the English rock band came in January 2010. "Listening to the Beatles and working through my email." Four during the month of March. "Working in the office and listening to the Beatles." And so on.

No one noticed them as they bobbed in the Twitter stream, lost amid tens of millions of other updates.

But for Jack, who had sent all of those Beatles-related tweets, they were the very beginning of a thousand-mile journey, a reinvention of self and a transformation that would see the man from St. Louis, who just a few years earlier had arrived at Odeo wearing a T-shirt with his phone number across his chest, go through a metamorphosis into a buttoned-up, suit-wearing, perfectionist, design-guru CEO whom everyone believed resembled the greatest businessman in America: Steve Jobs.

Jack had always been an admirer of Jobs, collecting the venerable CEO's quotes, researching his favorite designers, and trying to understand his business style—just like most young entrepreneurs in Silicon Valley. But unlike (most) other young CEOs, Jack started to take the admiration a step further.

In 2009, as Jack started building Square, he wasn't just looking at
Jobs with admiration; he was emulating him. It started simply enough
by letting everyone know he was listening to the Beatles, the Apple
chief's favorite band—Jobs once told *60 Minutes* that his "model for
business is the Beatles." But as time went on, Jack started to emulate
Jobs's appearance too. He experimented with Jobs's round glasses and
cloned the mantra of a daily uniform. One day he showed up to the office
in blue jeans, a white buttoned-up shirt, and a black blazer. And from
that moment on, he rarely wore anything else in public.

Jack began talking about Mahatma Gandhi, the nonviolent leader of
Indian nationalism, after he discovered that Jobs had traveled through
India for several months in 1974 in search of enlightenment. Jack made
a portrait of Gandhi the screen saver on his computer and then tweeted
the picture. He also started walking new Square employees along a path
through San Francisco that would begin at a statue of Ghandi.

He copied many of Jobs's decisions. He referred to "rounding the
edges" in design meetings, a term Jobs began using in 1981 when he
designed the Macintosh operation system. He set up the same weekly
schedule for product meetings at Square that Jobs had commanded at
Apple. And he started using Jobs quotes in his own speeches.

Then Jack started hiring former Apple employees at Square. But
their interviews were different from those of other candidates. "Did you
have the opportunity to work with Steve Jobs?" Jack would ask. "Can
you tell me a little about his management style?" During one discussion
with a well-known Apple designer who had been hired at Square, Jack
heard that Jobs didn't consider himself a CEO but rather an "editor."
Soon Jack started referring to himself as "the editor, not just the CEO"
of Square. During one talk to employees, he announced: "I've often spoken to the editorial nature of what I think my job is. I think I'm just an
editor."

Jack started saying "No one has ever done this before" about his
products, an exact quote from a Jobs interview in early 2010 at a conference. Jack then adopted Jobs's terms to describe new Square features,

words like "magical," "surprise," and "delightful," all of which Jobs had used onstage at Apple events.

Before long, like someone undergoing minor plastic surgeries until he resembles his idol, Jack no longer looked and acted like Jack Dorsey: He began acting like the second coming of Steve Jobs. The Beatles, the Gandhi references, the "editor" title, the design ethos, the daily uniform, and the quotes all contributed to what happened next.

The tech blogs, now believing that Jack had founded and built Twitter on his own, that he had come up with the idea when he was just a child—which Jack insinuated to dozens of media outlets—and that he possessed the same principles as Jobs in both design and management, started asking: "Is Jack Dorsey the next Steve Jobs?" (They inevitably answered: "Yes.")

It wasn't a grand master plan by Jack to copy Jobs. Rather it was dozens of little plans that added up to a re-creation.

In many respects it was Steve Jobs who helped create Jack Dorsey. Jobs was notorious for denying access to reporters. He had trained the media to behave exactly how he wanted them to—when he spoke, they listened, which was his best magic trick of all. So when he took a leave from Apple after falling ill in 2009, the media went in search of the next Steve Jobs. Jack walked like that duck, used the same quotes as that duck, wore the same glasses, had the same principles, and the same astounding theories on design as that duck. He even listened to the Beatles!

But for Jack the carefully orchestrated invention of Steve Jobs 2.0 wasn't just about creating an aura of visionary; it also had the unintended consequence of lighting a fire that Jack had been trying to start since he had been ousted from Twitter. A fire that would smoke Ev out of the company too.

On a late afternoon in mid-2010, Mike Abbott, who was vice president of engineering at Twitter, asked Jack if he could stop by the Square offices to chat. Abbott had no idea that Jack's title as chairman of Twitter was a veneer. Along with the rest of the world, he believed Jack was powerful in high-level decisions at the company. And like most of Silicon Valley, he believed that Jack Dorsey was the heir apparent to the Steve Jobs mystique.

They began meeting on a regular basis, discussing design and projects within Twitter. And then one afternoon the opportunity presented itself.

"I need your help," Abbott told Jack. "We have no direction at Twitter, and I don't know where the company is going." Abbott explained that he didn't like working with Greg Pass, now Twitter's chief technology officer, that he didn't think Ev had solid direction, and that he needed Jack's help and guidance. "I don't know what to do," Abbott admitted.

It was the moment Jack had been waiting for. Fenton had always been on Team Jack. But the other board members, specifically Fred and Bijan, were still very wary of Jack, believing that he had almost sunk Twitter with his inability to lead in the early days of the company.

Now a senior executive at Twitter was asking Jack for help. Like Jobs, Jack understood that he could whisper in one person's ear and those murmurs would turn into shouts somewhere else. So Jack began speaking softly.

"I consider the vice president to be the equivalent to the CEO, and if you've spoken to Ev and it's not going anywhere, you need to go to the board," Jack told Abbott. "Talk to Fenton, talk to Bijan, to Fred—whoever—about your concerns. Talk to the other senior execs."

Abbott did just that, calling the board to raise his concerns about Ev and Goldman and voice his fears that the company wasn't heading simply in the wrong direction but in no direction at all.

Abbott started telling other vice presidents at Twitter to meet with Jack too. The whispers eventually made it to Ali Rowghani, who had been hired as the chief financial officer at Twitter and was also frustrated by Ev's slow decision making. Ali set up a meeting with Jack at Blue Bottle Coffee near Square's offices. There, amid the aroma of five-dollar cups of coffee, Ali lamented the state of the company. Adam Bain, who was building revenue at Twitter, traipsed off to meet with Jack too. And then Dick followed too.

It wasn't that the company was falling apart. Quite the contrary. Twitter had secured the search deal with Google and Bing and was also now experimenting with advertising ideas, creating a new type of business experience where people could turn tweets into advertisements. The site was also finally on the mend. The engineering team had come up with an extensive long-term plan to rebuild the entire back end of Twitter, fixing the legacy problems that had plagued the company since its inception.

The problem was Ev. He was still unable to make a decision. He communicated infrequently with the board and senior staff. Some, like Mike Abbott, took it personally when they were not included in high-level conversations and decisions.

Ev was running a company that even the most experienced executive would have struggled to manage. What had been small problems at a tiny start-up like Odeo were big problems in a company that had grown as quickly as Twitter. Those big problems, when shown to the board under Jack's magnifying glass, would prove to be fateful for Ev.

At the time, Ev had set out to completely redesign Twitter, giving it a much-needed face-lift. He recruited his most trusted employees and set up what they nicknamed the war room in one of the conference rooms to brainstorm ideas. Each day, Ev huddled up with his small group of designers and programmers, with pictures and inspirations hung all over the wall, redesigning the site.

Ev buried his head in Twitter's redesign, ignoring most of the daily chores of a CEO. And across town, just a few blocks from the Twitter offices, Jack was offering friendly advice to the people not involved in the project: You should talk to the board. You should talk to Fenton. Tell Fred. Bijan. Tell them all that Ev isn't doing a good job. Tell them your fears for the future of Twitter. Jack even ensured that some people voiced their concerns to Campbell, Ev's coach.

Although it was not normal for a CEO coach to come to board meetings, Campbell would often arrive unannounced at Twitter board meetings and insert himself into the goings-on of the company. People were confused by the spectacle, but given that he was not a normal CEO coach, they simply stood back and watched.

With the whispers now entering Campbell's ear, he too was starting to voice concerns about whether Ev was the right CEO for the job. But he didn't tell Ev; instead he spoke to Fenton about the private coaching sessions going on between Ev and Campbell. Fenton then told Jack about those sessions. Like a snowball rolling down a mountaintop, accumulating every speck of dirt it encountered and growing darker and larger with each tumble (with each meeting, with each call to the board), the case against Ev started to gather an unstoppable momentum.

Russian-Roulette Relations

The snipers started showing up in the early morning. Dressed in all black, they climbed to the roof. Then, standing on gray concrete slabs, they unpacked long metal rifles and fine-tuned their scopes. Walkie-talkies could be heard giving off spurts of static as the masked men spoke to each other in Russian.

For two weeks, black suits had been sporadically appearing at the Twitter offices at all times of the day. They swarmed around cubicles like ants in search of food, checking every nook and cranny of the building. Their shiny sunglasses concealed their eyes; handguns were shrouded underneath dark blazers. Some had ferocious-looking dogs that sniffed the building for explosives.

They peeked out of windows, quietly pulling back the blinds to peer down at the busy San Francisco streets below.

"We will need a map of all of the exits and elevators," one of them said in his thick Russian accent to a Twitter employee. The elevators would need to be shut down for the visit. "We will put the metal detectors at the entrance of the offices."

After Dick had joined as COO, the company had gone on a hiring spree. By late 2009 Twitter had grown its workforce from 30 to almost 120 employees, including freelance contractors. So in November of that year the company moved into a new office at 795 Folsom Street, occupying the sixth floor of a large beige building that had been the home of several start-ups. By June 2010 that office housed almost 200 employees.

At a recent Twitter conference called Chirp, which was organized by the company, Ev had announced that more than one hundred million people had signed up for Twitter and three hundred thousand new people were joining the site each day. Ryan Sarver, who ran the company's third-party tools, told the audience that one hundred thousand applications were on Twitter too. Those apps, he said, were interacting with the site three billion times a day. The cherry on top of these Twitter numbers had also started to scare Google: People were now searching Twitter six hundred thousand times a day.

Sara had been recruited to redesign the new office space. The funky look featured a large red @-shaped light that hung above a blue, modern couch, lots of bird-related stickers, and hip designer accents like three wooden deer heads. There was even a DJ booth in the company's dining room.

Increasingly, government officials had been making the rounds at Twitter. John McCain had come in on a weekend, taking a tour of the office and meeting with executives to understand more about Twitter's role in government—and how to use it to not lose elections. Gavin Newsom, then mayor of San Francisco, had started showing up on a regular basis, coming for town-hall discussions and meetings with Ev. And Arnold Schwarzenegger had stopped by for a Web chat.

But June 23, 2010, was different. Dmitry Medvedev, the president of Russia, would be arriving at Twitter's headquarters to take a tour of the office and, as he put it, to "see with his own eyes" the hottest start-up in Silicon Valley. He also planned to send his first tweet.

It was a stark example of how the world's stage was changing. On previous visits to the United States, leaders of other nations would meet with newspaper and magazine editors. Now, rather than fly into New York City and make the rounds at *Esquire*, *Time*, or *Newsweek*, officials were dropping in to Silicon Valley to see the companies that were changing the way the world communicated.

Twitter would be the first part of a three-day trip to the United States by President Medvedev to bolster relations between America and Russia. He planned to stop by the Valley for a few meetings, including one with Steve Jobs. (Medvedev's hope was that he could explore how to build a Silicon Valley equivalent in Russia.) Then, after meeting with the nerds, he would be off to Washington to meet the suits: first President Barack Obama, then Secretary of State Hillary Clinton, Vice President Joe Biden, and other high-level U.S. generals and economic advisers, to discuss national-security issues, counterterrorism efforts, nuclear treaties, and the global economic crisis.

But first, before anything, Medvedev had something more important to do: He had to tweet.

There was, however, one slight problem.

For the past few months Twitter had been drawing more attention than ever before. The office had become Grand Central for celebrities, who often arrived unannounced, then proudly tweeted their locale for all to see. Visiting the company's offices had become a pilgrimage. As a result, Twitter's every breath was being picked up by press outlets from San Francisco to the Vatican. There was barely a publication on earth that hadn't mentioned Twitter.

Just a couple of weeks before the Russian president had announced he was stopping by the company for a visit, Twitter had been the cover story in *Time* magazine. The article had been titled, "How Twitter Will Change the Way We Live."

Steven Johnson, the bestselling book author who wrote the piece for *Time,* used the cover story to put to rest the common misconception that Twitter was only a place to tell all of your friends your favorite "choice of breakfast cereal."

Rather, Johnson noted, "as millions of devotees have discovered, Twitter turns out to have unsuspected depth."

"Partially thanks to the move from asking people to talk about their status to talk about what's happening [Twitter has become] a pointing device instead of a communications channel: sharing links to longer articles, discussions, posts, videos—anything that lives behind a URL,"

Johnson wrote. "It's just as easy to use Twitter to spread the word about a brilliant 10,000-word *New Yorker* article as it is to spread the word about your Lucky Charms habit."

As a result of all of this attention, hundreds of thousands of people were joining Twitter every single day. At the peak, more than twenty thousand were signing up for Twitter accounts in a single hour. (It had taken eight months to reach the twenty-thousand-user milestone in 2006.) Even the best-engineered Web site on the Internet would have had trouble handling such attention. But for Twitter, which was still being held together by chewing gum and masking tape, the crowds had been like a whale trying to fit into a goldfish bowl.

There were several reasons the site would disappear into its own black hole. A Twitter engineer could upload bad code that would completely disable the site. A server could fail and, like dominoes, bring down a dozen other servers. But there were more severe problems too. After the revolutions in Iran, in Syria, and elsewhere in the Middle East, Twitter was now a zone for rogue governments to attack, and bad guys with good computers were now trying to overthrow Twitter. Some hackers, proving to be deft at their trade, managed to hit the bull's-eye on several occasions, knocking the site completely off-line. As luck would have it, the moment President Medvedev's entourage of black cars pulled up to the beige building on the corner of Folsom and Fourth streets, one or all of the above had happened to Twitter.

The surrounding streets were now blocked off in all directions, with San Francisco police cars and dump trucks being used as road-blocks to foil potential assassination attempts. The Russian agents and United States Secret Service emerged onto the street, surrounding the president's car as his black, shiny loafers stepped out onto the street.

Ev paced upstairs. He had been nervous about the president's visit and had even dressed up for the occasion, wearing a beige button-down shirt and black blazer. Biz stood off to the side with Mayor Newsom, who was sipping from a Starbucks coffee cup so large it looked as if it would last a week.

"Nice of you to dress up," Ev had joked to Biz in the morning when he walked into the office. Biz was wearing disheveled sneakers, baggy, worn-in jeans, and a zip-up cargo jacket. He looked as if he had just run to the deli to pick up a carton of milk, not come to meet the president of Russia and an entourage of global press.

Goldman, the vice president of product, was situated on the third floor with the engineering team. As one of the most senior people at the company, he had agreed to manage any problems that arose while the president sent his first tweet.

Out on the street, President Medvedev looked up at the building as he was directed inside by his security detail. He walked past the Subway sandwich shop to his right, through the open glass doors, and across the marble-floored lobby and into the elevator. He didn't need to wait for an elevator, because for the next several hours the only person who would be able to enter or leave the building or travel between floors would be him.

Goldman stood like a general surveying the team of engineers who were watching over the site. As the president slowly rose through the building past the third floor, an engineer looked up at Goldman and said three dreaded words: "The site's down."

"What do you mean, the fucking site is down?" Goldman asked. Like someone who had just fallen into a pool of icy water, he went numb. He started to mentally envision the worst-case scenarios.

There had been meetings over the previous few weeks with the White House, the State Department, the San Francisco mayor's office, Governor Arnold Schwarzenegger's office, and the Russian embassy to play through the meticulously planned visit. The plan: After the Russian president sent his first tweet, the White House would retweet it. Barack Obama would reply, congratulating him on his tweet, as would the mayor and governor, all welcoming the Russian president to Twitter and to the United States.

But that wasn't going to happen without a Web site. Worse, as Goldman was confined to the third floor until the president left the building, he couldn't run up and tell Ev and Biz. He tried to text them both, but without knowing what was going on three floors above, Goldman didn't know whether the president was there or if they could see their cell phones.

As the elevator door opened to the sixth floor, the president emerged, shaking Mayor Newsom's hand. He was then introduced to Ev, Biz, and Dick.

As Biz reached out to shake Medvedev's hand, his phone vibrated in his pocket. It was a message from Goldman, explaining the situation and urging Biz to do everything in his power to delay the first tweet.

Biz showed his phone to Ev, who peered at the screen with a fake smile. "Shall we?" Mayor Newsom said as he led them down the hallway. Biz tried to delay, walking as slowly as possible as everyone went ahead. At one point a public-relations employee who had found out the site was off-line tapped Dick on the shoulder and said the same words that he had read from Goldman. "The site's down."

Dick turned with a look of confusion and shock. "Like, totally down?" he asked as his eyes widened. Biz continued walking glacially, trying to come up with any excuse to delay the group from tweeting. "Oh, we should show him the electric bike!" Biz said as they zigzagged like lost drunks through the office.

Twitter employees stood to the side as the group made its way through the cubicles, Biz's feet moving with the speed of an infirm ninety-year-old man, doing his best to slow the inevitable arrival in the cafeteria, where the first tweet was scheduled to leave American soil.

They continued strolling, slowly. Very, very slowly. They walked past some of the artwork Ev and Sara had chosen for the office, at one point catching a glimpse of one of Ev's favorite pieces of art, which sat in a black frame and, in a bit of irony, was hung upside down. It read: "Let's make better mistakes tomorrow."

Ev loved that poster. He had tweeted about it when it first arrived in mid-December, late on a Thursday afternoon, showing off a picture to his Twitter faithful with the title "New sign at Twitter HQ." But with the site down and the Russian president just a few feet away from the cafeteria, they could do without today's mistake. Or tomorrow's.

Goldman dripped with sweat as he paced behind the engineers, who were doing everything they could to get the site back up, frantically talking to servers and code consoles. "What's going on, guys?" he said. "Talk to me; tell me we've got the site back online." The engineers were trying every trick in the book, trying desperately to figure out what was wrong.

Upstairs, Biz and Ev were unable to hold off the president any longer. They walked into the cafeteria unsure of what they'd find on the computer. It all happened in slow motion, the pops of flashes from the media in tow as the president approached the podium, his fingers reaching out to touch the keys of a laptop set up for the first tweet. Ev looked over at Biz, who had no idea what was going to happen. Would the site work? Would this be the biggest embarrassment possible for the company, a media storm from San Francisco to St. Petersburg calling Twitter and American technology a joke?

Then the gods intervened. "We're back!" an engineer yelled as he leaned back in his chair, looking at Goldman. A sigh of relief enveloped the room.

"Hello everyone!" Medvedev typed slowly in Russian into the Mac computer at the podium, "I'm on Twitter, and this is my first tweet." Ev had a microphone in his hand, narrating to the employees and the media what was happening. As Medvedev pressed "send," he looked up to the projector in front of him and smiled. The president then gave a thumbs-up with his left hand, beaming like a child who had just figured out a complicated puzzle. Biz, who was standing behind them both with his hands cupped in his jeans pockets, smiled as the screen's reflection glimmered on his glasses.

"Holy fuck," he whispered to Ev as the president walked forward to talk to Mayor Newsom. "That was close."

Secret Meetings

The front door to Jack's apartment swung open and Dick walked in. He wandered down the hallway to the kitchen, which opened out onto the living room, then continued around the corner and over to the fridge. He pulled the handle back and then nodded as he peered inside. "Yep, just as I figured," Dick said to Jack with a smile as he looked back at the fridge, empty except for a couple of bottles of water and beer. "It looks like a bachelor pad, all right."

As Jack laughed, Dick turned and strolled into the living and dining area to shake hands with Fenton and the few others who were in attendance, including an outside public-relations consultant Fenton had hired to help with any media-related issues that might arise from the meeting they were about to have.

Jokes then ceased as the meeting got under way.

It was the second of two secret meetings that had taken place in Jack's Mint Plaza loft over the summer of 2010. It had been a few months since Jack had started to convince the board and senior Twitter employees that it was Ev's turn to be fired as the CEO of Twitter.

Jack had had no problem convincing Fenton that Ev was the wrong person to run the company. Fenton had happily slurped up the Jack Kool-Aid since day one. But Jack had found it much more difficult to convince the rest of the board.

Yet after Abbot, Ali, and other senior staffers complained to the board about Ev's recent management choices, the near miss with the Russian president, Ev's slothlike decision-making process, and his insistence on hiring friends, the tide had turned.

Ensuring that the right things landed in the right people's ears, Jack had spent the summer moving people around like pawns in a chess match against his nemesis. The problem was, Ev had no idea he was playing. These secret meetings taking place at Jack's apartment, at Blue Bottle Coffee, and at Square's offices? Ev had no clue of their existence.

After Jack had left a year and a half earlier, Fred and Bijan had believed that Ev was the right person to run Twitter. And Ev had quickly proven himself to them. But now, with revenue growing slowly and an entirely new set of problems having arisen with the massive growth spurts Twitter had experienced through 2009, the first investors were both questioning whether he was the right leader to take Twitter to the next level, which would include making the company consistently profitable—then, if all went according to plan, taking Twitter public. Their fears had been heightened when Jack had indirectly whispered in their ears that they could lose hundreds of millions of dollars in investment money with Ev at the helm.

Of course, Ev didn't have a chance to assuage anyone's fears. As far as he knew, everything was just fine at Twitter. He held his weekly meetings with Campbell, receiving his boisterous pep talk. "You're doing a fucking great job!" Campbell would bellow. At board meetings Campbell would appear to listen to Ev's presentations on the state of the company. After Ev's sermons were done, the coach would clap loudly and hug his protégé, proclaiming again to everyone in the room that Ev was "doing a fucking great job!" and asking them to clap (none of this was a usual occurrence in a corporate board meeting). Then, after Ev left the room, proud that his mentor thought he was doing such a great job, Campbell would shout at the group: "You gotta get rid of this fucking guy! He doesn't know what the fuck he's doing!"

For some of the senior Twitter staffers, including Ali, the entire ordeal had come down to one major issue that could take Twitter out at the knees.

Over the past year a company called UberMedia had been building and buying a number of third-party Twitter applications, including some big-name Twitter apps called Echofon and Twidroyd. UberMedia was managed by a shrewd businessman, Bill Gross, who was on the verge of buying another app, arguably one of the largest, called Tweet-Deck. But Gross had a much bigger plan in mind than just buying up third-party Twitter clients.

Gross's plan was to build a Twitter-network clone that could be used to divert people away from Twitter to an entirely new service, one where Gross could make money on advertising. He had also developed a business relationship with Ashton Kutcher and hoped to bring him into this new venture.

When Ali and Dick found out about the TweetDeck deal, they realized that such a sale would give Gross ownership of 20 percent of all Twitter clients. Ali and others at Twitter wanted to buy TweetDeck before UberMedia did. But Ev couldn't make a decision. He wondered if the tens of millions of dollars TweetDeck would cost would be worth it. One moment Ev agreed to buy the app, and the next he changed his mind, stalling the decision again.

At Jack's loft during the first of the secret meetings, the group that met had made a pact on three things: first, that they would agree to stand together against Ev and Goldman no matter what happened; second, that they would remove Ev as CEO; and third, that they would ask Dick to become the interim CEO until they found a suitable replacement. Finally, they would bring Jack back to the company. Although Jack wanted to be CEO, he knew he couldn't do it while running Square at the same time, but just returning would be enough. At least for now.

Then there was the second meeting, where they told Dick part of the plan. He was being picked, they explained, because the employees trusted him and he could help as a transitional CEO until they found a permanent replacement. This they couldn't do until Ev was out.

Back at the Twitter offices, Ev was oblivious to the coup. He was brimming with pride about the latest Twitter numbers: People were sending more than two billion tweets a month on the service, and millions of new accounts were being created each week. He was also exhilarated by the new and improved, redesigned version of Twitter he was planning to launch on September 14, 2010; it had been code-named Phoenix internally. Externally it would be called #NewTwitter and would take short snippets of media and embed them directly within a tweet. No more clicking off to other Web sites to see photos, videos, or links people were sharing; they would all exist within Twitter in little side panes. The 140-character tweet was becoming an envelope with more information inside.

Although Twitter was now making more money with its advertising products, Ev wasn't as concerned with the revenue side of the operation, which was more fuel for the board's desire to oust him as CEO. Dick, on the other hand, had been leading the charge to make Twitter profitable, which contributed to the board's decision to ask him to be the interim CEO when they thrust Ev out of the company.

For Ev life was going according to plan. He and Sara were starting to try for a second child. He had cashed out a small amount of his Twitter stock, giving him millions of dollars to buy a new house in San Francisco and a second home in Tahoe, three hours northeast of the city, to go skiing with his family. Ev had continued to try and help the people close to him, giving money away in undisclosed ways. At a friend's art opening, he anonymously purchased the artist's work. He had also started to give vast sums away to charities, secretly donating hundreds of thousands of dollars. And taking care of his friends and family by paying off debts for those closest to him.

Ev didn't know anything about the secret meetings or his lieutenants talking to the board or that his conversations with his coach would make their way back to Fenton and then Jack.

As far as Ev knew, he was "doing a great fucking job!"

The Clown Car in the Gold Mine

It was mid-September 2010, the sun shining brightly through the window as Ev stood in his office, scribbling Twitter-related ideas on his whiteboard. Outside his office door, rows of cubicles were pulsating with the quiet murmur of keyboard taps and mouse clicks. The street below bustled with cars floating by.

He looked up to see Campbell filling the doorway like a linebacker.

Ev smiled, happy to see the Coach for their weekly session. Ev was in particularly good spirits; #NewTwitter was garnering good reviews from the tech critics. He was especially looking forward to a party planned that evening to help celebrate the employees' months of hard work. The *New York Times* was also working on a large Sunday business profile about him: the billionaire farm boy who helped invent Blogger and Twitter. The man behind two companies that had changed media and the way people communicate.

But Campbell looked troubled. "Have a seat," he said solemnly to Ev. "This is going to be hard. We're going to have a hard conversation."

Ev fell onto the couch, not sure what he was about to hear from Campbell. His mind started to race with possibilities. And then, like the thud of a bird flying into a clear glass window, Campbell told him. "The board wants you to step up to the chairman role."

Ev was confused. "What do you mean?"

"The board is going to make Dick CEO," Campbell said. "They want you to step down."

At first Ev thought Campbell was kidding around, and he laughed nervously. But Campbell wasn't joking.

"You're being serious?" Ev asked, his heartbeat revving up. "I'm confused. What, what are you talking about?" he said, the smile now completely erased from his face. "I don't understand what you're talking about."

Then Campbell said it again. "The board doesn't wasn't you to be CEO. They want you to step down. They want you out."

Campbell continued talking, rambling about the board's decision, about their belief that Ev wasn't the right person to run Twitter. That he took too long to make decisions. That he couldn't execute. "Look, these fucking guys. These fucking New York investors," Campbell said, trying to show he had nothing to do with the decision.

As Ev started to grasp that what he was hearing was actually real, he interrupted Campbell. "Are you for this too?" Ev asked. "Do you agree with the board?" Campbell started hemming and hawing, looking away from Ev, unable to properly answer him. "And are you for it too?" Ev asked again in a fierce tone, his disbelief now turning to anger.

Again Campbell dithered, cursing about the board, the investors. "These fucking guys!" he said.

Eventually Ev had heard enough and asked Campbell to leave so he could call the board and find out what was going on. He quickly started dialing.

"Hey, I'm really sorry, man," Bijan said. He sighed and told Ev that he thought he was a great CEO. "We want you to stay on in a product-advisory role," Bijan said. "We don't want you to leave the company. We think you're really valuable to Twitter." But, he explained, the company needed a new type of CEO who could focus on revenue and take Twitter public.

Ev was stunned at what he was hearing. He hung up. He then called Fred Wilson, who was not remotely as friendly or apologetic as the others had been. Fred told him bluntly that he believed he had always been a terrible CEO, that he had no product sense. Fred said he hated the new Web site design, that it was the wrong direction for the company.

"What the fuck are you talking about?" Ev said to Fred, his voice now shaking. "This is how VCs fuck up companies."

"Where is this coming from? Every time I ever gave a product presentation to the board, you were always like, 'Yeah, this is amazing, this is awesome,'" Ev said to Fred. "I know we weren't executing well, but . . ." He paused, lowering his voice, and solemnly stated, "I really don't know how you can do this to a founder of a company."

"I never considered you a founder," Fred responded snidely, offended by Ev's slur against VCs. "Jack founded Twitter."

Ev's eyes widened. "What the fuck are you talking about?" he said. "You fucking fired Jack! This is insane. This is. Fucking. Insane."

"This is not a discussion," Fred said. It had been decided by the board. Ev was not going to be CEO anymore.

Ev was infuriated. He had no idea whom to trust. How long ago had the board decided to fire him? *Could* they fire him? After all, Ev still owned the largest majority stake in Twitter and owned two voting board seats.

Ev tried several times to reach Fenton, repeatedly hearing his voice mail rather than his voice. He wanted to talk to Goldman and Biz. Were they in on this too? Campbell, Fred, Bijan, and Fenton all wanted him gone as CEO—that much was clear amid the fog of confusion—but what about "his boys"? Dick, his friend of many years, had to be a part of the coup if he was being made CEO, Ev reasoned.

But not Goldman? or Biz? Ev thought, there was simply no way. Ev rushed out the door of his office and headed toward the third floor. He kept his head down to avoid talking to employees.

"You okay?" Goldman said as Ev walked up, a worried look on his face. Ev pointed to the rear conference room. As they went inside, Goldman closed the door behind them and sat at the table, looking up at his best friend and boss inquisitively. There were no windows, just dim lights shining down from the ceiling. Outside the room, hundreds of employees buzzed away. Ev leaned back against the wall and told

Goldman what had just happened. It was immediately apparent that Goldman had not been in on the boardroom rebellion.

"You're fucking kidding me," Goldman said in confusion. "What did they say?"

Ev walked him through his conversation with Campbell, then the phone calls with Fred and Bijan, broadly explaining what each had said.

Goldman was shocked.

———

It was dark outside as the rain pelted Dick Costolo's car relentlessly. He gripped the steering wheel with both hands, trying to concentrate on the dark road. He was exhausted after the long flight from Indianapolis, where he had been speaking at a conference about Twitter. *A few more miles*, he thought, *and I'll be home, out of these wet clothes.*

He had crossed the Golden Gate Bridge and begun navigating the dark, winding roads that led to his home in Marin when his phone rang. He fumbled to answer it with the Bluetooth in his car.

Ev and Goldman were sitting in another windowless conference room at Twitter on the sixth floor when the speakerphone finally clicked on. "Dick speaking," they heard over the sound of buckets of water smacking the window and roof of the car.

"What the fuck, Dick!" said Goldman. "So you're going behind Ev's back to be CEO of the company! I can't believe—"

Dick cut him off. "What the fuck are you talking about? Who is going to be CEO?"

Ev slowly leaned in to the phone. "The board tried to fire me today and said they're putting you in charge to run the company," he said in a placid tone, then repeated: "They told me to step up to the chairman role and that you're taking over."

"What the fuck are you talking about? That's news to me," Dick said, sounding as surprised as Ev had been when he had heard the same news from Campbell earlier in the day. "Was anyone going to tell me?" he joked, his deep laugh bouncing from his car into the Twitter conference room.

"You mean you didn't know about this?" Goldman asked.

"Noooo!" Dick said, shocked. "This is literally the first I've ever heard of it." This wasn't true, but it wasn't completely untrue, either.

Although the board had asked Dick to become interim CEO earlier that summer, Dick had asked that they execute it in a tactful way and that they determine how to tell Ev so it didn't seem that Dick was pushing him out of the company to take control, which he was not. That plan had vanished into a plume of smoke when Campbell had shown up in Ev's office earlier that day and delivered the wrong speech. Campbell, who had known about Ev's approaching ousting for months (even during the coaching sessions), had suggested to the board that he tell Ev to step down, but he wasn't supposed to mention the Dick part of the equation. That was supposed to come later.

Dick had been caught between ethics and business amid the ousting of his friend and boss and he often found himself at a loss for what to do. He had assumed the board would handle it tactfully. But now it had all gone awry.

As Dick drove through the dark along the wet road, he explained to Ev and Goldman that he was going to tell the board he wouldn't take the job without Ev's consent—and since that clearly wasn't being given, he wouldn't do it.

As they hung up the phone, Goldman looked over at Ev and asked if he believed Dick. "I have no idea," Ev said. "I really have no fucking idea who to believe anymore."

———

Over the following days, events started to play out exactly as they had with Jack two years earlier.

Ev called Ted, Twitter's lawyer, who repeated almost verbatim the words he had said to Jack when he was fired. "There isn't much you can do," he said. "It comes down to a vote by the board." Then, reading from the next line in the script, Ted explained that he was sorry, that he really couldn't talk to Ev about it because first and foremost, he was Twitter's lawyer.

Goldman then went on the offensive, telling the board that they clearly didn't understand Ev if they thought he would simply step down. "This isn't just going to happen like that," he said. "If you push him out, I'm going to leave. So is Biz. So are half of the employees. You're going to lose all of us." He was right. Most of the Twitter employees loved Ev. More than half would have gladly put their few digital belonging onto thumb drives and walked out with him if Ev had asked them to. He had gone to great efforts to be the best boss he could be, and he had been successful. But while he was adept at managing down, managing up and sideways to his senior staffers was an entirely different story.

The conversations started to turn into a merry-go-round. "Fuck this." "Fuck that." "Fuck you." Fenton came into the office to try to push things along. "I told you to manage Campbell," Fenton told Ev as they talked in his office. "I'm really sorry about this, but I told you to manage his ego."

"How the fuck is this up to Campbell?" Ev asked, cursing repeatedly, his hands shaking with anger. "Look, I totally acknowledge I'm not the best CEO, but you can't put Dick in as CEO. He's not a product guy; he's an operations guy."

"We'll sort the product stuff out later," Fenton told him.

"How?"

"I don't know; we'll just figure it out. You'll be involved at a high level; maybe Jack can come back and help out."

And there it was. Like a punch to the stomach. The word "Jack" hung in the air. "Wait, what did you just say?" Ev asked, his hands now still, his eyes hyperfocused on Fenton. "You're going to bring Jack back?"

"No, no. I don't know if Jack will come back. That isn't my decision; it will be the decision of the new CEO," Fenton said.

———

Another few days went by and there was a closed meeting of Campbell, Ev, and the rest of the board. Dick was sitting downstairs at his office, working away on daily operations.

After talking to the lawyers, Ev had realized he would indeed have to step down as CEO, but he also knew he could slow the transition and find the right replacement for Twitter.

"Should we hire someone outside the company, do a search for an executive, or should we just make Dick the CEO?" Campbell, who had commandeered the meeting, asked Ev.

Ev said Dick had done great work for the company, but "he's not the right guy to be CEO."

"So if he's not the right guy, should we let Dick go?" Campbell asked Ev.

Ev paused. "If I step down as CEO, I will likely be taking Dick's role, so yes, we should let him go."

"Okay!" Campbell said as he slapped the table then stood up as people started beckoning him to stop. "Shouldn't we talk about this?" Fenton said frantically.

"No. Guys, we're running a start-up here!" Campbell said as he stormed out of the room, leaving a shocked boardroom in his wake. Moments later Campbell was sitting in Dick's office and telling him he was fired and needed to call the board and resign without severance.

"What, what are you talking about?" Dick said, utterly and completely confused. "Are you joking?" One minute he was being told he was going to be the next CEO of Twitter, the next he was fired from the company.

Dick sat, mouth agape, unsure what to do as Campbell walked out after his speech where he told Dick that they would find another company in the Valley where he could become the CEO.

As soon as the board heard, Dick's phone started ringing, with Fred and Bijan telling him, "Don't go anywhere! You're not fired!"

When the weekend arrived, Dick and Ev decided to meet for brunch in Marin County. Dick had spent countless nights trying to decide what to do, and here he was again, stuck between the ethics of a friendship and his desire to see Twitter, with all of its employees, grow into a successful company.

"Listen, you brought me in here, and I told you when I started that I would never go behind your back, and I won't," Dick told Ev as they sat across from each other eating breakfast. "So you tell me what you want me to do and I'll do it."

"I need you to quit so I can focus on a CEO search," Ev said.

"Okay, great," Dick said, gently tapping his hand on the table between each word. "Great. I'll e-mail Ted and ask him to draw up papers and sort out my severance." He was trying to do the right thing by Ev, and he reasoned this was it.

But as soon as the board found out Dick was resigning, his phone started ringing again. "Don't quit!" Fenton told him.

"Jesus," Dick said, "what the fuck do you want me to do?"

"Don't do anything!"

———

Finally Fred had had enough.

An e-mail had arrived in everyone's in-box saying that Fred and Bijan were getting on a plane and flying to San Francisco for a meeting. Attached was a legal document noting that the entire board would be present. "Apologies for the formal notice, but I am told this is required," Fred said in the e-mail.

"Notice is hereby given to the members of the Board of Directors of Twitter, Inc. ("Twitter") of a Special Meeting of the Board of Directors. This Special Meeting is being called pursuant to Article II, Section 2.4 of the Bylaws of Twitter. The Special Meeting will be held in person on Friday, October 1, 2010, at 2:00 p.m., local time, at the offices of Fenwick & West, 555 California Street, 12th Floor, San Francisco, California."

It was signed by Fenton, Bijan, Fred, and Jack.

———

Although Biz knew the gist of what was happening with Ev and the board, he didn't know the full extent of it. Nor did he care to. He had never wanted a seat in Twitter's boardroom. Company warfare wasn't his thing. He preferred to build moral fences around corporate castles. But whether he liked it or not, he was about to become a foot soldier in the latest battle.

As the legal letter went from Fred to the board, Biz had set off to Japan for some press and meetings. The trip was going smoothly until, one afternoon, while he was walking through the hallway of the Twitter office in Japan, his phone rang. He looked down, saw the name Jack Dorsey pop up, slid his finger across the screen, and lifted the phone to his ear.

"Ev's out as CEO," Jack said without skipping a beat. "You have to come back so we can tell the company tomorrow." Biz was standing in a hallway, Japanese Twitter employees milling by as he heard Jack talking. "Hold on, hold on," Biz said as he peered from side to side looking for a quiet place to talk without people overhearing him. He quickly opened the first door he saw and ducked inside, closing it behind him.

"What are you talking about?" Biz said. Jack explained what had happened—the letter from Fred, the scheduled meeting at the law office— and that the plan was to announce that Ev was leaving the company the following day, Friday. (Ev didn't know about this plan either.)

"You can't do this without me," Biz said, looking around the room, which he now realized was a computer closet filled with racks of servers that were powering Twitter's Japanese office. Rivers of blue Ethernet wires crisscrossed the floors and walls.

"I know we can't. That's why you need to come back now. You need to get back here by tomorrow," Jack said. "Just get on a private jet and get back here."

"I can't get a fucking private jet from Japan," Biz said, also noting that he had an important press conference to attend. "That'd cost like a billion dollars."

"Cancel the conference and get a private jet," Jack said. "The company will pay for it."

"Let me think for a second," Biz said. He paused for a moment in the closet, the server lights blinking around him, the fans whirring. He knew if Jack was calling, it was real and Ev was going to be forced out of the company the next day, but this was one of those rare moments when Biz could stall the events about to happen.

"Look, you can't do this without me," Biz said to Jack. "If you stand up there in front of the company without me, the employees are going to think you pushed Ev out and you did it behind my back because I'm not there."

"I know! That's why I need you to get back here," Jack said.

"Well, I can't," Biz said in an uncompromising tone. "I can't get back until Sunday, so we'll have to announce this to the company on Monday."

After he hung up, Biz called Goldman to strategize. Jack called Fenton to do the same. It didn't matter; Jack was going to return to the company the following day, with Biz by his side or not.

———

Jack barely slept on Thursday night. He tossed and turned thinking about what he would say to the 300 Twitter employees he was going to address the following morning, 290 of whom he had never met before. But the plan had been set in motion, or so he thought. After the meeting was over, the deed done, Jack would go to Twitter's offices with Dick and the board. There he would triumphantly announce that he was coming back to the company. The exiled executive returning to his throne. Dick would be the new temporary CEO and Jack would serve another role at Twitter, likely running product, pushing his agenda of mobile-first status messages, not Web-first newslike messages.

He woke up on Friday morning, practicing what he would say to the employees as he dressed in his expensive daily uniform. He slipped on his dark Earnest Sewn jeans, tucked in his crisp white Dior shirt, then rubbed gel in his hands and scuffed his hair to perfection. His story about being the inventor of Twitter had been perfected over the past two years, and now he would get to tell it in the house that Jack built.

The day moved almost glacially. Jack was constantly distracted. As the time of the meeting approached, he scanned his in-box and saw a message from Ev. The two hadn't spoken privately in months. He began reading: "Jack: I know we haven't gotten along in the past but I really want to try to work this out . . . if I stay as CEO I'll figure out ways to bring you back into the company . . . I want to remind you that if we do this, make this change, then I take your seat and you're off from the Board."

Like Ev two years earlier, Jack didn't respond.

———

Ev barely slept on Thursday night. He tossed and turned thinking about what was inevitably going to happen the next day. When he awoke, he was almost in a daze. The day moved quickly, almost in a blur, and as the early afternoon set in, he knew his time had come.

He walked through the city streets alone, approached Fenwick's offices, and looked up at the large glass building. He had arrived early for a meeting with Fenton to try to sort out a compromise and negotiate a role running product at Twitter, or so he had been told.

The receptionist greeted Ev and showed him into the boardroom, where he immediately saw Fred and Bijan sitting next to Fenton. "What's going on?" Ev said to Fenton, confused by the sight of them all. "I thought you said it was just us meeting first."

"I'm sorry, we're not. We just have to get this done," Fenton said.

Ev looked over at Fred and Bijan and asked them to leave the room for a moment. They obliged.

"You fucking lied to me," Ev blustered at Fenton. "What the hell is going on?"

Then the conversation was muffled as the door closed behind Fred and Bijan.

———

Some time passed and everyone was told to go into the conference room. There were the seven board members: Fred, Bijan, Fenton, Dick, Jack, Goldman, and Ev. The two lawyers, Amac and Ted, were also in attendance.

The door closed. Tension filled the room as they sank into their seats. The meeting was called to order.

And then fifteen characters came out of Ev's mouth: "I resign as CEO."

"Someone needs to create a motion," Ted said. Then he asked for two people in the room to confirm the motion. Ev looked around the room to see who would vote, and the first hand shot into the air.

"I first," said Fred, frustrated by the past week's maelstrom.

Then there was a brief moment of silence. Fenton didn't raise his hand. Neither did Bijan. Or Dick. Instead, Jack's hand slowly rose into the air.

"I second," said Jack.

It was in that moment that Ev started to realize what was happening. Jack had been behind it all. Moving chess pieces, ten moves ahead. This was Jack's revenge.

The numerous lawyers Ev had consulted had told him, not in so many words, that he was fucked. The board had spent months preparing to oust him as CEO of Twitter, ensuring that once the gears began moving, there was nothing Ev could do to stop them.

As the lawyers explained, there were seven board seats at the time. Fred, Bijan, and Fenton were clearly going to vote to have Ev ousted. Goldman, Ev, and even Dick would vote against his being fired. Which left the one deciding vote: Jack.

As Ev looked around the room, realizing that Jack had conspired against him, he thought about the time two years earlier when he had paced back and forth in his living room, his feet brushing against the rug and hardwood floor as he debated with Fred and Bijan about what to do with Jack after he was fired.

Ev had agreed to make Jack the silent chairman as a consolation prize for all his hard work. A prize Ev didn't have to give out. No legal or corporate obligation to hand it over. Just a moral one.

There had been numerous times since then that he had thought about removing Jack from the board. Jack's press junkets. Jack very publicly telling people in the industry that Ev had kicked him out. Jack changing his Twitter bio to "inventor." Their fundamental disagreement over the product. But although Ev had come close on several occasions to removing Jack, once his friend, now enemy number one, he had always decided against the conflict. That act of mercy was to be Ev's demise.

Jack and Ev looked at each other for a moment in the boardroom. At that moment neither realized that they were both fundamental to what Twitter had become. The perfect equilibrium of two different ways of looking at the world: the need to talk about yourself, compared with the need to let people talk about what was happening around them. One could never have existed without the other. That balance, or battle, had created Twitter. A tool that could be used by corporate titans and teens, by celebrities and nobodies, by government officials and revolutionaries. A place where people with fundamentally different views of the world, like Jack and Ev, could converse.

Their stares were interrupted when a vote was presented to make Dick the company's interim CEO. First. Second. Done. And then another motion.

"We're rotating the board seats," Fenton said. "We're making Jack executive chairman."

Goldman and Ev looked at each in utter confusion. "What do you mean, you're rotating the board seats?" Goldman asked.

Ev had assumed that because he was no longer CEO, he would take the seat that Jack had been keeping warm as a silent chairman. With the move, Jack would be off the board. But the board had anticipated this. They had checked every character. Ev was being pushed further down the ladder and Jack was being made the executive chairman of Twitter. When Jack learned this, he was in shock at the brute force the board was using against him.

Then Dick, the new interim CEO, spoke up. "Okay, so we're going to go to Twitter and announce—" and he was quickly interrupted by Ev.

"No, we're changing the messaging," Ev said.

"What are you talking about?"

"Fenton and I agreed that I'm going to stay on as president of product," Ev said. "So I want to reconsider the messaging. So we won't be telling the company today." And, he added, he didn't want Jack to be there for the announcement. This, he explained, was part of the deal Ev and Fenton had made before the meeting.

The meeting wrapped up, Jack fuming that he wasn't going to return to the company to give his impassioned speech. As soon as he got back to his office at Square, he started making phone calls. "What happened?" he roared at Fenton. "This wasn't part of the plan!"

"I know, I know. We'll fix it."

A Sunday Storm

The first time any of Biz's coworkers saw him fight for something was with the mice.

It was late 2006 and Odeo had recently moved into 164 South Park, the office that would soon become the place of Twitter's inception. The space was relatively eccentric when the equally oddball group of programmers moved in. Little rooms off to the right and left, different levels, and a small kitchenette.

As they settled in, picking desks like children fighting over the best bedroom in a new house, the small kitchenette area became the heart of the office. On some mornings Noah would make pancakes and sing "The Pancake Song." To make the place feel a little more like home, snacks and a bowl of fresh fruit sat out on the countertop. But the Odeo programmers didn't nibble on the apples and bananas that sat there. Instead it was little mice that each night left tiny teeth marks that looked like mini Grand Canyons carved into the fruit.

"This is so fucking gross," employees would say when they saw the ransacked fruit each morning.

So it was decided: The mice had to be exterminated—with traps, poison, whatever it took. When Biz found out about the plan to have the mice killed, he arrived on the scene like a hostage negotiator at an elementary school.

"You are not killing those mice," he said. People looked at him, unsure if he was joking. "I'm not kidding; no one is touching them."

Everyone tried to reason with him that the mice were eating the fruit, that they were dirty, that . . .

"I don't give a shit. There is no fucking way we are setting traps and killing mice," he said sternly, tears welling in his eyes, his hands shaking with anger, his fists clenched, baffled that anyone would harm an animal, especially one as small and helpless as a little mouse. "It's not going to happen," he repeated. "No one is killing the mice!"

It was the first time anyone had seen Biz erupt like that. Though it wasn't the last, over the next four years it would happen only a handful of times.

On the morning of October 3, 2010, two days after Ev had been fired as CEO in the law offices, Biz woke from a groggy, post-Japan, jet-lagged sleep, and although he didn't know it yet, it was about to happen again. This time it would be about protecting not mice but instead Ev, his boss and closest friend of nearly a decade.

Biz tended to the pets in the house. Made his morning coffee. Kissed Livy good-bye, apologizing that he had to work on a Sunday, and set off into San Francisco.

Twitter's offices were still and windless in the early morning. The lights were off. Computers sleeping. Motionless. Outside, the occasional empty taxi passed by as early risers walked their dogs. Small, puffy clouds crept across the sky like sleepy turtles covered in cotton balls. A few blocks away AT&T Park was stretching awake, getting ready for game day, when the San Francisco Giants would take on the Padres.

But the calm in the office was about to be broken, another storm about to erupt. In a couple of hours, Twitter would come alive with cursing and tension that the office had never seen before. And the first cracks of thunder could be heard in the distance, from New York, when an e-mail from Fred arrived in everyone's in-box at 9:57 A.M., addressed to Ev but including the entire board and Biz.

"Ev," it began, "Peter, Bijan, and I will not be at the Company on Monday as we all discussed." Then he highlighted six bullet points that should be communicated to Twitter employees and the media, most of which Ev already knew: Dick is becoming interim CEO; the board will eventually perform a CEO search to replace him; Ev will still be on the board, have an office at Twitter, represent the company externally, and contribute to product strategy. But there was a new addition to the announcement. "You will no longer have an operating role in the Company," Fred wrote.

Ev read the line a few times, confused. When he had agreed to step down on Friday, he had been told by Fenton that he would be the president of product at Twitter, ensuring the site continued on a design-based trajectory, not a money-minded one. Now, as he made his way into the office to plan the company announcement that he thought would simply state a change of roles, he was being told that there had been a bait and switch.

Like Jack two years earlier and Noah two years before that, Ev was officially out of a job at Twitter. And like his two cofounders, he was completely powerless to do anything about it. Which the board knew. He had officially stepped down as CEO, so any previous deals that had not been inked on paper or pixelated over e-mail were null and void. The decision now lay with Jack, the executive chairman, and Dick, who was officially and legally Ev's boss at Twitter.

One by one, Ev, Dick, Biz, Goldman, Amac, and Sean Garrett, who ran the public-relations team, streamed into the office. The lights clicked on. Computers gasped for air as their fans whirred to life. The executive assistants arrived, ready to help their bosses.

The meetings began.

The executives shuffled in and out of three different conference rooms. And although they were holding meetings that would decide the fate of Ev, they looked like children who had come into an empty office with their parents and been left alone to play hide-and-seek.

But the mood wasn't jovial. There was no laughing. There was only tension that could have been sliced with a tweet and sadness, even among the winning team.

Goldman was despondent as he sulked into the office, especially after reading Fred's e-mail. They had lost, and Ev was out. It was over. All that was left to do was write the press release that would go into the history books describing a made-up version of how the battle ended.

But Biz was genuinely confused. "I don't understand how they can just throw away this guy's entire career," he said to Goldman as they talked about Fred's e-mail. "Don't these people have feelings?" Although Biz was a cofounder of Twitter, he had never really had much power at the company. He had never understood what drove the "money guys." The e-mail from the board seemed utterly unfair.

As they shuffled between the conference rooms, one of the public-relations employees sat on the couch in the hallway, her laptop open as she wrote different variations of the blog post that would go up on the site on Monday morning. The first version was going to announce that Ev was leaving the company for good and Jack, the exiled founder, was returning. But as the day progressed, the plan and blog post would change several times.

Kris, Ev's assistant, had been asked to go through Dick's tweets, highlighting any that could be perceived as controversial. As she scrolled through his thousands of 140-character updates, she stopped midscreen and rolled her eyes as she called people over to look at the message he had jokingly sent a year earlier: "First full day as Twitter COO tomorrow. Task #1: undermine CEO, consolidate power."

———

First Ev went into the Puffin conference room with Dick and tried to pitch Dick on allowing him to stay at the company.

"It's not up to me, it's up to the board," Dick said.

"You're the CEO, you have to decide," Ev pleaded.

The conversation continued and then grew heated. "I'm not doing it," people heard Dick yell from the hallway. "I'm not fucking doing it!"

Moments later Ev emerged, his head hanging low. Biz walked into the room. "Ev just left here looking very disappointed," he said to Dick. "What happened?"

Dick explained that Ev had proposed taking a lead product role, with Dick's becoming the permanent CEO, but he once again refused to accept the proposal, telling Biz, "I'm uncomfortable doing it because it will look like I did a trade to get this position."

Biz shook his head, defeated like Ev, and walked out.

Dick had been told by the board to stand firm in the decision that Ev was out of a job. Even if Dick wanted to keep Ev in the company, the verdict was out of his hands; the people above him had already made their decision.

People talked on phones to board members. There were private meetings about private meetings. And then they all shuffled into the main conference room—Dick, Sean, Amac, Goldman, Biz, and Ev—to hash out how Monday would transpire.

"So here's the deal," Dick said. "Ev's out and I'm interim CEO. . . ." He continued to talk, explaining what the messaging to the world would say. Ev sat silently, helpless in the company that two days earlier he had been running.

"And then Jack will be here. . . . ," Dick continued as he spoke about the plan, which included Jack being present at the announcement that Ev was leaving the company.

Then Biz quietly interrupted in a sort of whisper. "I'm sorry, but I'm confused. Why can't we just say Ev's going to be in charge of product?" Biz asked Dick as he sat across from him.

"I'm not doing that," Dick said matter-of-factly.

"Why not?" Biz asked, genuinely bewildered by what was happening.

"I'm not going to do a trade; I'm not going to have it come out later that the only reason I'm CEO is because I horse-traded," Dick said, slamming his fingers repeatedly on the table as he spoke. Biz again looked at him with confusion, partially because he didn't understand what the term "horse-trade" meant but also because he couldn't comprehend that the board was capable of just pushing Ev out of Twitter without compromise. Dick repeated himself: "I'm not going to have my whole thing be that the reason I'm CEO is because I did a deal."

Biz's face twitched slightly as he listened.

"Everybody stop for a second!" Biz said as he held his hand in the air like a traffic cop. "Just stop, for one second." He looked directly at Dick as everyone sat silently and watched Biz, whose voice was now shaky.

"Dick!" he said loudly. "Please explain to me—let me see if I have this right—you will not agree with the idea that Ev is head of product and you are CEO because you're uncomfortable?" Biz said.

"That's exactly right," Dick replied tersely.

"Well!" Biz started to shout. "Well! How about you fucking be uncomfortable in reference to the entire fucking career of this guy?" Biz said, his arm now pointing at Ev. "How about you be fucking uncomfortable?"

The room was dead silent. Not a squeak as Biz glared directly at Dick. Then Biz lowered his voice, hopelessness in his tone. "You can't be uncomfortable for the sake of Ev's entire career?"

Everyone looked at Biz, stunned expressions on their faces. Biz sat there, half-irate, half-exhilarated by his own outburst.

Dick stared back at him, silent for a moment, his brain weighing the ethical decision versus the business one. "All right, fine," Dick said. "Fine. I'll do it. Fine, fine, fine." He stood up and walked out of the room as he spoke. "I've gotta go call Fenton and talk to him."

Dick walked into the cafeteria as he put his cell phone to his ear, leaning against the window of the cavernous, empty room, where in less than twenty-four hours employees would greet him as the new CEO of Twitter.

Biz and Goldman followed behind, cutting in the other direction and heading into a different conference room. The executive assistants in the hallway watched in confusion as people zigzagged all over the place. Kris sent a series of text messages to Sara, who was home with the baby, and gave her updates about what was going on.

Biz's hands were shaking with adrenaline as he called Bijan, who was greeted by a confident, forceful Biz on the other end of the line as Biz laid into him. "Look, if Ev doesn't come in on Monday, I'm not coming in on Monday!" Biz said emphatically. "And you can deal with this announcement on your own, without me, without Goldman, and without Ev, which is going to be a giant fucking disaster."

Goldman sat quietly as he listened to Biz talk to Bijan as if he didn't have a care in the world. Bijan didn't need much convincing. He felt bad about the way things had transpired but also knew that the investors needed to ensure they didn't lose the hundreds of millions of dollars that were at stake if Twitter failed. Like Dick, he was caught between morality and business interests. As Bijan started to speak, Biz cut him off. "And you guys need to make Dick the full-time CEO—none of this 'interim' bullshit." He explained that the company and its employees had already been through enough, and the current plan, which would mean firing one CEO, bringing in an interim CEO, and then searching for a third CEO, would destroy the employees' confidence in Twitter.

"Okay, I get it, I get it," Bijan said. "Let me call Fred and Fenton and talk to them."

———

After the calls wrapped up, they all reconvened back in the conference room and put together what would be the final plan—a plan that Jack was not happy about, as it meant he would not be in attendance for the Monday-morning announcement; a plan that would allow Ev to keep a job at the company as director of product. But Jack knew it was a plan that would last only a little while. Ev did not.

October 4, 2010, 10:43 A.M.
The Twitter Office

"Get out," Ev said to the woman standing in his office doorway. "I'm going to throw up."

She stepped backward, pulling the door closed, a metal clicking sound reverberating through the room as he grabbed the black wastebasket in the corner of his office with hands that were now shaking and clammy.

It was Monday morning, forty-seven minutes before Ev would deliver his speech to the company. A company that, outside that door, had no idea what the day would bring.

The office had opened as usual. The coffeepots were filled. Employees trundled in thinking it was just another Monday morning at Twitter. Maybe a celebrity would arrive unannounced again. Or a politician. Maybe there would be a tasty delivery from a food truck or a local ice-cream parlor, thanking the company for all it had done to help their business grow.

There were links being shared on Twitter about the latest issues of the *New Yorker*, the *Economist*, and the *New York Times*, each with an article about Twitter's role in the revolutions now taking place in the Middle East, revolutions that were beginning to spread to more countries in the tumultuous region, all thanks to Twitter.

Goldman had arrived early on that Monday morning. He had taken a couple of very trusted employees aside and told them a variation of the story that would be told to the media later that day. Then Ev and Sara had come in, walking into his office as he prepared for what was coming next. "Are you okay?" Sara asked, as he responded that he wasn't feeling well. He didn't know if it was his nerves, or if he was coming down with something, but either way, his stomach churned. Sara left the room as one of the public-relations employees walked into Ev's office to review the speech he would give in forty-five minutes. And then he interrupted her.

The door closed as Ev fell to his knees to the rough carpet floor.

This was it. His last act as the CEO: staring at the bottom of a garbage can, searching for how he had gotten there. Searching memories that had been blogged, photographed, and tweeted over the past decade but still lingered somewhere else, lost in a sea of tens of billions of tweets.

He searched the emptiness for answers. How was he forty-five minutes away from being thrust out of the company he had started, the company he had financed with his own money, the company he loved, the company he had hired his friends to help run? Some who had betrayed him.

He searched his memory looking for answers. But even when you bury those memories on the Internet as tweets, you have to remember which box you hid them in. And when you put them there. If there's no X to mark the spot, there is no spot.

Even on the Internet, the elephant that never forgets, memories are still forgotten.

Ev had known all along that it had never been about the money. A billionaire still throws up into a garbage can. It was about making a dent in the universe. About power, the power that had been sucked from politicians and Hollywood, from celebrities, revolutionaries, corporations, and the media, then siphoned through this bizarre fucking thing called Twitter. This accidental thing that had tipped the world upside down.

Now it was time for Ev's world to tip. And in that moment, staring at the floor, alone, he felt it. The feeling of regret.

The door to his office opened and Sara walked in. "How are you feeling?"

"Fuck."

Dick was on the phone next door, peering down as he paced in his office, talking about Jack's return to the company. A new plan was being hatched.

Biz sat down at his computer and typed out an e-mail to the company telling everyone to meet at 11:30 A.M. in the cafeteria. No outsiders allowed; put them in the lobby until after the meeting; there will be no hummus, just important news.

And then it was time.

Employees stood up from their desks, walking through the labyrinthine halls of Twitter as they shuffled into the cafeteria, a quiet and confused hum echoing through the room. They found their seats.

Then Ev appeared, Biz and Goldman in tow.

Then Dick.

Ev walked out, a microphone in his hand, and delivered his own eulogy, telling employees that he had decided to step into a product role and had asked Dick to take over as CEO. A solemn few words said in an upbeat tone. Then he stepped aside, handing the microphone to the new CEO of Twitter. The third CEO in two years.

At 11:40 A.M., as Dick took the helm, a woman from the public-relations team, who sat in the audience with her laptop open, hit "publish" on the blog post announcing that Dick Costolo was the new CEO and that Evan Williams, of his own volition, had stepped down to focus on product.

"If we want to get Twitter to a hundred-billion-dollar company," Dick said to the audience, "Ev and I agreed that this is the best move for the company."

Within seconds the press started scrambling to cover the announcement. An announcement that didn't mention the vicious mutiny that had taken place in the boardrooms of Twitter over the past months. An announcement that didn't mention that Ev had almost been completely out of a job. And one that didn't mention that Jack Dorsey would be returning to the company. That was all still to come.

V.
#DICK

No Adult Supervision

D o you smell that?" a round-faced Twitter engineer said as he peered up from his cubicle. It was late in the afternoon on a Thursday. Moments earlier the office had been as serene and calm as a summer lake, the only sound a faint white noise coming from employees' computers.

"It smells like weed," the engineer said to his cubicle mates as he took a deep whiff to be sure his nose was being honest. "Right? That's weed?"

Another engineer sat up, now sniffing too. "Wait, is that rap music?" he asked.

They looked at each other, trying to figure out what was going on.

They didn't know it, but two hours earlier the metal elevator doors on the sixth floor of Twitter's office had quietly slid open and, like a scene from the beginning of a rap video, an entourage of a dozen large men, most of them black, had poured into the lobby.

"I'm Nick Adler," a man with a shaved head said confidently as he approached the doe-eyed, petite receptionist, who, sitting behind the low counter, looked back at the posse with utter confusion. "We're here to meet with Biz Stone. Omid sent us."

The receptionist looked back and saw, towering above everyone, in the center of the group, like a queen bee surrounded by its lieutenants, the rapper Snoop Dogg. His head swayed slightly from side to side as he looked around the lobby, his sunglasses concealing his bloodshot eyes. A large, droopy hat covered his cornrowed hair.

"Yes, um, let me call him," the receptionist said, smiling awkwardly as she tried to reach Biz. But there was no one to call. There were no vice presidents or senior executives or any adult supervision at all in the building.

One of Dick's first tasks when he had taken over as CEO had been to remove Goldman as head of product at Twitter. Dick wanted to clean up the board, get out the old and bring in the new, make Twitter his company. Removing Goldman was the first step. Yet at the last moment there had been a compromise: Rather than being fired, Goldman was "allowed" to quit.

In early December Goldman set out for the LeWeb show in Paris, and while onstage with M. G. Siegler, a *TechCrunch* blogger, he broke the news publicly.

"You've been with Twitter for a while. So what's next for you personally?" Siegler asked.

"I've just announced to the entire company last Friday that I'll be leaving Twitter at the end of the month," Goldman said. "I'm not going to say I need to spend more time with my family—as it only consists of my girlfriend and two cats—but I just need a bit of a break." (He was still dating Crystal.)

Ev, too, was nowhere to be found. After handing the CEO role to Dick and processing the initial shock of being pushed out of the company, he was actually excited by his new job, realizing that it freed him from the stresses of the business side of the company. Now he could focus on the product. So in November he got to work designing new features for Twitter. But things quickly soured.

When he presented these new product ideas to Dick, they were brushed off and mostly ignored. Before long Ev was being ignored too. There were executive-level discussions that he wasn't invited to, senior off-site meetings he was not privy to. Like Jack in his "silent" chairman role, Ev was now a "silent" product director.

Over the Christmas holidays, Ev set off to Hawaii with his family—a vacation he had taken with Dick many times before, but not this year. While away, sitting by the pool, thinking about the psychological trauma of the past several months, he realized he didn't really have a role at Twitter after all. He had been fired without being escorted out of the building.

On January 2, 2011, he sent an e-mail to everyone in the company, announcing that it was time to take a break. "I've decided to extend my vacation even longer—through March," he wrote. "Why? I've been needing a break for a while, and the timing seems ideal. I'll still be available and monitoring email, attending board meetings, talking to Dick and other folks regularly, doing some press if needed, and keeping a close eye on things. But I'll also be spending a lot more time with Miles and Sara." He signed the e-mail, "Mahalo, Ev."

With Goldman gone and Ev on leave, Biz wasn't coming into the office either. He felt like an intruder in Dick's company and had been spending his days trying to figure out if he would leave Twitter too.

"Hi. Um. Biz isn't around right now," a short, white, geeky Twitter engineer said to Snoop Dogg's entourage as he appeared in the foyer with a laptop in his hands. "He's on his way back to the office, but . . . I can show you around until he gets here," the engineer said.

The employee nervously led the group through a door to the right that emerged into the center of Twitter's offices. As the men flowed into the silent cubicles, a ruckus immediately ensued.

"Whad up, honey, you look fly-a-liscious," Snoop said to a young, attractive female employee as he wandered by. "Damn, girl, you be dope on a rope. What's your name, honey bunny?" he said to another, hovering over her cubicle in his oversized blue Adidas jacket with "L.A." emblazoned across the front. "Oooh, oooh, ooh," he added, pursing his lips and shaking his head from side to side as if he were about to eat from a buffet.

The sound of the entourage was so distracting to employees, it was as if someone had just set off a bottle rocket in a public library.

"Um, excuse me, Mr. Snoop Dogg," the engineer skittishly said as he looked up at the six-foot-four-inch rapper. "We're going to go, um, go into this conference room."

Snoop, along with his entourage, which included Warren G and several other rappers, were in San Francisco for a show they were performing that evening. Nick Adler, who managed Snoop's digital presence, had organized the meeting and been told that Biz would be there to meet with the Snoop entourage. There was a slight problem, though: Biz had not been told. Nor had any of the other Twitter executives, who were all at an off-site meeting.

Snoop's visit had been set up by a new employee of Twitter's emerging media team, a group that had been developed to build relationships with more high-level stars, including actors, athletes, and musicians. These people were called VITs, or Very Important Tweeters, inside the company.

It also signaled a change in music culture. Although top-of-the-charts musicians had visited Twitter in the past—including Kanye West and P. Diddy—these stars were no longer visiting a certain other media: radio, ironically the thing Ev and Noah had originally set out to reinvent in 2005.

Instead, musicians wanted to see Twitter. Enter Snoop Dogg.

But this particular "tour" wasn't going as planned.

After Ev's ousting, Dick had organized a number of off-site meetings to reorganize the company. As a result, most execs were missing from the office as the slight, white engineer tried to entertain Snoop Dogg and his posse. It wasn't going well; he was like a substitute teacher trying to manage a group of unruly kids.

"So this is our new analytics tool," he said to the group. "It can show you which tweets are performing better than others."

"Oh, really, dude? That's really neat, dude," Snoop said, imitating a white-person voice. "That's your new analytics tool. Dude, that's really cool." Laughter erupted from the rest of the class as they all sat playing with their phones, barely paying attention.

But the engineer continued to speak. "So you can see, whenever you tweet about weed, you get a huge spike from your followers," he said. At this Snoop sat up, staring inquisitively at a graph on the screen.

After some time in the conference room the entourage quickly sat for a short video interview to help publicize a new feature on Twitter, and they were then led out through the Twitter cafeteria and back to the lobby. As they wandered past a DJ table and microphone set up in the cafeteria, Snoop stopped in his tracks. "Yo, yo, yo," he said, his arms outstretched on either side. "I can get on that?" he asked, pointing to the turntable. But before the engineer had a chance to answer, Snoop had a microphone in his hand and music was blasting out of the speakers. The sound flowed through the hallways, and employees quickly started to venture into the cafeteria. Before long people's phones were out, taking pictures, shooting videos, and, of course, tweeting.

Then, like a magician pulling a rabbit out of thin air, Snoop Dogg had something else in his hand: a large blunt the size of a Sharpie pen. Then a lighter. And a few seconds later he was smoking weed, ferociously. Seeing this, his entourage assumed it was okay to light up in the Twitter offices, so naturally they pulled out joints that had been in their pockets or tucked behind their ears.

In a matter of minutes, the cafeteria had become the stage for an impromptu Snoop Dogg concert, with a dozen large blunts being passed around among famous rappers and Twitter employees, most of whom were dancing, some grinding on each other. A few girls stood on cafeteria tables, their arms waving in the air as if they were atop a large speaker in a nightclub, not at work. They were all partying while their parents were away.

Eventually a Twitter lawyer appeared. Asking Snoop Dogg and his entourage of rappers to stop smoking weed in the office wasn't an easy affair, but all parties must come to an end, and eventually they left, bequeathing a haze of smoke, dozens of stoned employees, and hundreds of tweets in their wake.

A note was sent around to employees by the lawyer reminding people that they were not allowed to use drugs at work. People were asked to delete tweets. Photos were removed from the Web. The only incriminating videos left online belonged to Snoop Dogg.

Dick was furious when he found out about the weed, the dancing, the partying employees. He vowed that this was the last time anything like that would happen. It was time for Twitter to grow up, he said.

Jack's Back!

I t was light outside and dark inside. Jack was pacing back and forth in front of the bright projector screen as cracks of daytime hidden behind the blinds crept in. His brown dress shoes slid against the carpet like a ballet dancer's slippers. A white employee badge with the name Jack Dorsey and the word "Twitter" dangled from his waist, swaying from a thread clipped to his jeans.

"We're calling this Twitter 1.0," he said to the several hundred Twitter employees who sat watching him. "We're going to abbreviate it 'T1.'" Then he explained to them all that before that moment, until Jack had arrived back at the company, Twitter had been incomplete. "Pay attention to the direction, not the details," he said confidently. This was the new Twitter. He didn't praise the previous iteration of the product—Ev's version—but rather took a couple of slight swipes at it. It was a beta and incomplete, he said.

He had started his preamble by playing the song "Blackbird," by the Beatles, where a bird with broken wings learns to fly. Fitting. Some of the employees were excited, but many looked around, upset, as Jack disparaged the work they had spent the past two years on.

It was the moment Jack had been waiting and planning for—the moment that should have happened months earlier when Ev was forced down. Now Ev was being forced out.

After discussions with Dick and the board, Jack had arrived back at his castle in late March, a banished king returning from exile.

When Dick introduced him at a Tea Time, he was greeted with a standing ovation from most of the now 450 employees at the company, many of whom believed he was the rightful heir returning home. But there were a few who didn't stand up: a small handful of people who knew what had really happened with Jack's return.

As Jack stood there basking in the glow of applause, Ev sent an e-mail to all of the employees at Twitter.

"I've been doing some serious soul searching," Ev wrote about his past two months away. "Obviously, Twitter is the biggest thing I've ever played a significant part in or likely ever will. And, though I couldn't be more proud of what we've accomplished together, it is clearly not finished. If it reaches its potential, Twitter will be around for many, many more years, and we'll look back at 2011 as one of the quaint early years.

"I've decided, though, that my role in Twitter from here on out will not be day-to-day," he wrote. "I'll be doing what I can to help, as a co-founder, board member, shareholder and friend of the company (and so many people in it)."

He concluded, "I'm by no means disappearing," and signed the letter, "Continue changing the world. Your friend, Ev."

Three days later, on Monday morning, the company officially announced that Jack was back. This was followed by his tweet confirming his return. "Today I'm thrilled to get back to work at @Twitter leading product as Executive Chairman. And yes: leading @Square forevermore as CEO," Jack wrote.

Then came the press. Piles of it. Fenton stepped in to make sure Jack was painted as the hero. "It was a tragedy for the period of two years when he wasn't involved with the company that we were missing the founder," Fenton told the *New York Times* in an article about Jack's return.

In public talks and news interviews Jack continued to channel Jobs, using terms like "magical" and "delightful" and "surprising" and "best" to describe products, along with almost exact vernacular used by Jobs at conferences and on television, including "we're just humans running this company" and hawking the concept that Jobs shared, when he told people he was "most proud" of the things the company hadn't done.

Then, as he started to move into a greater orbit, he was featured in a huge profile in *Vanity Fair* on April 1, 2011, titled, "Twitter Was Act One." Next to the several-thousand-word article was a picture of Jack in a black suit and tie, his chest pushed forward, a little blue bird resting on his shoulder.

The article touted Jack as the "inventor" of Twitter and noted that this was one of the first times he had spoken publicly about his ousting as CEO. "It was like being punched in the stomach," Jack told David Kirkpatrick, the reporter who wrote the piece for *Vanity Fair*. The quote was picked up thousands of times on social and news networks.

Yet to a few the quote sounded eerily familiar. Like many of the things Jack had been saying for the past year, it was an unattributed quote by Steve Jobs. When Jobs was ousted from Apple in 1987, he told *Playboy* magazine: "I feel like somebody just punched me in the stomach."

Two weeks later, for the first time in several years, someone else appeared in the press: Noah. Nicholas Carlson, a blogger for *Business Insider*, had tracked Noah down and interviewed him for a piece on the real story of Twitter's founding. Carlson wrote that "all of the early employees and Odeo investors we talked to also agree that no one at Odeo was more passionate about Twitter in the early days than Odeo's cofounder, Noah Glass."

Ray, Blaine, Rabble, and others spoke on the record and said Noah was the "spiritual leader" of Twitter. Noah, though reluctant to talk about the old days, did too.

"Some people have gotten credit, some people haven't. The reality is it was a group effort. I didn't create Twitter on my own. It came out of conversations," Noah told Carlson in the interview. "I do know that without me, Twitter wouldn't exist. In a huge way." But Noah's real gripe was with Ev, whom he still believed had pushed him out of the company.

The same day the article came up, Ev tweeted: "It's true that @Noah never got enough credit for his early role at Twitter. Also, he came up with the name, which was brilliant."

But none of this stopped Jack. As the media's Next Steve Jobs, he was too big and too powerful for anyone to dent his version of history that had appeared in thousands of press outlets. And as the months rolled by, Jack's image and fame only grew. He started spending more time with celebrities. He partied at ritzy affairs in Los Angeles and New York City. He flew on private jets. He appeared in gossip outlets, partying on boats with celebrities and models. He metamorphosed with the help of coaches and stylists and drastically grew the public-relations team that would get him featured on more television shows and in more magazines.

Biz was the last cofounder to leave. On June 28, 2011, he announced that he was leaving a day-to-day role at Twitter. But really he was leaving *because* he didn't have a day-to-day role. His collaborators were already gone.

The day after Biz said he was leaving the company, an e-mail went out to all the Twitter employees announcing that the following day the White House would make public its plans for the first-ever "Twitter Town Hall" with President Obama. The event would be held in the East Room of the White House and streamed live to millions of Americans on the Web, and on Twitter, the e-mail said. It also noted, "Jack Dorsey will be the moderator."

Biz was sitting up in his bed when he read the e-mail, his back resting on his pillow. Seeing Jack's name, he started to fume. Over the years, he had never really grown too upset about Jack's media blitz, unless it crossed the ethics he and Ev had worked so hard to infuse into Twitter's culture. That had happened when Jack's name had been included in the Iran revolution story in the *New York Times* and when Jack had spoken about Twitter and China. And now it was about to happen again.

Biz quickly wrote an e-mail, his thumbs tapping the screen of his iPhone as the hair on the back of his neck stood on end.

"When Amac first explained this to me he said that nobody from

Twitter would be the moderator specifically to highlight the fact that we are a neutral technology," Biz wrote in an e-mail that he sent to the entire company. "I very strongly disagree with anyone from Twitter being involved as the moderator especially a founder." He went on: "This goes against three years of work to stay out of the narrative and remain neutral. Amac, what happened? This is the complete opposite of what you pitched me and it was the one thing I said to avoid to which you wholeheartedly agreed. The only thing I said to avoid. Please, please, please don't do it this way. We should not get involved in this manner."

And then, like a light switch turning off the last dimming bulb in a once brightly lit room, Biz's e-mail was disabled from e-mailing the entire company. His voice was muted.

Jack Dorsey was going to interview the president of the United States, cast across the media spotlight for all to see. Ev, Biz, and Goldman wouldn't be able to stop him now.

Make Better Mistakes Tomorrow

The nearly six hundred Twitter employees spent most of the week of June 4, 2012, placing their belongings in cardboard boxes. Books, keyboards, computer wires, little trinkets were all sent to sleep in the confines of cardboard. Then, as the week drew to a close, they walked out of the office that Ev had built, 795 Folsom Street, for the last time.

Over the weekend a swarm of men arrived, lifting the boxes and computers and transporting them to trucks that lined the street below. A light wind rustled the trees on Folsom Street as the engines coughed to life. Then they drove along the quiet streets, turning left onto Third, then down Mission, right, left, and finally arriving at a beige building the width of a city block on San Francisco's Market Street: Twitter's new home.

Along with the boxes and computers, the movers also carefully transported the artwork that Ev and Sara had carefully picked out, a beautiful neon sign that read TELL YOUR STORIES HERE, and the @ symbol that hung in the cafeteria.

The following Friday, Dick stood up in front of the employees in the company's new cafeteria. Compared with the old office, this new space was gargantuan. To the right of the entrance there was a huge outdoor roof deck where employees could lie on faux grass and work encircled by the San Francisco skyline. Snack stations were set up on each floor. There was a game room with table tennis, couches, and old and new video games. Wood-slab tables. A yoga room. Parking. And the dining area, where Dick was about to speak to employees, was a cavernous space, with a ceiling that rose up into the sky like a wave about to crest.

Although Jack's image on the outside was mushrooming, internally his aura had quickly started to fade. In late July 2011, he had fired four product managers who were part of Team Ev and had been (somewhat) privy to Jack's role in the ousting of Ev. Gone. Then he pushed Sean Garrett out, partially as revenge for Sean trying to muffle Jack's media frenzy a year earlier. Twitter employees also started to complain to Twitter managers that Jack was difficult to work with and repeatedly changed his mind about product ideas.

Jack's twenty-four-hour-a-day press tour had started to affect his relationship with Dick, who was often assumed to be an employee of Twitter in interviews, not its CEO.

When Jack went on TV to do interviews, he was sometimes introduced as the CEO of Twitter and Square, and he made no point to correct the mistake. The misinformation that Jack was CEO spread to leaders of other companies, to the media, and even to taxi drivers in the city.

One afternoon Dick was taking a cab back to the Twitter office from a meeting.

"Where to?" the driver asked.

"The corner of Market and Tenth," Dick replied. "The Twitter offices."

The cabbie explained that he would have to drop his passenger around the corner, because there was nowhere to pull over on Market Street. "It happens every time I have to drop someone off here," the cabbie proclaimed. "There really should be a place to pull over near the Twitter office."

"I might be able to do something about that," Dick said, understanding the man's plight. "I'm the CEO of Twitter."

The cabbie turned around with an excited look on his face and said, "Whoa! You're Jack Dorsey?"

Dick just sighed.

Though the public didn't know it, the employees of Twitter did: Dick was in charge.

He had worked extremely hard over the past year to boost company morale from the tumultuous years of different CEOs. Twitter employees clearly loved Dick, and in turn he genuinely cared about the company and the people who worked there. He had also gone to great lengths to ensure that the company kept the ethical values instituted by Ev, Biz, and Goldman and continued to stand up to government requests for information about users. And he also knew he had a responsibility to make Twitter into a profitable and successful company. Dick and Ali Rowghani also started shutting down third-party feeds to ensure that competitors, including Bill Gross, couldn't siphon people away from Twitter to a competing network.

Early one morning, after the employees had unpacked their boxes, placing books, keyboards, computer wires, and little trinkets on their desks in their new home, Dick called his first Tea Time meeting in the Market Street office. He stood in front of the employees in the cafeteria to welcome everyone to their new home—a home that felt like a large corporate company. A company that under Dick's leadership had grown to a ten-billion-dollar valuation in 2012. A company that had begun making one million dollars a day in advertising revenue from sponsored tweets and other ads and by the end of the year would become consistently profitable, pulling in hundreds of millions of dollars a year from advertising. A company that, under Dick, would also soon fix its outage problem, staying up and stable nearly 100 percent of the time. A company that planned to go public in less than two years. A company that investors hoped would eventually be worth one hundred billion dollars.

As the employees sat, hushed, Dick paced in front of them with the microphone in his hand and told a story about their recent move.

He said that when he had directed the movers to transport the artwork from the old office, he had instructed them to leave one piece of art behind. It had hung in the Folsom Street office since late December 2009. The piece of art was in a black frame with a white border. In a bit of irony, it had been hung upside down. And in bold white letters on a dark background, it made a statement in thirty-six characters: "Let's make better mistakes tomorrow."

The new office, Dick explained, meant that it was time for Twitter to grow up as a company. To end the rolling site outages and a long list of other problems that had plagued Twitter's infancy.

"We're leaving the motto of making better mistakes tomorrow in the old building," Dick said. "That's not the type of company we are anymore."

What's Happening?

Each day, Chris Hadfield, the commander of the International Space Station Expedition 35, peers out the domed window of his spaceship, holds up his digital camera, and captures small, square snippets of Earth. He then swims through the air back to his sleeping pod, loads the images onto his computer, and tweets them. These are images that most of the seven billion people spinning below him will never have the opportunity to see in real life.

He captures images of the Middle East, where protests against dictators are still organized using Twitter. He captures Rome, where the pope now talks to millions of Catholics in 140-character sermons. He captures Washington, where the president of the United States regularly addresses Americans in tweets. He captures Israel and Gaza, where a war as old as religion itself now rages online, on Twitter. He captures images of hundreds of millions of people who tweet to one another billions of times a week, in every language and from every corner of the globe.

On January 24, 2013, he happened to be passing over San Francisco and snapped a picture of the city where Twitter was born. Then he tweeted the image. If you look closely at the photo, you can see the Golden Gate Bridge, its vast red columns reaching into the sky, surrounded by San Francisco Bay. The same bay where a few years earlier, a group of friends who worked at a small, failing podcasting company called Odeo sailed across the water to share a drink at Sam's Anchor Cafe. That group of nearly a dozen people who would all contribute, in their own special way, to the creation of Twitter.

If you were able to look closely enough at Commander Hadfield's photo, zooming into the intricate web of city streets, houses, and office buildings, the parks and beaches, you would be able to see Jack, Ev, Biz, and Noah wandering the city—separately, together.

———

In the summer of 2012, Noah anxiously walked into a doctor's office with his girlfriend, Delphine. They approached the counter, told the nurse who they were, and filled out the appropriate paperwork. They then sat in the waiting room, hands clasped together, holding each other's hearts.

Noah had moved back to San Francisco in mid-2011, realizing it was time to get back to life. Back to a different life from the one he had left two years earlier. He had placed everything in cardboard boxes in LA and driven north where he had once gone south. Although Twitter wouldn't have existed without Noah, Noah now didn't exist because of Twitter.

Time heals all wounds, but some leave very visible scars. So he settled back into the same city, differently, renting a loft apartment with Delphine in a different neighborhood from the one he had lived in years earlier. He made new friends who didn't work in technology. People who wouldn't become business partners.

Then, in July 2012, they received the news and made an appointment with the doctor.

Their name was called and they walked down a hallway, opened a door, and entered a relatively dark room. There were screens everywhere. Blinking lights. Beeping noises. Delphine was told to lie on the bed and lift her shirt as Noah watched nervously. The doctor reached over and pressed a number of buttons on one of the machines, then started to gently rub gel on Delphine's stomach. Noah grasped her hand tightly.

There was a long pause as the doctor looked at the screen on the machine, then back at Noah and Delphine.

"Congratulations," the doctor said with a smile. "You're going to have a little baby girl." Noah looked at Delphine as tears welled up in his eyes, then started to trickle down his face. She looked back at him and smiled, an affectionate, happy smile. A loving smile. Then Noah buried his head in his hands and wept. He had cried hundreds of times over the years, cried a million tears. He had cried alone. In his bed. In his truck. But this was different. This time he was crying out of joy. He had always wanted a baby girl, dreamed of a little girl he could hold in his arms and cuddle and kiss and care for. And love. A little girl he could love. And here she was.

It was in that moment that he realized this was what he had been searching for in mid-2006, when he sat at his computer and typed a short blog post about the name of the latest project he was starting with his friends: Twitter.

He had explained what this new project could do: "The fact that I could find out what my friends were doing at any moment of the day made me feel closer to them and, quite honestly, a little less alone."

That feeling he had been searching for when he helped start Twitter was a hope that a technology could connect him to people. Yet it was the hand he was holding at that moment, Delphine's, that was the real connection he had always been searching for. The technology in that room, the screens, the beeps, had also done what Twitter had never been able to do for Noah. They had allowed him to feel a connection to someone who wasn't there. The technology had connected him to his baby who wasn't born yet.

Noah collected himself, wiping the tears away from his eyes as he looked at Delphine and kissed her. They walked out of the doctor's office, the warm sun drying his moist face, and peered up at the sky as birds floated by, lightly chirping, flapping, and tweeting in the warm San Francisco sun. He looked down at Delphine's hand, grasping it as they walked, together. Compared to his former cofounders, Noah made very little money from Twitter and Odeo. One day in the future he hopes to take the small sum he has saved to try his hand at another start-up.

On April 6, 2013, Noah tweeted for the first time in more than two years: "Cheeks stained with glorious tears of joy and absolute humility I celebrate the birth of my daughter Oceane Donnie Marie-Louise Poncin Glass."

———

Some mornings, Biz and Livy wake up in their two-thousand-square-foot home across the bay in Marin County, their heads resting atop puffy pillows as the sun streams in through their windows. "Hey, Livy!" Biz says as they look each other in the eye. "We're rich! We're rich!" At which they both giggle like children who have a secret pile of candy under their bed. They remind each other that as Twitter was just hatching, they lived a very different life. On some mornings they recite the story of a certain day, five years earlier, at the Elephant Pharmacy in Berkeley.

It was a late weekend afternoon, and Biz and Livy wandered into the kitchen of their small, box-shaped home and opened the fridge. It was completely empty. Just a cave of white plastic. They wandered to the cabinets: empty. Their wallets: empty too. Livy looked at Biz and with a sad smile asked what they were going to do. They were tens of thousands of dollars in credit-card debt at the time. Bills landed with a thud on top of more bills. They had already borrowed money from Ev twice, which had since dissolved. Their tweets lamented their current state: "we're paying bills."

They were broke and had no options. Well, almost no options.

"I bet you there's a lot of change in this can," Biz said as a he grabbed the coffee can the two had been using to collect spare change. It was your typical homemade piggy bank, round and metal with a plastic top. Each day the Stones came home and dropped dimes, nickels, and pennies inside—sometimes a few quarters would mix in too. *Clink. Clink. Clink.* The echoes grew quieter over time as the piggy bank filled up. Now, broke and hungry, they decided it was time to cash in. They walked down Cedar Street, the coffee can in hand as if it were made of glass, and arrived in front of the Elephant Pharmacy in the Gourmet

Ghetto. They walked inside, through the glass doors, and stood in front of the green Coinstar machine.

Biz began tipping the coins into it, carefully grasping the side of the can as Livy stood behind him and watched. They had assumed that they could get thirty dollars—maybe even fifty!—from the coin collection, but the number displaying the total kept flipping higher and higher. Before long, they were approaching sixty dollars. Then past seventy. Eighty. And still it kept going.

"Oh my god! Oh my god!" Livy said, clapping her hands with pure excitement as she jumped up and down in place.

"Are we in Las Vegas?" Biz asked as he looked back and forth between her and the rising number.

"Oh my god! Are we going to pass one hundred dollars?" she asked as the numbers continued to flip. Silence fell over both of them as the machine continued to $90. Then $91. $92. Livy began jumping in place again, her hands in the air, and yelped as they passed $100, coming to rest at $103. They both wore smiles so wide they looked unreal. Happiness at the bottom of a coffee can.

Once they collected their winnings, they traipsed off to Trader Joe's, where they loaded up on food—chips and dips, bread, a six-pack of cheap beer—and they went home, happy. The crinkle of their grocery bags accompanied them as they wandered back up Cedar Street.

Years later, their lives had become very different. Biz can sometimes make upward of half a million dollars to give a fifteen-minute public talk. Their bank account, which once began with a negative symbol, now ends with seven zeros.

When people ask Biz about his wealth, he tells them that money rarely changes people; it often just magnifies who they really are. Biz and Livy still drive their old Volkswagen and Subaru to work. Biz still dresses as if he walked out of a thrift store. And the majority of the money they make goes to the Biz and Livia Stone Foundation (a non-profit they founded that gives money and support to organizations that make it easy for anyone to help students in need) and a number of animal-related sanctuaries. As a result, a few mice now have a warm home on a farm.

———

In early 2012 Jack sold his loft in Mint Plaza, saying good-bye to the nearby homeless glut of the Tenderloin, and moved to the glitziest part of the city. His new home, for which he paid almost twelve million dollars, isn't visible from the street. It sits behind a large wooden gate and down a steep driveway, hidden from view by old, swaying trees. The rear of the house, which is an endless wall of glass, sits atop a giant, jagged, rocky cliff face at the edge of the world.

Each night, when Jack comes home from work, he types his password into the keypad that opens his front doors, then walks inside his empty glass castle in the sky. The rooms in the house are all sparse. In the living room there are only a couple of pieces of furniture, including the same Le Corbusier couch and chair Steve Jobs once had in his home.

Through the living room there is a set of glass doors that open onto a balcony that sits out over the rocks like a magic carpet floating atop the moist air. Some nights Jack wanders out there alone and looks out at the bay. Below, the waves crash against the rocks, making a roiling sound like ferocious lions locked in a dungeon.

By 2013, with a net worth of a billion dollars, it might seem like Jack had "won." But to some of the people who knew him when he arrived at Odeo eight years earlier, it seemed quite the opposite. Back then he had joined the company as a quiet young programmer in search of friendships and a mentor. He had found the mentor, sort of, in his emulation of Steve Jobs. But he lost friends when he used those same people as a ladder to climb to the top.

Jack is often featured on the covers of magazines. He's been profiled by *60 Minutes* as a visionary and touted as a playboy billionaire who parties with the stars in gossip rags. He is often spoken of as the next Steve Jobs and the sole inventor of Twitter.

From his balcony, as he watches the dark ocean down below, he can hear the sounds of boats heading back from sea, their horns blaring as they return to port.

In early 2013, on the nights that Jack stands out there alone, as the smell of the bay drifts up the sides of the rocks, he looks out at the ocean and plots his next moves. His plans for Square, where he has become an adept leader, growing the company into a multibillion-dollar business. His plans for Twitter, where he one day might return as CEO. His plans to one day become the mayor of New York City.

But during those moments when he feels truly lonely—when the ocean, the sirens, the rocks stop calling to him, he walks back inside, closing the glass doors behind him, and reaches into his pocket, pulling out his smart phone. He slides his finger across the glass screen, then places it on the blue icon with the little blue bird. And he talks to Twitter.

———

On Monday evenings, just before five o'clock, Ev rushes out of Obvious Corporation, which he reopened for business after officially leaving Twitter. His office is in a nondescript building on Market Street, just a few blocks away from Twitter's headquarters. He dashes home to eat dinner with his family. Then they wander upstairs for their nightly ritual of reading together—their favorite part of the day.

Ev was despondent for months after leaving Twitter. He started to piece together what had happened to him, learning more about the secret meetings between Jack and others. He played back in his head over and over conversations where people who worked for him had acted surprised at the news of his firing. Some of those people had actually been involved in the coup.

On Tuesday evenings Ev works late, often the last person to leave the office as he sits sketching out ideas for new projects, the glow of a computer screen lighting his way.

His Twitter stock and other investments are now nearing two

billion dollars, sure to continue growing as Twitter pursues its goal of becoming a hundred-billion-dollar company.

On Wednesday evenings a cooking teacher comes to the house. Four-year-old Miles and Ev and Sara's second boy, Owen, now fourteen months old, learn about vegetables, soil, and farming.

In 2012, a year after Ev officially left Twitter, thinking of what had taken place behind his back, he sat down with Sara and they asked each other the following questions: How can we raise our children to never act this way? How can we raise them to be honest and caring? How can we make a road map for the kinds of parents we want to be and the type of family we want to raise?

They came up with two solutions. First, the money they have made over the years would go into a trust. When Miles and Owen grow up, they will be responsible for giving it away to charities, organizations that exist to try to make the world a better place. Second, they would develop a weekly schedule to adhere to, ensuring that family comes before anything else.

Weekends are special for Ev, Sara, Miles, and Owen. On Saturday mornings Ev makes waffles. They are often bizarre concoctions, with Ev adding nuts and seeds and other strange ingredients.

Miles, like his dad, is a daydreamer, and he often just sits and stares into space, thinking. On Sunday mornings the two daydreamers go on an adventure together, always taking the train through San Francisco to a museum, a park, or the bookstore.

Ev and Sara noticed early on that, like Ev, Miles is shy and sometimes socially awkward. As much as they want to change that in him, they know they can't. But they also know that technology won't change that either, so the kids are strictly forbidden to use iPads, iPhones, or televisions. Human interactions are encouraged. So are physical, paper books.

So Sunday nights, before the weekly schedule begins anew, it's time for the nightly ritual, the best part of each day.

On one side of Miles's bedroom there is a wide, oval, gray couch. It's big enough for the entire family to squeeze onto. Directly across the room there is a stacked bookshelf. On it there are dozens of print books of all shapes and sizes. Children's books. Books about butterflies and pirates. Encyclopedias.

Each night, as Ev drops down onto the couch, Sara next to him with Owen in her arms, Miles runs across the room, his feet briskly flying across the gray carpet to grab his favorite book: *The Astronaut Handbook*, a story about a group of kids who want to become astronauts when they grow up. Miles bounds back across his bedroom, handing the book to his father. Then together, as a family, they read as Miles stares out the window, just as Ev did on his father's green tractor as a child, up into space.

———

From time to time the astronauts on the space station host a question-and-answer session on Twitter. People ask 140-character queries that are sent via cyberspace into real space, where astronauts who live for sixth months at a time in small spaceships that circle Earth do their best to explain what it's like to live in a glass capsule hundreds of miles away.

In one recent session, a woman on Earth asked whether it was lonely in space.

"In the centre of every big city in the world, surrounded by noise and teeming millions of people, are lonely people," Commander Hadfield wrote. "Loneliness is not so much where you are, but instead is your state of mind." Then he explained that the few people who live on the space station can contact their families through a number of technologies designed to connect people, including radio, telephone, and social media.

As the sessions on Twitter concluded, someone else asked how these astronauts tweet from space. Hadfield explained that he has a laptop inside his sleep pod. As he floats around the spaceship, checking on experiments that could cure diseases or enable people to grow scarce resources in space or answer previously unanswerable questions, he often takes short breaks and slips into his bay to check Twitter. There he talks to millions of people who are floating 240 miles away. People who can talk to him but can't touch him. People who can make him feel just a little less alone.

Acknowledgments

On Twitter people can only send 140-character updates at a time; printed books have their own character limits, too. So for those I do not thank individually, please understand that it is a matter of constraint, not appreciation.

A special thanks to the hundreds of people who provided me documents and e-mails and took the time to sit for interviews for this book, especially Ev, Biz, Jack, Goldman, Noah, Bijan, Fred, Fenton, and Dick. Although some of these people agreed to speak to me reluctantly, I am eternally grateful for their time. There are some people I cannot thank by name—sources who put their job and friendships on the line to help me find the truth—they know who they are when I offer a heartfelt and respectful bow of gratitude.

Thank you to my editor, Niki Papadopoulos, who seemed to telepathically know when I was stuck on a sentence or theme, reaching out, sometimes via Twitter, to push me along and in the right direction. (And immense appreciation for her listening to me ramble for hours on end about the book.) To my agents, Katinka Matson, John Brockman, and Max Brockman, who helped me find this project and a publisher that believed in it. And to Natalie Horbachevsky, Jennifer Mascia, Adrian Zackheim, and Drummond Moir for their involvement in, help for, and dedication to this book.

To my friends and coworkers: Nora Abousteit, Jill Abramson, Melissa Barnes, Ruzwana Bashir, Lane Becker, Veronica Belmont, Danielle B. Marin, Ryan Block, Tom Bodkin, Danah Boyd, Matt Buchanan, David Carr, Brian Chen, Mathias Crawford, Tony and Mary Conrad, Tom Conrad, Paddy Cosgrave, Dennis Crowley, Damon Darlin, Anil Dash, Mike Driscoll, Aaron Durand, Josh Felser, Tim Ferris, Brady Forrest, David Gallhager, Michael Galpert, John Geddes, Shelly Gerrish, Ashley Khaleesi Granata, Mark Hansen, Quentin Hardy, Leland Hayward, Erica Hintergardt, Mat Honan, Arianna Huffington, Kate Imbach, Larry Ingrassia, Walter Isaccson, Mike Issac, Joel Johnson, Andrei Kallaur, Paul Kedrosky, Kevin Kelly, Jeff Koyen, Brian Lam, Jeremy LaTrasse, Steven Levy, Allen Loeb, Kati London, Om Malik, John Markoff, Hubert McCabe, Christopher Michel, Claire Cain Miller, Trudy Muller, Tim O'Reilly, Carolyn Penner, Nicole Perlroth, Megan Quinn, Narendra Rocherolle, Jennifer Rodriguez, Evelyn Rusli, Naveen Selvadurai, Ryan and Devon Sarver, Elliot Schrage, Mari Sheibley, MG Siegler, Courtney Skott, Robin Sloan, Andrew Ross Sorkin, Suzanne Spector, Brad Stone, David Streitfeld, Gabriel Stricker, Arthur Sulzberger Jr., Kara Swisher, Clive Thompson, Deep Throat, Baratunde Thurston, Mark Trammell, Sara Morishige Williams, Nick Wingfield, Jenna Wortham, Aaron Zamost, Edith Zimmerman.

To my family: Terry and Margie, Betty and Len, Eboo, Weter and Roman, Sandra and David, Stephen, Amanda, Ben and Josh, Matt and Sam, and, of course, Michael, Luca, Willow, and Crazy Lotte, who housed and fed me (and Pixel) while I wrote at their dining room table.

To the readers who, in a world of never-ending media, took the time to read this book.

And last, but very far from least, Chrysta Olson, for her wisdom, support, and love. And, thanks in part to our discussions at Cecconi's and elsewhere around the storyline of *Hatching Twitter,* allowed us to hatch a relationship of our own. I love you.